Variations on Catastrophe

Variations
on
Catastrophe

Some French Responses
to the Great War

JOHN CRUICKSHANK

Clarendon Press, Oxford
1982

Oxford University Press, Walton Street, Oxford OX2 6DP

London Glasgow New York Toronto
Delhi Bombay Calcutta Madras Karachi
Kuala Lumpur Singapore Hong Kong Tokyo
Nairobi Dar es Salaam Cape Town
Melbourne Auckland
and associates in
Beirut Berlin Ibadan Mexico City Nicosia

Published in the United States
by Oxford University Press, New York

British Library Cataloguing in Publication Data

Cruickshank, John
Variations on catastrophe: some French responses to the Great War.
1. World War, 1914–1918—Influence and results
2. Europe—Civilization   3. France—Intellectual life
I. Title
940'.01   CB203
ISBN 0-19-212599-0

Library of Congress Cataloging in Publication Data
Cruickshank, John
Variations on catastrophe.
Bibliography: p.
Includes index.
1. French literature—20th century—History and criticism.
2. World War, 1914–1918—Literature and the war.
I. Title
PQ307.W3C7 1982   840'.9'358   81-22462
ISBN 0-19-212599-0   AACR2

Typeset by Cotswold Typesetting Ltd, Cheltenham.
Printed in Great Britain at the University Press, Oxford by Eric Buckley,
Printer to the University.

Preface

This book is the outcome of dissatisfaction. It has arisen from the fact that the secondary literature which I consulted a few years ago failed to provide adequate answers to various questions which the experience of the Great War quite clearly raised in France as elsewhere. These questions had mainly to do with the anticipation of war before 1914, the experience of war between 1914 and 1918, and efforts to understand its meaning for western man after 1918.

The question of intellectual responses to the catastrophe of war, viewed from these three standpoints, is obviously a complicated one. Not all aspects have been ignored and indeed certain topics – for example the phenomenon of French nationalism before 1914 – have been closely and thoroughly examined. On the other hand, subjects which remain relatively unexplored include the immediate response of writers while undergoing the horrors of trench warfare, or the great variety of response, expressed after 1918, to the significance of this experience.

This is a very large area of enquiry and I make no claim to comprehensiveness in the pages which follow. At best, I have tried to examine the ideas of a limited number of writers, some of whom are now largely forgotten. My purpose has been to open up some lines of investigation which may encourage others to deepen and extend the subject of response to the Great War in France between the approximate dates of 1912 and 1927.

Part of the material in Chapters 2, 3, and 9 appeared in earlier form in the following: C. E. Pickford (ed.), *Mélanges de littérature française moderne offerts à Garnet Rees par ses collègues et amis,* Paris, Minard, 1980; C. A. Burns (ed.), *Literature and Society: Studies in Nineteenth- and Twentieth-Century French Literature Presented to R. J. North,* Birmingham, J. Goodman & Sons, 1980; M. Bowie *et al.* (eds.), *Baudelaire, Mallarmé, Valéry: New Essays in Honour of Lloyd Austin,* Cambridge, CUP, 1982. I am grateful to the editors of these volumes for their co-operation.

1 January 1980   J.C.

v

Contents

PART ONE

The Prospect of Catastrophe

CHAPTER 1

Heroic Enthusiasm
Psichari and Agathon

The Great War of 1914–18, still relatively close as a historical event, appears much more remote as a psychological and moral phenomenon. It remains a living memory for many families and the anniversary of the armistice continues to be an occasion for some form of national self-recollection. Yet it contains features which seem to defy our understanding. For example, in view of many events and certain widespread attitudes in the first years of this century, we may wonder how it was that war came as such a totally unexpected event to so many of its ultimate victims. At another level, we find it increasingly difficult to understand the vast enthusiasm and confidence – 'the air was ringing with rousing assurances'[1] – with which so many involved originally set out to do battle. Nevertheless we need to come to terms with this experience of unpreparedness, and the reaction of heroic enthusiasm, if we are to appreciate the traumatic effects which the events of 1914–18 had on European attitudes and beliefs and the extent to which they ended an era of confidence and ushered in that 'age of anxiety' which has since been our lot in the twentieth century.

Our understanding of these matters is bound to be complicated by the fact that the attitudes and responses to which historians regularly refer were never total and never attributable to the entire population of a given country. When historians speak of aggressive nationalism in France, of European confidence in scientific progress and rational processes, of German militarism, or of international pacifism, they are referring only to sections of a given population or to intellectuals, ideologues, and politicians whose ideas were frequently unrepresentative of the nation at large or who exercised an influence quite disproportionate to their numbers. One is therefore obliged to admit, by the same token, that even the two problems mentioned above were not total. Not all Europeans were psychologically unprepared for war in

3

1914. Neither did all Europeans regard war, when it came, as an opportunity for heroic and patriotic virtue or as a 'great scavenger of thought' which 'cleans out the stagnant pools and clotted channels of the intellect'.[2] The sequence of almost complete unpreparedness followed by heroic confidence reflects a broad general trend to which individual exceptions may readily enough be found. It is virtually impossible, however, to find exceptions to the claim that this particular war, when it broke out in August 1914, far exceeded the anticipations of its participants in terms of its scale, its duration, and its savage horror.

The Great War was a catastrophe not only in the sense that it was a human massacre but also in terms of its sudden dislocation of what was widely experienced as an apparently calm, ordered, and relatively peaceful rhythm of life. For a hundred years, since Waterloo, there had been no general European conflict. There had been crises and confrontations but no major bloodletting. The first decade of the century was the Edwardian period in England, the 'Belle Époque' in France, the age of what came to be called *la douceur de vivre* or, in the words of an English commentator, 'stabilized tranquillity'.[3] Inevitably, and with the benefit of hindsight, later writers have shown us that these appearances of calm contentment were deceptive. Social historians remind us that class consciousness was growing among urban workers, that industrial disputes provoked sharp conflicts in several countries, that the Bonnot anarchists were active in Paris, and that in London in 1914 militant suffragettes practised direct action and attempted to attack Buckingham Palace. In a similar way cultural historians point to the violence and nervous tension pervading artistic life. In painting, primitive and barbaric elements became prominent while the Cubists outlined the obituary of something like 500 years of representational art. As regards music, Stravinsky's *Rite of Spring* provoked days of rioting in Paris in 1913 and what were perceived as cacophonic, nerve-jangling scores were being written by Berg, Webern, and others. Not least, political historians now speak of a long, slow fuse which made the conflagration of 1914 an inevitable one. They remind us that the famous *douceur de vivre* was accompanied by dangerous developments in terms of nationalism, colonialism, and the growth of the armaments industry.

Warning signs such as these were widely ignored at the period. This is particularly true of the middle-classes whose political awareness and foresight were not especially sharp. In writing of the situation in France at the time Pierre-Henri Simon is careful to present *la douceur de vivre* as a mainly middle-class phenomenon:

Le bourgeois européen de 1900 est un homme heureux. Sa vie matérielle est facile, sa fortune est stable, sa conscience est bonne. Il n'a pas le temps de s'ennuyer: on lui organise des expositions universelles où il se réjouit de voir rassemblées ses richesses et ses machines; ses ingénieurs lui construisent des jouets qui le passionnent, la bicyclette, l'auto, l'aéroplane; ses écrivains lui fournissent une littérature de consommation agréable où, selon le degré de sa culture, il trouve les divertissements de l'esprit boulevardier, les plaisirs plus raffinés de l'ironie et de l'humour, les derniers frissons du romantisme, les douces harmonies franciennes et néo-classiques.[4]

It is not surprising, in the light of such a description, that Schinz should write in 1920 that 'war took almost everyone by surprise'.[5]

And yet in France the signs on the international horizon now seem to us to have been particularly disturbing. French and German interests had clashed at Tangier in 1905 and at Agadir in 1911, providing propaganda for the nationalists of both countries. The French nationalists, still acutely conscious of the defeat of 1870, kept alive the question of the lost provinces of Alsace and Lorraine. The threatening growth of German industrial and military power was widely recognized in France as it was in Britain. In 1913 compulsory military service in France was extended from two to three years by the *loi de trois ans*. In the sphere of philosophical thought, as distinct from that of political action, there was much support in Germany – and some in France – for the Hegelian idea that peace means stagnation and that moral order between states must be replaced by *Realpolitik*. And yet even the assassination of the Archduke Franz-Ferdinand at Sarajevo on 28 June 1914 was not regarded by most Frenchmen as a likely cause of war. J.-J. Becker's magisterial analysis of the written sources of the period fully supports his claim that the French attitude was one of 'insouciance', followed by considerable surprise at the turn of events, despite ten years of discussion and prediction of war before 1914.[6] Public preoccupation at the time was not with the likelihood of international conflict but with the summer holidays and the trial for murder of Mme Caillaux, wife of the then Minister of Finance and President of the Radical party.

Various attempts have been made to account for this apparent insensitivity to important events outside France's frontiers. For example, chronology has been invoked and it has been suggested that the more vengeful manifestations of nationalism and patriotic fervour greatly lessened during the decade before 1914. Writing in 1921 and looking back at the pre-war period, Georges Guy-Grand claimed that much of the Alsace-Lorraine element in French nationalism disappeared with the generation of 1870: 'La génération de la Revanche, qui avait subi la défaite, ne pensait qu'à elle . . . avait en partie disparu.'[7]

Revenge against Germany became the theme of 'de rares exaltés' only. It has also been argued that the nationalism of Barrès and Maurras had become much more defensive and conceived of nationalist fervour as a focus of internal and highly conservative values rather than as the basis of an aggresive foreign policy.[8]

A rather different explanation of this French 'insouciance' in the summer of 1914 points to the growing confidence which the country experienced, within a wider context of European belief in inevitable progress, as the memory of 1870 began to fade and the conviction of French pre-eminence became common currency. The belief that France had undergone a form of regeneration was increasingly expressed.[9] In some circles, of course, this belief in national revival gave a certain impetus to the expression of military and patriotic themes. Elsewhere, a few intellectuals remained aware of dangerous trends in Europe and expressed unease at the decline of the birth-rate in France and at the country's relatively poor performance in economic and industrial terms. But a majority responded to the mood of self-confidence. At the same time, it is clear that self-confidence can be expressed in either offensive or defensive terms. While some groups attempted to organize patriotic fervour against what they conceived of as 'the German threat', it appears that the vast majority of the population, in so far as they had a view at all, favoured the more complacent expressions of self-confidence and assumed, after forty-four years of peace, that 'things would be arranged' and indeed that war had become an anachronism. This latter view seems to have been encouraged both by pacifist propaganda and by the conviction, inherited from nineteenth-century *scientisme* and now filtering through to much of the population, that human beings could control their destiny through scientific rationalism and that social and moral progress were inevitable. Discussing the attitude of the French people in the immediate pre-war period K. W. Swart writes: '. . . of a cheerful disposition and hardly aware of the increasingly serious international situation, they did not yet see any reason for abandoning their former belief in progress and their often overly optimistic, complacent estimate of the strength of France. Outbreak of war was held to be improbable in the enlightened twentieth century and the trend toward greater political and social equality seemed irreversible.'[10] The logic of progress is succinctly expressed by Jacques Barzun: 'All events had physical origins; physical origins were discoverable by science; and the method of science alone could, by revealing the nature of things, make the mechanical sequences of the universe wholly benevolent to man. Fatalism and progress were as closely linked as the Heavenly Twins and like them invincible.'[11] As regards the view that war had become an outdated and highly unlikely means of solving international disagreements, Roger Martin du Gard wrote that in 1914 'la majorité du monde civilisé avait vécu longtemps dans l'illusion que la guerre était un phénomène périmé.'[12] At the same time, while belief in inevitable progress and a general materialist confidence characterized the outlook of many ordinary people, a spiritual and often specifically Catholic reaction had set in, in intellectual and literary circles, against late nineteenth-century 'scientism'. The philosophy of Bergson proved a powerful influence against belief in determinism, whether of an optimistic or pessimistic kind. In the two decades before the outbreak of war a series of well-publicized conversions to the Christian faith took place and included such important names as those of Claudel, Jammes, Rivière, Péguy, Jacob, Cocteau, and the Maritains. It seems fair to add, however, that the religious reaction did little to strengthen efforts to avoid war. Its effect, in many cases, was to reinforce moral, social, and general intellectual traditionalism. We shall see later in this chapter, for example, that renewed spiritual zeal among the intellectual youth of the nation, on the threshold of war, went hand in hand with patriotic, authoritarian, and militaristic attitudes.

In spite of the explanations proposed above, it remains easier to describe the general unpreparedness for war in 1914 than to account for it in convincing detail. Something similar happens once we attempt to examine the confidence and enthusiasm so widely expressed by the troops who first set out for the front in early August. Both phenomena, in fact, give rise to similar problems of interpretation. It is possible that a psychological link exists between them. It can be argued, for instance, that a show of enthusiasm was a way of compensating for the fact of having been taken unawares. J.-J. Becker seems to lend some support to this view in the course of distinguishing between the somewhat shocked and relatively low-key response to mobilization and the positive excitement expressed a few days later as the troops left home for the battle line.[13] Reaction to the mobilization notices was essentially calm, orderly, serious, and public-spirited. But with descriptions of the departure of the troops (in prefectorial reports, local newspapers, etc.) the tone changes quite noticeably. It is as though the initial shock had ended and a subsequent emotional release was taking place. This is the occasion when rifles were decorated with flowers, streets were hung with flags, bands played the *Marseillaise,* and cries of 'Vive la guerre!', 'A Berlin!' or 'On les aura!' rang out. Documents cited by Becker use such terms as 'allégresse', 'enthousiasme exceptionnel', 'frisson patriotique', and 'chaleureuses acclamations'.[14]

In general psychological terms these early days of August also confirm in some measure Alexis Philonenko's broad account of the sequence of responses to the outbreak of war. He regards the proclamation – in this case the notices of mobilization – as the point at which the fact of war, and its intoxicating potential, are first revealed to the population at large. The military parades which follow provide a ritual language giving expression to the unconscious impulses (of participants and spectators alike) initially stirred by the proclamation. Finally, the formulation of slogans such as 'A Berlin!' conveys the *vox populi*, helps to link soldiers and civilians, and offers rallying-points for the departing troops. But Philonenko significantly and rightly adds that 'la question se pose de savoir si l'on se bat pour une réalité ou pour quelques formules.'[15] This is a question which some of the most articulate combatants were to ask themselves increasingly as the war continued.

At a somewhat different level, it has often been suggested that the sudden war enthusiasm of 1914 was the inevitable result of instinctive patriotic fervour combined with the pressures of public opinion and governmental propaganda. It is said that these last two pressures proved so effective precisely because they touched the inherent aggressiveness in human beings. Put in a different way, the prospect of war appeared as a desirable and indeed necessary release from tensions which had built up intolerably during a long period of peace in a society characterized by triumphant materialism operating within a set of particularly strong social constraints and moral inhibitions. This is what E. J. Leed calls the 'drive-discharge' model and it has frequently been invoked as a psychological explanation of enthusiasm for war.[16] What the drive-discharge theory says, in effect, is that war fulfils the function of 'discharging' drives which cannot be ignored yet which equally cannot receive satisfactory expression within the placidities of peacetime living. Another form of jargon makes a very similar point when it describes war as 'libidinal release' from 'the tradesman mentality'. Although it is part of Leed's purpose to argue against this type of explanation, at least where the Great War is concerned, he accepts that it was 'a deeply rooted cultural assumption intrinsic to the sense of liberation that many experienced in August of 1914'.[17]

The belief that war would provide a release from the dissatisfactions of civilian life does indeed seem to have been fairly widespread. While only a small minority positively wanted war before 1914, many who were strongly critical of their society expressed desires and impulses which war alone appeared likely to satisfy. For the more romantically traditionalist critics of the age war and military life promised a superior ethic of discipline, authority, courage, self-sacrifice, and comradeship. They deplored the decline of such values in a society increasingly devoted to mean-minded materialism. For the more anarchically inclined, war was to be welcomed to the extent that it was likely to break down social barriers, increase social mobility, create the conditions for what was seen as a more natural, healthy, and democratic society. There was also some anticipation among the more politically conscious participants in the war that those who served at the front would return with the ability and the desire to lead a post-war social and political revolution. Such ideas were expressed by individuals in all the main countries involved in the Great War.[18] In France in particular, relatively young men like Péguy and Psichari were already committed to belief in the psychologically liberating and morally reforming potentiality of army life, and even of war, before 1914. In 1911, for example, Péguy asserted that 'l'homme n'est jamais libre qu'au régiment. Hors des servitudes civiles; hors des émoussements civils.'[19] And Psichari wrote in 1912, in a liminal note to his *Appel des armes* of 1913:'Lorsque l'auteur de ce récit fit ses premières armes au service de la France, il lui sembla qu'il commençait une vie nouvelle. Il eut vraiment le sentiment de quitter la laideur du monde et d'accomplir comme la première étape d'une route qui devait le conduire vers de plus pures grandeurs.'[20] We shall see later that Franconi and Barbusse were among those who discussed in their work the possibility of a post-war revolution being led by the returning soldiers, their eyes opened to political realities by their experiences.

In the event, the Great War developed rapidly into an unparalleled exercise in technological and industrialized slaughter. It took on an increasingly nightmarish quality, and far from creating or fostering high moral values it seemed to intensify, and apparently legitimize, some of the worst and most inhuman features of the age. The tyranny of machines over men and of technology generally was more complete and more lethal in war than in peace. The war was certainly widely regarded as being fought in defence of important moral ideals, yet it turned out to be of such a nature that it offered little scope either for chivalric action or libidinal release. What the Germans were to call the *Materialschlacht* exploited technology for destructive ends and made it an instrument of terror rather than a means of more comfortable and more 'civilized' living. The suspicion grew that modern wars may reflect all too accurately some of the basic features of the industrial societies which wage them. Leed goes so far as to say that 'in the trenches men learned that mechanized destruction and industrial production were mirror images of each other.'[21]

There is still room for some debate on these points, but the fact remains that the 'poor fork'd animal' that is man was exposed to a new and murderous fire-power. Material and mechanization became increasingly efficient in the laceration of human flesh and the destruction of human life. As a result, whole armies sought relief by digging holes in the ground and trench warfare was born. The result was 'a new dimension of foulness, a tunnel life lived in a troll kingdom in which immobility never brought peace and activity scarcely ever brought mobility.'[22] Consequently, the actual human enemy was sometimes unseen for weeks on end although his artillery wrought terrible damage. This impersonal war of material means allowed little in the way of chivalric deeds and heroic self-realization. Orders often had to be obeyed without any opportunity of understanding their purpose or assessing their moral and tactical justification. Leed puts the point well when he says that what was first conceived of as a release from the constraints of civilian life was gradually transformed for many into a form of permanent estrangement.[23] It has also been suggested, incidentally, that precisely because modern industrial war blocked the release of personal aggression, this aggression found ultimate expression in an increasing hostility towards officers, the general staff, the 'profiteer' on the home front, etc.[24]

All this, however, is to anticipate. The fact remains that in August 1914 enthusiasm for the war was widespread, encouraged by a sense of participation in a great crusade which would restore moral values to the world and bring about social and political renewal.

The two reactions to the outbreak of war, surprise followed by initial enthusiasm, have been presented so far in what is perhaps too isolated a way. While the aggressive nationalist sentiments of certain intellectual groups, strongly influenced by Barrès or Maurras, have been mentioned, it is probably true to say that some members of the generation after theirs were to have a more direct impact on many of the young men who marched to war in 1914. Three leading members of the post-Barrès generation were Péguy, Psichari, and Massis. Péguy, some years older than his two colleagues, set an example and provided a kind of generational link between them and Barrès. The admiration of all three for the military life, and their growing conviction that war was both inevitable and necessary, were based less on the political calculations of some of their elders than on high-minded moral convictions tinged with a certain amount of mysticism.

Péguy had the strongest liberal credentials among the three in the sense that he had been a socialist militant, a *dreyfusard,* and came of humble peasant stock. In his own unique way he held together a number of apparently conflicting causes: patriotism and international-ism, republicanism and conservatism, a measure of anti-clericalism and a devout and mystical Catholicism. The story of his disillusionment with Third Republic political and intellectual life is well known, as is his opposition to those whom he saw as having reduced a pure *mystique* to a timeserving and trimming *politique.* Péguy was one of the few (along with Bloy and Sorel notably) who had anticipated war at least since 1905 and his belief in an eventual conflict with Germany dom-inated many of his attitudes. He attacked the 'lourde barbarie latente' of his contemporaries (what others saw, on the contrary, as 'la douceur de vivre') and was particularly severe in his condemnation of crude materialism, social injustice, and a narrow, pedantic rationalism. His attitude on the eve of the Great War comes out clearly in his criticism, in 1913, of the reorganized Sorbonne and the École Normale Supér-ieure.[25] He accused the Sorbonne of sterile pedantry and deplored its failure to give genuine intellectual leadership to the country. Above all, he saw both the Sorbonne and the École as anti-French and dangerously pacifist centres of pan-Germanism. In 'L'Argent (suite)', for example, he upbraided the Sorbonne and the 'parti intellectuel' for opposing the extension of compulsory military service to three years. He also accused them of hypocrisy, partisanship, blindness to the way affairs were dev-eloping, and a highly selective liberalism which claimed to be inter-nationalist and humane but which was only extended to those who merited ideological approval. 'L'Argent (suite)' contains sarcasm at Lucien Herr's antimilitarism in the Rue d'Ulm and notes ironically the apparent pacifist conversion of journals with such ringing titles as *La Guerre sociale* and *La Bataille socialiste.* Péguy sums up his criticism in characteristic style:

Il y a en Sorbonne (actuelle) et dans la nouvelle École Normale un noyau de gens qui ne veulent pas du nationalisme, à moins qu'il ne soit allemand; et du militarisme, à moins qu'il ne soit allemand; et du capitalisme, à moins qu'il ne soit allemand; et de l'impérialisme, à moins qu'il ne soit allemand; et du colonialisme, à moins qu'il ne soit allemand. Nous demandons seulement que ces gens et que ce noyau ne fassent point un corps de l'État français.

Ce n'est peut-être pas trop demander.[26]

This interpretation of the views of his intellectual enemies gave Péguy further opportunities to attack pacifist attitudes and to claim that the outcome of pacifism was a desire for peace at any price – even a preference for 'une paix dans l'injustice' over 'une guerre pour la justice'.[27] Finally, he broadens his attack further by listing four *sornettes* or 'bits of nonsense' which he attributes to the socialist party: their call to 'arm the people', but for what purpose?; their claim that war has no practical results and decides nothing; their assertion that wars are plots against people laid by capitalists, kings, and governments generally – the view that 'les rois n'ont qu'une idée, entre les repas, qui est d'embêter les peuples';[28] finally, their belief (against all the evidence which they are prepared to suppress) that the socialist parties of France and Germany, working in concert, will ensure that neither country goes to war against the other. In sharp contrast, Péguy is the spokesman of those who remain 'résolus à tout prix à ne pas retomber dans le ridicule de 1870.'[29] War is inevitable, despite the categorical assurance of the historian Charles Seignobos to the contrary. War will be the unavoidable outcome of a moral, intellectual, and political tension which has increased steadily since 1905. It will also provide an opportunity for the regeneration of the nation.

This idea of the regenerative power of war, but with the additional logical conclusion that war is therefore positively desirable rather than merely unavoidable, finds particularly clear and complete expression in Ernest Psichari's novel, *L'Appel des armes,* published in 1913. Significantly, Psichari dedicated his novel to Péguy.[30] Ironically, both men died on active service within a few weeks of the outbreak of a war which they had accepted with enthusiasm and high hopes. Two days before his death Psichari wrote confidently to his mother: 'Nous allons certainement à de grandes victoires et je me repens moins que jamais d'avoir désiré la guerre qui était nécessaire à l'honneur et à la grandeur de la France.'[31]

Psichari, born in 1883, was a grandson of Renan. He was brought up in the secular, republican tradition and initially shared many of the intellectual attitudes, and some of the scepticism, associated with his grandfather's name. He was also a progressive and a fervent *dreyfusard* like Péguy. He inclined towards humanitarian socialism and taught for a time in the working-class *universités populaires.* Around the age of twenty, however, he underwent a deep personal crisis, led a miserable existence for something like two years, and eventually sought a solution to his difficulties by joining the army in 1905 and serving in Africa. While in the army he began to wrestle with religious problems

and after a lengthy intellectual struggle he was finally converted to
Roman Catholicism in 1913. This latter phase of his life was given
fictional form in his posthumously published novel *Le Voyage du
centurion* (1915). While we now think of Psichari as above all a deeply
conservative and traditionalist defender of the army and the church, it is
well to remember that he arrived at this position in spite of his background rather than on account of it. He is one of a considerable list of
French intellectuals – already mentioned above – who underwent a
dramatic religious and intellectual transmutation in the face of the
prevailing secular orthodoxies of the Third Republic in the period
before 1914.

L'Appel des armes is the story of Maurice Vincent, the son of a
pacifist and anticlerical village schoolmaster. In part through the
influence of an older friend, a regular army officer Captain Nangès,
Maurice eventually joins the army despite his father's opposition. He
serves in North Africa, is wounded, and returns to France with a
pension and a part-time job in a government ministry in Paris. The
novel clearly reflects the main intellectual currents in France at the
period, including a strong sense of generational conflict. Vincent *père*
is the archetypal Third Republic *instituteur*: rationalist, republican,
antimilitarist, anticolonialist, and anticlerical. The nineteen year-old
Maurice has naturally been brought up to accept these ideas, but his
friendship with Nangès awakens hitherto dormant ideas and emotions.
Maurice is moved by the account which Nangès gives of his experiences
of war in the Sudan and is strongly and spontaneously attracted by the
austere and disciplined way of life which he describes, as well as by the
idea of military glory. This experience naturally sets up an inner
conflict in Maurice and he fights against these new thoughts and
feelings: 'Mais aussitôt il se reprenait, s'indignait de ce mouvement du
cœur et, en bon élève, maudissait la guerre.'[32] Two pages later,
although impressed by Nangès's simplicity and moral strength, he
reminds himself that his response to such 'medieval' ideas is thoroughly
unhealthy. Nevertheless he has given clear signs of being what Psichari
calls an *âme choisie,* and after a protracted struggle he enlists.

Psichari obviously regarded this conflict between the generations as
being of the utmost importance and he makes a number of interesting
comments on it. We shall see below that it was also the phenomenon
which Massis and Tarde investigated in 1912. Indeed, it seems essential
to any understanding of the attitude of so many young intellectuals of
military age in 1914. In *L'Appel des armes* Psichari points out, for
example, the surprising reversal of roles at the heart of the conflict

since it is the young man, Maurice, who eventually defends tradition while his father appears as the more 'liberal' and 'progressive' figure. And Psichari comments: 'Ainsi l'ordre ordinaire des facteurs se trouvait-il renversé, le père se disant nouveau, et l'enfant, au contraire, faisant office de vieil homme' (p. 163).[33] This is partly explained by the fact (according to Psichari) that many of the ideals expressed by Vincent *père* and his generation are no longer living ideas rooted in genuine emotional and intellectual conviction. Maurice finds, for example, that his father 'parla longuement de l'armée, et il put le faire sans qu'un mot original, qui vint de son âme à lui, effleurât ses lèvres' (pp. 166-7). The rebelliousness of youth is therefore stimulated by the unconvincing (because only half-heartedly held) doctrines of its elders. Furthermore, because these latter doctrines are liberal and rationalist in appearance, the natural rebellion of the younger generation will be in the direction of what is seen by its parents as illiberalism and irrationality. The materialism of the middle-aged, apparently inseparable from their rational liberalism, made this generational reversal of roles all the more inevitable.

Again, Psichari inevitably regarded the progressive ideas of his elders, and not least the increase in pacifism, as certain to undermine the moral fabric of the country, to make it unprepared to meet approaching dangers, and generally to bring about a decadent state of affairs characterized by abdications, defections, defeats, and 'l'affaissement progressif et irrécusable des vieilles vertus' (p. 207). There can be no doubt that some of the most articulate members of the 'generation of 1914' held these views in total sincerity and regarded the army as the only source of national salvation. Psichari expresses them most directly in a curious dreamlike passage late in the novel when Nangès, at a moment of exhaustion in the desert, appears to meet the spirit of Lieutenant Timoléon d'Arc, a minor character in Vigny's *Servitude et grandeur militaires*. In the course of their conversation Nangès says:

Ce que l'armée a été pour vous, Monsieur, elle l'est aujourd'hui pour beaucoup de Français. Beaucoup ont ressenti l'ennui de vivre 'dans un monde trop vieux', – comme c'est vrai: 'Où trouver, se disaient-ils, une raison d'être? Où trouver un règle, une loi? Où trouver, dans le désordre de la cité, un temple encore debout?' Ils cherchaient, en tâtonnant, une grande pensée. Avec plus de foi, ils seraient entrés au cloître. Mais aujourd'hui les cloîtres servent de musées. J'ai connu ces heures-là. (pp. 306–7)

In other words, the army and army life are a kind of surrogate church and religion for those like Psichari who, at this stage, was not ready to embrace the Christian faith. Indeed, like Vigny whose spirit presides over so much of *L'Appel des armes,* Psichari argued for renewed belief in what Sainte-Beuve, referring to Vigny, termed 'une antique vertu chevalresque'.[34] Hence the crucial importance for Psichari at this time of military values and virtues.

Psichari's view of the army, then, is coloured by his need to possess a faith and to find an institution which will impose a rule of life and combat decadence. Belief and authority, one might say, shape his conception of military life. As Micheline Tison-Braun puts it: 'Il a fait de l'armée un objet de vénération et de la discipline militaire la base d'une éthique.'[35] Hence the doctrine preached by Nangès, and absorbed by Maurice Vincent, which emphasizes an ethical and indeed a semi-religious interpretation of the soldier's profession. Because of the sense in which 'l'armée est un article de foi' (p. 22), militarism and monasticism are not far apart in Psichari's thinking. As his experience of military life grows, Maurice increasingly sees links between the symbols of sword and cross, *ense et cruce,* which become 'auréolés de surnaturels rayons' (p. 168).

One is reminded of monasticism by Psichari's conception of the army as a serious and austere way of life inspired by 'une sorte de mysticisme singulier'. The soldier is presented as a kind of secular monk who accepts a hard, repetitive routine because he is in love with certain moral absolutes and believes in a 'mystérieuse destinée'. He also recalls the monk in the sense that he seeks no material recompense. His satisfaction is derived from a consciousness of duties performed and honour obeyed. In short, asceticism and adherence to enduring values characterize what is best in the army as in the church. The outlook attributed to Nangès early in the novel sums up these points:

Il sentait qu'il représentait une grande force du passé, la seule – avec l'Église – qui restât vierge, non souillée, non décolorée par l'impureté nouvelle. Les soldats ne sont pas des hommes de progrès. Le cœur n'a pas changé, ni les principes, ni la doctrine. Cette pureté, cette simplicité barbares qui sont à eux et leur bien, Nangès les retrouvait là, merveilleusement préservées de toute contamination. Le progrès, c'est une des formes de l'américanisme, et l'américanisme le dégoûtait.
– Ce n'est pas difficile, le progrès, disait-il. Je n'admire pas. Ce qui est difficile, au contraire, c'est de rester pareil, d'être le roc battu de tous les orages, mais qui reste debout et qu'aucun ouragan n'ébranlera. (pp. 32–3)

There are other aspects which suggest parallels between the ideal soldier and the ideal man of religion. Both perform a vocation rather than a profession and therefore the apparent servitude which their way of life demands is in fact a form of deep, inner freedom and fulfilment. Again, both live in a world which largely rejects, or is indifferent to, their values and beliefs. But in Psichari's view they conserve a precious heritage of moral truth, living not by secondhand ideas suggested by the prevailing intellectual fashion but by authentic ideas which they have found and tested in their own experience. Not least, the ideal soldier and the ideal monk are prepared, should it prove necessary, to die for their ideals. Indeed, Psichari seems to suggest that death for a noble cause is the crowning glory of the soldier's life.

This last point leads inevitably to the question of war. Psichari has no desire to avoid the subject. On the contrary, he makes it the central issue of an important debate between two of his fictional officers as they carry out their duties in the North African desert. One of them, nicknamed 'le Marsouin', is prepared to fulfil his duty as a soldier, but he makes it clear that he is not one of those who actively desire war; he is much too conscious of 'toutes les misères' and 'les conséquences effroyables' which a future war will inevitably entail. Another officer, Labastière, takes the opposing view and has no difficulty in accusing le Marsouin of apparent illogicality. Le Marsouin, he says, accepts every aspect of military training yet he is opposed to its unique and ultimate purpose which is war. 'Vous posez gaillardement des prémisses, mais la conclusion vous effraie' (p. 303). The lengthy debate which is carried on at this point suggests two things. It shows us that Psichari understood the case against war, particularly a war of aggression, and that he was not prepared, like some of his contemporaries, to dismiss this case out of hand. But it also suggests that Psichari held the case in favour of war to be of such importance that he was determined to set it out in a detailed argument rather than assert it dogmatically. As we know, he came down clearly on the side of war – and particularly of war against what he held to be an aggressive, expansionist and barbaric Germany. This is clear from his correspondence and is reflected generally in *L'Appel des armes* as well as by such specific phrases as 'la guerra qui purifiera' or 'la guerre qui sera sainte' (pp. 115, 116). Later in the novel Nangès recalls the phrase by Joseph de Maistre – 'la guerre est divine' – and Psichari comments: '. . . il s'apercevait que, vraiment, de toutes les choses divines qui nous restent, celle-là est la plus divine, la plus marquée du sceau divin. Et elle est la plus inaccessible dans son essence, et aussi elle est la plus voisine des puissances cachées qui nous mènent' (p. 314). If the first sentence here strikes us nowadays as unhealthy mumbo-jumbo, the second sentence suggests the argument, still widely used, that war is good in so far as it gives natural expression to inherent human aggression. Psichari's defence of war, however, depends mainly on his semi-religious, mystical view of the military condition which we have already briefly described. His basic argument, as expressed by Labastière in his debate with le Marsouin, is that a clear distinction must be recognized between what is moral for the nation and what is moral for the army. As Labastière puts it: 'La morale applicable à la nation ne l'est pas à l'armèe. Les principes qui valent pour l'une ne valent pas pour l'autre. L'armée comporte en elle-même sa morale, sa loi et sa mystique' (p. 197).

The quite unacceptable applications to which this distinction has sometimes given rise hardly need to be pointed out. The purpose here is not to argue against Psichari's ideas – or indeed to defend them – but to understand their nature and therefore to understand something of his militarist ideals. These were widely accepted in 1914 before their practical consequences had become part of the experience of several million men. It is worth adding, however, that Psichari was writing from the viewpoint of the professional soldier. The later widespread antagonism to the ideas he represents came primarily from men who were civilians temporarily caught up in a war. Also, it is only fair to say that he allows le Marsouin to point out the dangers of 'césarisme' or military dictatorship inherent in such a doctrine (p. 203). The fact remains, however, that Psichari accepted the risks contained in his argument on behalf of war. Many of his contemporaries either failed to appreciate these risks or accepted them with equal determination. Hence the mixture of intense ardour and total unreality with which they set out for war.

It is clear from what has just been said that much of the interest of *L'Appel des armes* lies in the fact that it embodies and dramatizes some extreme ideas of the period. But this, of course, can also be a drawback. The type of novel which attempts to give fictional expression to a set of moral absolutes is not in favour nowadays. It is likely to strike most readers as excessively contrived and unacceptably didactic. A modern critic, referring to *L'Appel des armes,* speaks of the 'ton volontiers sermonnaire' adopted by Psichari.[36] The adverb is important. There can be no doubt that Psichari wrote this novel not simply to entertain but quite deliberately to instruct and persuade his readers concerning the moral quality of military life and the necessity of war. In a letter of 1912, written before the novel was published, he described it as 'un livre d'actualité qui propose un remède pratique au mal dont nous souffrons.' He added, on the subject of the 'remedy' of war: 'Remède qui pourrait être néfaste à telle autre époque, mais qui est appropriée à ce temps-ci.'[37] Psichari seems to be saying that desperate situations demand desperate remedies and, in a way that recalls Péguy, he regards the potential menace of Germany and the decadent materialism of France as aspects of the desperate situation of his times. Hence the relevance of his insistence on austerity and the disciplined fulfilment of duty, as well as his acceptance of war. He related these two attitudes closely, insisting that inner spiritual growth, and therefore the strength to sustain war successfully, depend on hard work and unyielding austerity. This is why he regarded the aridity of the desert as a source of essential moral values. The desert imposes a way of life which he described in the novel by such words as 'simple', 'nue', 'frugale' – the antithesis of 'douceur de vivre'. One of the artistic achievements of *L'Appel des armes* is the skill with which the desert is used both as an appropriate physical backcloth and as an essential moral presence.

On 30 September 1912 Psichari wrote to Henri Massis congratulating him on a series of four articles which had appeared in the Parisian daily *L'Opinion*. These articles, written by Massis and Alfred de Tarde[38] under the joint pseudonym of 'Agathon', reported on their enquiry into the attitudes of young people in higher education. Psichari commented: 'Je tiens ces pages pour très importantes et je souhaite que tu continues cette psychologie d'une génération qui restera comme un jalon important pour la connaissance de notre époque.'[39] In the following year an expanded version was published by Agathon under the title *Les Jeunes Gens d'aujourd'hui*. It showed that this part at least of the 'generation of 1914' emphasized the need for action, regarded deeds as the criterion of morality, expressed a strong patriotism, was considerably affected by the 'catholic renaissance', and gave evidence of political realism and a ready acceptance of the likelihood of war. Psichari was moved to write enthusiastically:

Il me semble que tous les traits que tu notes doivent nous mener un jour à de la gloire guerrière, et, pour tout dire, à une revanche dont avant tout nous ne devons jamais détourner nos regards. Je le souhaite de tout mon cœur, mais il est certain qu'à ce moment-là, nous nous retournerons avec gratitude vers ceux qui auront démêlé les premiers symptômes de notre relèvement moral, encouragé nos espoirs et préparé à leur façon la victoire.[40]

These comments confirm that in 1912 Psichari saw war as both inevitable and desirable . However, while his views, and those reported by Agathon, confirm and partly explain the heroic enthusiasm of 1914, they do nothing to account for the sense of being taken unawares which was also strongly expressed at the moment of mobilization. Nevertheless, as already suggested, these two responses are not totally contradictory. They serve to remind us, indeed, that Psichari and the young men investigated by Massis and Tarde represented a minority sensibility and opinion, though an important and quickly – if briefly – influential one. The majority of the nation did not share such views or such anticipations in 1912. When war came, however, they moved rapidly towards these views under a variety of pressures. A number of such ideas were maintained on the home front, by dint of propaganda and control, but scepticism and disillusionment grew fairly rapidly at the battlefront itself.

What Massis and Tarde were claiming was something of considerable interest and importance. In their view a crucial mutation in attitudes and ideas was taking place among the intellectual élite of the nation aged between eighteen and twenty-five. These young people looked upon their fathers as representing a generation that had betrayed the highest values of French culture, had yielded to the worst features of materialism, was sceptical, lacking in ideals, and cut off from genuine experience by an abstract intellectualism. Generational conflict is hardly unusual, but as Psichari was pointing out around this same period it was unusual for the younger generation to stand so firmly for a return to many traditional (and sometimes intellectually disreputable) values such as those of discipline and authority. Here again one must remember that the enquiry by Agathon was limited to young intellectuals of mainly middle-class origins. And it is important to add that Massis and Tarde were perfectly well aware of this themselves. They wrote in their introduction: 'Il ne s'agit ici que de la jeunesse cultivée . . . de la jeunesse d'élite', and added that an enquiry among 'ceux des ateliers, des faubourgs et des champs' might have given very different results.[41] Nevertheless, they justified their procedure by arguing that this was a case where quality was more significant than quantity. They took the view that it is always the doctrine of an intellectual élite which gradually filters down to the masses and becomes accepted by them. The process is usually a slow one, but in this case its rhythm was suddenly accelerated by the actuality of war. It is worth adding, perhaps, that while Massis and Tarde reported rather than explained the phenomenon into which they enquired, the accuracy of their observations was not denied even by their most distinguished opponents such as Romain Rolland and Martin du Gard.[42]

Les Jeunes Gens d'aujourd'hui is an early and non-quantified example of the now familiar opinion poll. The fact that it has survived as a significant document, as against a whole series of *enquêtes* being carried out around the same period, is largely due to the approach of its joint authors.[43] Massis, born in 1886, was all but a member of the generation which he was analysing. Tarde, born in 1880 and holding rather different views, was distinctly more detached. Massis was inclined to colour enquiry with advocacy. Tarde approached the whole question from the less emotional position of a professional social psychologist. Massis was tempted to mould opinion. Tarde was concerned to measure it.[44] Their joint effort resulted in a piece of reporting which combined liveliness with a considerable degree of accuracy.

This collaboration between Massis and Tarde had already proved successful in 1911 when they published their *L'Esprit de la Nouvelle Sorbonne* under the same pseudonym of 'Agathon'. Here, in common with Péguy and others, they accused the Sorbonne of falling into the worst forms of Germanic pedantry, of poisoning France with Germanic ideas generally, and of failing to provide intellectual and moral leadership for the youth of the nation. It was to this youth that they now turned in *Les Jeunes Gens d'aujourd'hui,* claiming that young people were severely critical of their academic teachers and were saying in effect:

A cet âge où l'on est avide de notions dont on puisse faire de la vie, alors que nous cherchions dans nos maîtres le prestige d'une autorité spirituelle, leur demandant de nous découvrir à nous-mêmes, qu'avons-nous trouvé? Une science vide qui ne tenait compte que des besoins de l'intelligence, un matérialisme pédant, une investigation sceptique qui abîme et diminue. (p. 57)

This is one general expression of the gap between the generations which Massis and Tarde emphasized by picking out five main characteristic ideas or attitudes of their young contemporaries.

The first of these attitudes is the taste for action shown by the new generation. Their fathers, according to Agathon, were a prey to self-doubt, humiliation and pessimism in the wake of the events of 1870. The older generation also experienced an irreducible conflict between thought and action. The claim now made is that the new generation had broken through this apparent contradiction and achieved a synthesis between being and doing. They had come to regard the world as an arena containing obstacles to be overcome by active effort and not simply 'thought out of existence' by ironical reduction. Agathon says of these young men: 'La seule spéculation digne d'intérêt, à leur gré, est celle qui dit: "Qu'y a-t-il à faire?" et "Comment faut-il le faire?" ' (pp. 20–1). In one of the various appendices to *Les Jeunes Gens d'aujourd'hui* an *agrégation* candidate is quoted as saying of his fellows and himself: 'Nous préférons les réalités du sentiment et de l'action aux idées abstraites et aux systèmes' (p. 155).

The second attitude singled out as characterizing the new generation is one of patriotic enthusiasm. Around the turn of the century humanitarian internationalism and antimilitarism had attracted many supporters. In particular, the universities were strongly pacifist and generally antipatriotic. After 1905, however, more and more students began to believe in the reality of 'the German menace'. A professor in Dijon is quoted as saying: 'En province comme à Paris, les sentiments de la jeunesse actuelle sont tout autres que ceux qui nous animaient à vingt ans, et le réveil de l'instinct national a remplacé la passion de tant de chimères' (p. 29). In an appendix François Poncet confirms in 1912 that while, until quite recently, the *Internationale* was often heard in the corridors of the École Normale Supérieure, the situation had changed radically; the strains of the *Internationale* had been drowned by the notes of the *Marseillaise*.

It is also Poncet who says that Agathon failed to pay enough attention to the importance of sport for the youth of the period. He describes, for example, the way in which he was dragged along by his young brother, ten years his junior, to watch a rugby match each Sunday afternoon at the Parc des Princes. He emphasizes the fact that virtually all his brother's schoolfellows were present, and we are presumably meant to understand that they were frequent participants in sport, even if they were spectators on Sunday afternoons. In fact, sport became more popular and more important after 1918, but in any case Massis and Tarde do mention it, if only rather briefly, as a feature of 1912. They also express the view that it helps to encourage and maintain the military virtues. Several of those who comment, in an appendix, on the growing enthusiasm for sport relate this fact to increasing anti-intellectualism. It seems clear that a concern with action and a turning towards patriotism, together with a very pragmatic view of morals (a third main attitude), encouraged or at least accommodated a new anti-intellectualism among the young. To some extent also, a form of anti-intellectualism was encouraged by the philosophy of Bergson. Massis and Tarde were no doubt putting the position accurately when they wrote that 'ces jeunes gens n'ont point cette ivresse de la raison pure qu'éprouvèrent leurs aînés' (p. 56). It is worth remembering, however, that this is the one aspect of the

Agathon *enquête* which greatly disturbed Psichari. In the letter to
Massis quoted earlier he wrote:

Il n'est qu'un point qui m'inquiète un peu. Cette nouvelle génération veut-elle
réellement nous proposer un idéal *à l'américaine* si éloigné du vrai génie
français? Faut-il réellement fair grand cas de ce mot affreux que tu cites: 'Mes
fils vivent très peu avec les livres'? Il me semble pourtant que tu n'es pas très loin
de cette génération que tu comprends si bien et que tu es une preuve éclatante de
ce que peut faire notre vieille culture, unie à la générosité du cœur. Dieu nous
préserve de la *vie intense* et du *rooseveltisme*. Ce serait singulièrement rabaisser
la foi patriotique que de la croire fonction de la barbarie et de l'inculture. Ce
serait aussi vouloir nous ramener au point de l'Allemagne actuelle, où tout est
sacrifié aux entreprises de la vie pratique. Ce n'est pas un idéal enviable.[45]

Massis and Tarde themselves quote other comments by Psichari,
including the following characteristic observation: 'Quoi que nous
fassions, nous mettrons toujours l'intelligence au-dessus de tout. Il est
possible que la pureté du cœur vaille mieux. Mais un Français croira
toujours que le péché est plus agréable à Dieu que la bêtise' (p. 193).

A fourth distinguishing feature of the young generation, as analysed
by Agathon, is its contribution to the revival of Roman Catholicism
taking place at this time. In the École Normale Supérieure, for
instance, something like a third of the students (i.e. around forty) were
practising catholics in 1912 as against a mere three or four ten years
earlier. The same change was evident in the Sorbonne and in such
major Parisian *lycées* as Henri IV, Louis-le-Grand, and Condorcet.
The whole atmosphere had changed dramatically from that of a
generation earlier when scientific rationalism was believed in as
'l'unique maîtresse de vérité' (p. 74). The general picture is summed
up by Agathon who emphasizes the commitment and active
conception of Christianity expressed by the young: 'Rien n'est plus
étranger à la nouvelle génération que le "mysticisme sans Dieu", la
"dévotion athée" d'un Maeterlinck, si ce n'est le dilettantisme
esthétique d'un Renan pour qui le christianisme devait cesser d'être un
dogme pour devenir une "poétique" ' (p. 90).

Finally, what Agathon calls political realism is attributed to the new
generation. The term 'realism' as used here involves both national self-
interest and a rejection of the party politics of the Third Republic. The
first of these interpretations is expressed by the insistence that 'c'est du
point de vue français que [la nouvelle génération] aborde la question
politique' (p. 94). The second is justified by the conviction that 'le
gouvernement des partis n'est que le règne de l'accident et de
l'incohérence, il s'oppose à tout dessein continu dans le

développement national, il abaisse la moralité individuelle en détruisant toute responsabilité' (pp. 94–5). Both quotations reflect the strong, underlying patriotism of the young men interviewed by Massis and Tarde. The second is reminiscent of many statements made on behalf of the *Action française* and accepted by the young monarchist members known as the *camelots du roi*. The 'political realism' singled out by Agathon seems to have involved the acceptance, if not the advocacy, of violence at home and of war abroad. Nevertheless, Massis and Tarde found that many of the students to whom they spoke were more strongly attracted by the 'democratic' violence of the syndicalists than by the 'reactionary' violence of the *Action française*.[46] Among the many who required a strong moral underpinning of their political beliefs there existed a large number who held the doctrines of the *Action française* to be politically cynical and intellectually amoral. Hence the verdict by Agathon that political realism had given rise to two distinct reactions among the young:

En résumé, le réalisme politique des jeunes gens suit deux voies divergentes: l'un, confiant dans les vertus de l'agencement politique, bâtit sur d'audacieux syllogismes une France non parlementaire, antidémocratique, logiquement ordonnée autour de la personne centrale du roi; l'autre prend son point d'appui dans les aspirations individuelles et dans le sentiment démocratique qu'il ne veut point refouler, mais redresser et élever. (pp. 109–10)

It is noticeable throughout Agathon's enquiry that it was directed towards a section of youth and not, as so often in France, towards literary intellectuals. The accent is placed on youth and the sense of a new, distinctive generation is strongly articulated. There is also an implication that the educated youth of the country is being seen more clearly as a significant element in national life. Wohl says of Massis and Tarde: 'Perhaps they intuited that youth was a social category that was increasing in number and gaining in power and prestige.'[47] As regards the literary intellectuals of the period, Wohl regards them as having been much less in touch with the prevailing mood and much less in tune with the character which it would increasingly assume: 'Writers both lacked a sense of what was going on in French society and despaired over their ability to represent social realities to a broader public.'[48]

However, once the intellectuals sensed the general post-mobilization mood of heroic enthusiasm they were quick to respond to it. Wohl says that 'everywhere in Europe intellectuals militarized themselves'[49] and R. N. Stromberg begins an article on the intellectuals and the coming of war with the statement: 'The enthusiastic approval accorded by almost all intellectuals of all sorts to the war of 1914 seems to be one of history's better kept secrets.'[50] The 'mobilization of mind and conscience' was under way and philosophers, historians, poets, novelists, and many others set out to justify their country's participation in war. They did so with a striking mixture of determination and enthusiasm. The avant-garde responded no less than the traditionalists; the political Left approved as vigorously as the political Right. Romain Rolland – one of the minority of writers who resisted the worst temptations of chauvinism – put an awkward question, directed in particular at the older generation, on 15 September 1914: 'Cette élite intellectuelle, ces Églises, ces partis ouvriers, n'ont pas voulu la guerre . . . Soit! . . . Qu'ont-ils fait pour l'empêcher? Que font-ils pour l'atténuer? Ils attisent l'incendie. Chacun y porte son fagot.'[51] In particular, Rolland brought together in an uncomfortable, even guilty, relationship the intellectuals of his own generation and the young people reported on by Agathon and now bearing the brunt of the war. He held the former to be largely responsible for the sacrifice of the latter:

Osons dire la vérité aux aînés de ces jeunes gens, à leurs guides moraux, aux maîtres de l'opinion, à leurs chefs religieux ou laïques, aux Églises, aux penseurs, aux tribuns socialistes.

Quoi! Vous aviez, dans les mains, de telles richesses vivantes, ces trésors d'héroïsme! A quoi les dépensez-vous? Cette jeunesse avide de se sacrifier, quel but avez-vous offert à son dévouement magnanime? L'égorgement mutuel de ces jeunes héros! La guerre européenne, cette mêlée sacrilège, qui offre le spectacle d'une Europe démente, montant sur le bûcher et se déchirant de ses mains, comme Hercule![52]

It was to take some time, however, for the reality of the 'égorgement mutuel' and the 'mêlée sacrilège' to break through and destroy the heroic enthusiasm of August 1914.

PART TWO

The Experience of Catastrophe

CHAPTER 2

Saying the Unsayable
Problems of Expression

Initially then, the outbreak of a major war in 1914, especially after so many years of virtual peace between the leading states of Europe, shocked the majority of the French population. They had believed in progress and trusted the capacity of human reason to avoid catastrophe. They had failed to interpret events correctly and failed, even more thoroughly, to anticipate the outcome of those events. The war, when it came, was enough to throw them – temporarily at least – off balance. As for the minority who foresaw war or welcomed it as a possibility, they too were soon to be badly shocked. If the mere fact of war did not surprise or dismay them, its horrifying reality quickly did so. Ironically, neither Péguy nor Psichari survived long enough to see the ideals of heroic chivalry destroyed by the new industrialized form of killing, but many of their contemporaries did before paying with their lives. A few individual and unorthodox thinkers had also predicted war, but had done this positively and without heroic enthusiasm. Bloy and Sorel[1] are examples, but they belonged to a much older generation (they were born in 1846 and 1847 respectively). Yet even they, despite their greater realism about the mechanized nature of a future war and the suffering and destruction which it would bring, were also taken aback by the horrors of trench warfare. In short, whatever the prior assumptions or predictions of the various groups making up French society, the Great War proved as severe a shock to the *avertis* as to the *ignorants*.

As indicated in the previous chapter, the combatants of August 1914 set out in a spirit of resolution and optimism. With the benefit of hindsight we now know how deluded they were. The war turned out to be a traumatic experience which permanently changed, or indeed destroyed, values and beliefs as well as men and materials. Nevertheless, although we are familiar enough with the view that

27

events of 1914–18 marked a social, political and moral turning-point in the history of western Europe, we are perhaps less aware of the extent to which, at a literary level, a deeply rooted and generally accepted rhetoric of warfare was quickly undermined and eventually discredited. Initially the traditional vocabulary of war – confident, patriotic, proclamatory and morally aggressive – was widely adopted. Indeed, it was the only language readily available to express such matters, and it was used by many civilians, especially politicians and journalists, as well as by the military high command and a number of writers at the front. But as the war continued, with its growing recourse to trench fighting and industrialized, mechanized slaughter, fine words and resounding phrases were increasingly called in question. Many combatants in particular found that the official, public rhetoric no longer corresponded to the truth of their experience. Various writers discovered that they were trying to convey unprecedented events and sensations armed only with a vocabulary and literary techniques fashioned for other times and other circumstances. One critic, emphasizing the peculiar difficulty experienced by writers who, in 1914, already possessed a literary past and literary habits, went on to explain: 'Ce passé, ces habitudes de penser et de composer sont comme une infirmité quand il s'agit de traiter ce sujet tout neuf: la guerre.'[2] Perhaps this is one reason why few established writers wrote well about the war while it was actually in progress. The problem behind the failure of many was the coming together of an apparently unparalleled event and of inadequate means for its formulation. It was a particularly acute problem for those who wrote under the immediate impact of events rather than in retrospect. By no means all were aware of the difficulty when it first presented itself, but with time awareness increased quite sharply.

It has been suggested several times above that the Great War was a unique event which gave rise to unparalleled human experiences. This is a view which has been widely expressed, though one must add that it has not been universally accepted. Indeed, the general concept of a totally unprecedented event has given rise to a certain amount of philosophical debate. And it happens that in France, during the three decades leading up to 1914, both Bergson and Valéry contributed to this debate, though without having the phenomenon of war specifically in mind.

Bergsonism emphasizes the uniqueness of each moment of experience.[3] Bergson posited singularity but argued that it could be grasped by the faculty which he called 'intuition'. He saw intuition as the means of penetrating beyond the disturbing novelty of certain phenomena to an understanding of their individual uniqueness. Thus uniqueness should not leave the observer nonplussed. He has the means of understanding it and, presumably, of expressing it. This last point suggests, where war fiction is concerned, that the early war novelists were not faced with a totally incommunicable situation. They had simply not yet discovered the means, which existed somewhere, of expressing the unprecedented nature of their experience.

Valéry, on the other hand, was sceptical about the existence of genuine uniqueness and regarded Bergsonian intuition as an aberration. The strict rationalist within him posited a system of rationally deducible laws which would account for apparent singularity. In 1941, in *Mauvaises Pensées et autres,* he stated categorically: 'Ce qui ne ressemble à rien n'existe pas.'[4] His *Introduction à la méthode de Léonard de Vinci* (1895) had taken a fundamentally similar view. He described the world and the individual's experience of it as 'irrégulièrement semé de dispositions régulières.' It is this underlying regularity which allows the cognitive faculty (which he put in the place of Bergsonian intuition) to work by means of precedent and parallel. Valéry added a few lines later: 'Les événements les plus surprenants et les plus *asymétriques* par rapport au cours des instants voisins, rentrent dans un semblant d'ordre par rapport à de plus vastes périodes.'[5] This suggests that what appears to be unprecedented can be accounted for and related to the past provided a sufficiently long perspective is adopted. The 'événement neuf' can ultimately be reduced to a dimension of continuity and analysed in terms which link it to prior events. It has been suggested that Valéry modified this rejection of singularity in the marginal comments which he added to the text of the *Introduction* in 1930. The following comment certainly appears to suggest a change of attitude: 'L'isolé, le singulier, l'individuel sont inexplicables, c'est-à-dire n'ont d'expression qu'eux-mêmes.' Valéry gives the impression here that he later came to the conclusion that the unprecedented *does* exist and that it cannot be explained or expressed. Such a view would seem to be at variance with his categorical statement of 1941 already quoted. It is possible that he simply changed his ideas. But it is also not implausible to suggest that the 1930 comment was made in terms of mathematics, and particularly of mathematical incommensurability, not in terms of human experiences. There is a reference immediately afterwards to the problem of prime numbers.

In a comment on the views expressed by Bergson and Valéry, A. E. Pilkington writes: 'Valéry accepts that a high degree of complexity or novelty might prove refractory to reduction, by analysis, into elements of continuity and thus is *nominally* in limited agreement with Bergson; but he would maintain that singularity, if it is not knowable by analysis, is not knowable at all since he rejects the possibility of an appeal to intuition and empathy, central to Bergson's thought.'[6] The distinction here is an important one and we may have to agree, despite what was said earlier and despite the belief of many combatants themselves, that the Great War was unprecedented only in the loose sense of 'a high *degree* of complexity or novelty'. It was not unprecedented in the strict and absolute sense of 'singularity'. This means that the casualties were unprecedented only in the sense of being *quantitatively greater* than in previous wars; that the applied technology of killing was unprecedented only in the sense of being *more efficient and sophisticated* than in previous wars; that the reduction of individuals to numbers and objects was unprecedented only in the sense of being *more intense and widespread* than in previous wars.[7] In all these cases, the term unprecedented paradoxically implies a comparison. It therefore offers a basis for the wider perspective of continuity posited by Valéry. And continuity, however violent the degrees of change which it includes, can be expressed intellectually in terms of parallels, affinities, and approximations.

The Great War may not therefore have been 'unique', in the strictest sense of the term. But such aspects as the bloodshed, the applied technology and the reduction of men to mere ciphers were certainly more intense and more dramatic than in earlier wars. More importantly, the war of 1914–18 was *perceived* as an unprecedented event by the writers who fought in it precisely because there was no point of reference in their own prior experience to which it could be related. Some writers were tempted to ignore the distinction between perception and actuality and made sweeping claims. Jacques Rivière, for example, captured three weeks after the outbreak of war, wrote while still a prisoner: 'Rien de comparable entre la guerre actuelle et aucune de celles qui ont précédé.'[8] Léon Werth, in his pacifist novel *Clavel soldat,* took a less absolutist, more comparative view when he referred to the Great War as being 'loin de l'époque où les dangers de la guerre semblaient une généreuse aventure.'[9] However, whether or not they claimed total uniqueness for the war in which they fought, most writers tended to single out three features which they thought non-combatants would find it difficult to grasp adequately.

First there was the scale of the killing. In novels like *L'Appel du sol* of Bertrand or *Le Feu* by Barbusse, almost all the characters are eventually killed, often in a horrifying way. Piles of rotting corpses, hideously and grotesquely distorted by violent death, litter the landscape of war fiction. In fact, very heavy casualties occurred from an early stage. Although it is impossible to obtain precise figures, there is general agreement that the total number of deaths from military action, massacre, and starvation was something over 12.5 million. In France in particular 8.41 million citizens were mobilized between 1914 and 1918. Of these, 1.35 million were killed, and the minimum figure for missing and wounded is 3.5 million. The total of French dead, wounded, and missing was therefore at least 60 per cent of those mobilized. The corresponding percentages for Britain and Germany were 37 and 41 per cent. One is largely justified, where France is concerned, in speaking of a whole generaton of younger men having been virtually wiped out.[10]

The nature of this blood-letting was at least as horrifying as its scale. It resulted from the application of new and increasingly sophisticated industrial techniques to warfare. Traditional war had come to an end and, as one writer put it, 'one might almost term the war an industry of professionalized human slaughter.'[11] The machinery of killing and maiming became more and more effective. The 'machine-made horror of modern war' was born.[12] On the German side Ernst Toller expressed clearly the significance of the experience for those who fought at the front:

Instead of escaping the soul-killing mechanism of modern technological society, they learned that the tyranny of technology ruled even more omnipotently in war than in peace-time. The men who through daring chivalry had hoped to rescue their spiritual selves from the domination of material and technical forces discovered that in the modern war of material the triumph of the machine over the individual is carried to its most extreme form.[13]

Ironically, a society which had put its trust in materialism suffered a fearful fate at the hands of technological weaponry. The 'nature and scale of modern industry was asserted in the most unmistakable and belligerent terms.'[14] Alain, in *Mars ou la guerre jugée,* was to refer several times to what he called 'ce massacre mécanique'.

Léon Bloy had warned of these developments some years previously. He wrote: 'L'évolution moderne du monde, ce fut, et c'est chaque jour davantage, sa matérialisation, sa *mécanisation* progressive.'[15] In 1910 he had been scornful of the view that the aeroplane would prove to be, exclusively, an 'engin de paix'.[16] He saw the industrialized killing of 'le matériel humain' on the Western Front as the inevitable outcome of mechanization and materialism. Hence his prophetic reference in 1912 to 'cette guerre à laquelle nulle autre n'aura ressemblé'.[17]

What appeared to be without parallel – and what was emphasized by many writers – was the exposure of fragile human flesh to factory-produced metal travelling at high velocity. Appalling wounds and appalling deaths were a daily occurrence. One is reminded of T. E. Hulme writing from the trenches in 1916 and describing the psychological effects of ninety minutes' exposure to continuous shelling: 'It's not the idea of being killed that's alarming, but the idea of being hit by a jagged piece of steel.'[18] Novels of the period turned to such consciously literary images as 'une averse de fer', 'une pluie d'acier', 'un rideau de plomb'. Many memoirs emphasized the exposure of 'unaccommodated man' to 'expériences disproportionnées à la résistance humaine'[19] and underlined the 'effroyable disproportion entre les engins de mort et les petits soldats dont le système nerveux n'est pas à la hauteur de telles secousses.'[20] Shell-shock, and eventually gas-poisoning, became new hazards and new forms of suffering.[21]

In the face of such experiences the 'baptême du feu' became a *locus classicus* of wartime fiction. Adrien Bertrand's novel *L'Appel du sol,* serialized in *La Revue des Deux Mondes* of 1916 and published in book form in the same year, refers to the baptism of fire early in the first chapter. A company of *chasseurs alpins,* newly arrived at the front and subjected to heavy shelling for the first time, is ordered to lie flat on the ground. The men's reactions, uncertain and inexperienced, are closely observed:

On avait soif, on avait la gorge serrée; personne ne parlait. Les hommes ne savaient même pas ce qu'ils ressentaient. Ils tâchaient seulement d'habituer leur oreille à distinguer l'endroit où éclaterait l'engin. Un ou deux malheureux atteints par quelque éclat s'étaient levés, hurlant, pour s'éloigner. Ils avaient été recouchés à jamais par l'averse de fer. Cela avait servi de leçon. On ne remuait plus. Certains avaient des crampes. D'autres se croyaient blessés à la jambe, au bras; ils se tâtaient avec la main, mais sans oser faire de geste, prudemment. La section, étendue sur la plaine, semblait la carapace d'une tortue.[22]

These are men learning the difficult art of survival among wholly unfamiliar dangers. The total unpreparedness of a regular officer, Capt. Nicolaï, is emphasized a few pages later:

Nicolaï ne lui répondit pas. Ces obus, venus de si loin, le déconcertaient. Il connaissait à fond son métier. Jamais il n'eût pensé qu'on pût employer contre des troupes de l'artillerie lourde. Les Allemands inauguraient là une tactique nouvelle, qui l'inquiétait . . .
– Nous n'avons prévu l'emploi de canons lourds que contre les fortifications.[23]

The scale and the nature of the Great War, both experienced as unparalleled at the time, produced a further striking result. Individuals were reduced to the status of units in a complex logistic exercise. In this way a pre-war social and political tendency, clear to a minority of observers only, was confirmed and eventually dramatized. Léon Bloy, in the passage in which he noted the increasing materialism and mechanization of Europe, had also pointed to what he regarded as the growing menace of 'machines, rouages, agencement, administration, État'. These features were becoming, in his view, an integral part of a society yielding more and more to the demands of collectivism and the corporate state. Like Péguy, he saw them as the outcome of replacing God by Man – a process which paradoxically reduced ordinary individuals to the level of objects manipulated by corporate forces.

In 1914 this process was temporarily legitimized and permanently intensified by the phenomenon of total war. The Great War was the first manifestation of such total war. It was a new experience in the sense that it involved the mobilization of whole nations, rather than the deployment of relatively small and largely professional armies. And national mobilization meant the mass organization of individuals, their distribution within a set of sharply defined hierarchies, their ultimate existence as numbers and material rather than persons. Ten years before the outbreak of war Péguy had pointed to the dehumanization of man. He wrote: 'C'est justement à l'âge où l'homme croit être émancipé, à l'âge où l'homme croit s'être débarrassé de tous les dieux que lui-même il ne tient plus à sa place d'homme.'[24] For Péguy, in short, western man was rapidly undergoing the striking experience of dehumanization by humans. In the event, and predictably, human reason and political will proved incapable of preventing war. And war itself was increasingly responsible for reducing people to the level of *effectifs* and *matériel.*

This phenomenon is again frequently referred to in the literature of the war. Adrien Bertrand more or less accepted the fact that individuals had become 'les instruments involontaires de la volonté nationale' and that 'ils avaient perdu leur individualité; ils n'étaient plus qu'une cellule de la nation.'[25] More sharply and critically, in 1917 (the year of the army mutinies), Pierre Chaine wrote in *Les Mémoires d'un rat:* 'Le chef-d'œuvre de l'organisation consiste à faire accomplir par la collectivité ce à quoi chacun de ses membres en particulier répugne le plus.'[26] And Alain, looking back at a later date at his own war experience in the ranks, regarded the military machine itself as more profoundly destructive than the new array of arms which it deployed. He argues that the automatism of discipline and the experiences of mass living and mass emotions ensured that individual personality was the real victim of war.

In terms, then, of scale, intensity and collective pressure – the killing and maiming both of bodies and of individual personalities – the Great War was a unique experience, particularly for the mass of participants who were civilian volunteers or conscripts rather than regular soldiers. These civilian participants, suddenly translated from a normal existence to the total abnormality of the Western Front, included many writers and artists. They naturally reacted to this experience in different ways. Their attitudes developed along different lines and according to different rhythms. But whatever their response, they were obliged to seek or to invent forms that would enable them to convey the essence of their experience to those not directly involved. It is significant that the writers whom we find unreadable today are exclusively those who recognized no problem or who believed that unprecedented suffering could be satisfactorily expressed in terms of a traditional heroic and chivalric nineteenth-century rhetoric.[27]

It is impossible to summarize briefly or accurately the impact made by the unforeseen nature of the war from 1916 well into the 1920s. What one can say is that it burst upon a society which had growing confidence in the values of rationalism, progress, and general humanist reassurance. Many had come to accept the secular faith of man in man, based on trust in 'a luminous intelligence that selected and controlled and did not allow itself to be overwhelmed.'[28] The fact of war, especially in terms of mechanized killing and the massacre of a generation, threw this faith into total disarray at the level of immediate, personal experience. Stanley Cooperman writes with some justice: 'The experts were suddenly proved wrong by events which shattered the certainty of progress, introduced technological slaughter, manipulated mass propaganda to justify mass death, and produced a collective trauma such as the world had never known.[29]

This 'collective trauma', both as psychological experience and literary challenge, pervades fiction written contemporaneously with the war and constitutes much of its interest and value. If most of these novels lack the artistic quality of some later works, they gain in immediacy and authenticity, unhampered by hindsight and accumulated abstractions. It has rightly been said that 'we cannot understand the effect of World War I on literature, and the effect of World War I literature on the reading public, by limiting ourselves to the more objective work produced at the end of the twenties and during the early thirties'.[30] One is reminded of the argument and insight offered by Péguy in connection with painting. On the subject of Monet's famous series of water-lily paintings, Péguy asks the question whether the first or the last paintings of the series are the better and then gives his own answer: 'Le mouvement logique serait de dire: le dernier, parce qu'il savait (le) plus. Et moi, je dis: au contraire, au fond, le premier, *parce qu'il savait (le) moins.*'[31] In a similar way it may be argued that the early war fiction, written primarily as authentic testimony rather than intellectual analysis, has a power of conviction at the level of direct human experience which retrospective war novels lack. This makes it particularly distinctive and valuable and, in a certain sense, particularly 'true'.

The experience of 'technological slaughter', and the attempt to provide adequate literary expression for it, came together in 1914–18 in part because so many established or aspiring writers were involved in the actual fighting.[32] The literary dimension to the war was pointed out on a number of occasions and Edmund Gosse suggested an explanation:

No doubt, the reason why this has been, for France, so peculiarly a literary war, is that the mechanical life in the trenches, alternately so violent and so sedentary, has greatly enforced the habit of sustained contemplation based on a vivid and tragic experience. This has encouraged, and in many instances positively created, a craving for literary expression, which has found abundant opportunity for its exercise in letters, journals and poems; and what it has particularly developed is a form of literary art in which Frenchmen above all other races have always excelled, that analysis of feeling which has been defined as 'le travail de ciselure morale'.[33]

In fact, the number of authentic novels and collections of short stories written during and about the war is something around thirty. In the nature of the case it is often difficult to separate personal memoirs and genuine fiction.

If one were to accept H. M. Tomlinson's claim that 'the test for a book about the war is the same as for any other book',[34] most of these novels would have to be regarded as second-rate. In fact, Tomlinson was writing at the beginning of the 1930s and largely had in mind novels written at that time – not those written under the immediate impact of events. Novelists writing between 1914 and 1918 faced particular problems and the purpose of what follows here is to understand the nature of these problems rather than to pass critical judgement on individual novels.

Prior to what might be called the technical difficulties of writing about the Great War, there is a moral problem which the events of 1914–18 posed with some severity. To many who experienced the actual fighting there seemed to be something indecent in using the wholesale killing and maiming of their comrades as the subject-matter of an artistic exercise. Dorgelès, for instance, although he had accumulated a vast pile of notes ('déjà plus épais qu'un Bottin') and had written several chapters of his novel by 1916, did not publish *Les Croix de bois* until 1919. He commented later: 'Nous étions trop écrasés par la guerre pour l'envisager comme une matière de littérature' and he added, referring to his comrades: '. . . j'aurais eu honte de faire des phrases avec leur agonie, d'exploiter leurs souffrances, de trahir leurs secrets.'[35] There is no inconsistency, of course, in Dorgelès's unwillingness to publish a certain kind of material while the war was in progress and his readiness to make notes and write privately. He thought it appropriate to maintain a public silence of limited duration.

For many combatants indeed, the horrors they had witnessed were so terrible that they regarded a determined silence as the only decent response. Others were convinced that anything they said would either fail to convey reality adequately or would not be understood – and might indeed be misunderstood – by their hearers. Alain, for example, quotes a young soldier at the front as saying: 'Si simplement qu'on parle de la guerre, on l'orne trop; et les enfants qui nous écoutent ont toujours trop d'envie de la faire. Il vaut mieux n'en point parler.'[36] There was also a widespread and traditionalist view that the true soldier remains silent however severe his sufferings. On such grounds a sense of moral inappropriateness began to merge into a sense of literary impotence.

At the same time it would be wrong to fail to mention writers like Barbusse who reacted differently to the moral problem involved and were moved to utterance and assertion. They believed that the horrors of war must receive immediate and direct expression, however inadequate, for what were also moral reasons. Barbusse, for example, saw a need for witness and testimony in the midst of what was a propaganda war as well as a war of machine-guns and shells. For him silence would have been equivalent to a conspiracy of silence. Yet even among those who felt obliged to speak out at once, there were some (not Barbusse) who found that language as such – not simply the particular language at their disposal or the language they attempted to invent – falsified their experience of war. Alain wrote: 'Il y a donc deux guerres, celle qu'on fait et celle qu'on dit, et qui n'ont presque rien de commun. Il n'y a point de machiavélisme en cela; la difficulté de dire ce qui est nouveau par de vieux discours suffit bien.'[37] In the particular circumstances of the Great War, then, language often appeared to betray the dead. Even those who responded to the moral problem of utterance in a very positive way faced problems of literary inadequacy.

It so happens that scepticism concerning the capacity of language to embody experience in a satisfactory way – an attitude that is quite common nowadays, not least in France – was repeatedly expressed during the twenty-five years prior to the outbreak of the Great War. As early as his *Essai sur les données immédiates de la conscience* of 1889 Bergson had pointed to the inadequacies of language. The essence of his argument (which is concerned with the everyday use of language rather than with language as fashioned by outstandingly gifted writers) is that words, because they are a public medium, are an inadequate vehicle for the expression of private experience. In effect, ordinary language reduces individual experience to the lowest common denominator of public generalization and abstraction. When public medium and private experience come together in words, the former dominates to the disadvantage of the latter, except in the case of quite outstanding artists. Bergson puts the matter clearly when he writes: '. . . nos perceptions, sensations, émotions et idées se présentent sous un double aspect: l'un net, précis, mais impersonnel; l'autre confus, infiniment mobile, et inexprimable, parce que le langage ne saurait le saisir sans en fixer la mobilité, ni l'adapter à sa forme banale sans le faire tomber dans le domaine commun.'[38] This explains, at least in part, why the war memoirs of so many combatants, though provided with a subject-matter that was immediate, authentic and dramatic, strike one as surprisingly flat and inadequate. It may also explain the existence in so many of the early novels of stock situations, stock images and stock characters which vary little from one author to

another. And this same abstracting and generalizing tendency of
language, with its bias towards the public and away from the private,
made war propaganda an easier undertaking than truth-telling about
war.

In *Le Rire* of 1900 Bergson made more allowance for the
potentialities of literary language. He accepts that words can be so
arranged as to convey things beyond the reach of 'le mot banal et
social'. The war novelist, to the extent that he seeks to convey a moral
response to exceptional personal experiences, must find an adequate
balance between a banal, social language and a personal, artistic one.
Once he decides to write, which is itself a moral decision, he must bear
witness, communicate publicly, convey a personal truth and pursue
authenticity. To choose a wholly public language is to accept banal
generalities about war. To opt for a strictly private or experimental
rhetoric – as Apollinaire did in a number of his *Calligrammes* – may
be to sacrifice moral persuasion to aesthetic distinctiveness. This is the
dilemma which must explain, at least in part, why there have been so
few genuinely great modern war novels. To write a war novel of
outstanding quality requires both skilful, accurate reporting and the
capacity to demonstrate the superiority of art over journalism in terms
of ultimate truth. This is a challenge which the early war novelists in
particular were mostly unable to meet psychologically, morally, or
artistically. Many of them had a deep emotional commitment to
convey the horrible truth of war in as direct, journalistic, and public a
manner as possible. And most of them were in any case either too
inexperienced or insufficiently gifted as writers to meet the highest
challenge of artistic truth.

It is significant, then, that war fiction between 1914 and 1918 began
predominantly in terms of testimony and direct reportage. It was only
very slowly that it began to display major literary concerns. The
wartime novelists were mainly anxious to provide grounds for an
affirmative answer to the question: is my work true? By 'true', of
course, they meant: does it evoke the concrete experience of this war in
an adequate manner, and does it thereby provoke reflection, and
possibly action, on the part of the reader? Only later was this question
fundamentally modified to read: is this a great novel artistically
speaking?[39]

Apart from the moral problem involved in writing about war, and
the more general problem of language, there is a third difficulty which
might be termed the absence of an appropriate literary tradition. In a
passage quoted above Alain referred to the disjunction between 'ce qui

est nouveau' and 'vieux discours'. Nevertheless, despite the inappropriateness, many who underwent the totally new experience of trench warfare and industrialized slaughter, and who had literary interests or aspirations, turned instinctively to a French tradition of writing about war. Among their nineteenth-century predecessors alone, such authors as Stendhal, Vigny, Hugo, Mérimée, and Zola offered them points of reference in the midst of emotional disorientation.[40] This is one way of explaining, without cynicism, why a number of writers proceeded to describe the war having asserted that it was indescribable. Literary parallels and literary echoes contrived to give their experience something like that dimension of continuity of which Valéry had written. There is perhaps a principle here which enables us to divide wartime novelists into two distinct categories – those who subordinated their experience to an existing literary tradition and those who attempted to modulate the tradition in order to serve their experience better. The two categories can be represented by Bertrand and Barbusse respectively.

Bertrand's *L'Appel du sol* and Barbusse's *Le Feu* were both awarded the Prix Goncourt in 1916. The two novelists started from very different moral and political assumptions in their attempt to tell the truth about war. Bertrand did not avoid the brutality or deliberately minimize the horror, but he employed a traditional and very literary 'high diction' of war writing. In *L'Appel du sol* a patriotic sense is either 'l'appel du sol' or 'l'appel de la terre française'. Death is 'le sacrifice', wounding 'le martyre', and there is a pervasive Vigny-like vocabulary: 'grandeur morale', 'acceptation résignée', 'obéissance passive', 'grand sacrifice', 'abnégation', 'mission rédemptrice', etc. Within the general tone created by this vocabulary the main characters, despite the horror of their experiences, take a high moral view both of their patriotic duty and of military discipline. In this way the effort is made to allow the unspeakable facts of the Great War to enter and inhabit as subject-matter a refined literary tradition stretching back to Homer. There are those who admire this particular mode of writing. They find within it, in contrast with much fiction of the Second World War, a fruitful and persuasive tension between rawness of experience and restraint of expression.

For others, such 'high diction' betrays the nature of war, throwing a mantle of literary and moral deceit over what is fundamentally brutal and inhuman. Barbusse largely shared this view. While poetic and moral stylization are by no means totally absent from *Le Feu,* the general aim is a naturalistic and earthy tone. Conversations, for example, are given in common speech and army slang. The theoretical consequence is to reduce the sense of 'literariness' and hence to facilitate the transition from morally disorientating experience to realistic fictional expression. Ironically, the effect is often far from naturalistic. A certain accent or dialectal colouring do not transfer easily to the printed page. The cumulative effect of many sentences of the 'qu'est-c'qu' alle dit?' or 'c'est qu'i's peuv'tent pas' variety is actually to underline the fact of literary transcription. It may well be significant that Barbusse's later war novel, *Clarté* (1919), transcribes the characters' speech in more 'literary' language.

˙ The very limited concern with language and form shown by Bertrand and Barbusse suggests that adequate fictional techniques for the transcription of their war experience did not exist in 1914. Yet this can hardly be true since the modern movement in the arts had been exploring new ways of rendering cultural change and personal alienation since the 1880s. The fact is that Bertrand and Barbusse, and indeed all the early war novelists (in contrast with such poets as Apollinaire and Jacob) had little knowledge of avant-garde experiments and little sympathy with them. Furthermore, it would seem that the pressures of war, which encouraged a strengthening of certain traditional moral values (patriotism, duty, courage, etc.), called forth a corresponding artistic traditionalism. Some temporal distance from the events themselves was to prove necessary before they could become the subject of appropriate experimentation and invention. Time had to pass to make possible a shift from a virtually exclusive preoccupation with subject-matter to a positive concern with its expression. One thinks of Céline or Jules Romains applying new techniques to writing about the war in the 1930s.

One further factor prevented a technically imaginative and original response to the war by these early novelists. This was an (understandable) failure to realize its full implications. While the fact of horror and suffering, death or maiming, was recognized early because experienced early, the full significance of these things took more time to make itself felt. Tomlinson, writing in 1930, referred to 'the greatest disturbance of mankind since the glaciers pushed our hunting forefathers down to the south.'[41] From around 1917 onwards, partly encouraged by Spengler's *Decline of the West* (1918), there was a growing feeling that the Great War marked a fundamental crisis and historical turning-point in western civilization. The consequences were drawn for language and artistic form as their status as socio-cultural creations was more widely recognized. It was felt that the significance of a disintegrating culture could not be conveyed by its own moribund art forms. A break with artistic tradition was as necessary and as inevitable as social or political change. The modern movement, particularly in the 1920s, often invoked the social and moral consequences of war to explain the inevitability of new techniques which many interpreted as leading to the 'dehumanization of art'. Malcolm Bradbury has written: 'Pre-war modernism . . . tended to modernise form as such; later modernism, after the war, tended to see the new disjunction in history too, and modernised life, man, history as well.'[42] Novelists like Bertrand and Barbusse, who attempted in their different ways to say the unsayable, inhabited as best they could the essentially traditionalist aesthetic no-man's-land between pre-war and post-war modernism.

CHAPTER 3

Critical Approaches to Great War Fiction

There is much to be said for the view that the basic function of criticism is to understand and interpret rather than to classify. If such critical priorities are accepted, a good deal can be learned from the scrutiny of writers not generally regarded as outstandingly gifted or successful. It seems clear that most of the Great War novelists who had published by 1920 come into the 'not outstandingly gifted' category. Those who responded immediately to the experience of mobilization and trench warfare did not, on the whole, produce artistically memorable writings. The few works published at this time which are still read – Barbusse's *Le Feu* (1916), Duhamel's *Vie des martyrs* (1917), or Dorgelès's *Les Croix de bois* (1919) – are admired more as moral outcry than aesthetic achievement, more as documentation than art. But the truth of the matter is that the vast majority of the novels and collections of short stories published by 1920 have long been out of print. While this situation has been created in part by changes in literary taste, much of it must also be attributed to the limited talents of most of these authors. And yet they most certainly should not be ignored, particularly if we hope to catch something of the general atmosphere and flavour of the period. To concentrate exclusively on the major writers of a given period is often simply to impose upon it a shape and a significance at variance with historical reality. The literary experience of the reading public in, say, 1914 did not coincide with what we may now consider to have been the finest literary output of the time. Furthermore, the literary response to certain events is not to be identified solely with that of the outstanding figures of the age. More commonplace reactions, or the response of run-of-the-mill writers, can be equally important and significant. If we are to get an accurate impression of a given landscape we must take account of valleys and foothills as well as of mountain peaks. It is also of importance, where the Great War is concerned, that we should not confuse the response of novelists writing in the 1930s with that of those who reacted immediately to events between 1914 and 1918. Not least, as noted in the previous chapter, the work of the latter group is made distinctive and valuable by the immediacy and authenticity which they offer and which works published later are almost bound to lack. Flawed immediacy can be more valuable testimony than flawless but detached reconstruction.

We saw in the previous chapter that the writers of 1914–18 faced particular moral and technical difficulties. The basic problem was one of finding appropriate ways of articulating experiences which, at their worst, were totally horrifying and totally unfamiliar to the participants. The scale of the casualties, the nature of the killing and wounding, the increasing assault on human flesh by industrialized technology and machine-made ingenuity, the loss of personal identity and dignity in the names of discipline and military necessity – all these things were experienced and had to be absorbed not by a small professional army but by civilians suddenly uprooted by mobilization from normal life in villages and towns. The writers among them lacked an adequate rhetoric with which to express these experiences. The traditional language of war writing was not only inadequate but inappropriate. It suggested high chivalry, the heroic trial of valour, a confidence in resounding moral absolutes. But these are precisely things which the Great War finally denied and destroyed. The phenomenon of industrialized and total war was one which required time and some detachment for its proper understanding and expression. Significantly, the most successful and admired novels of the war were almost all written in the 1920s and 1930s.[1]

It has already been suggested that some of these later novels, because of their literary skill, lack the immediacy and also the authentic imperfection of less fully realized works of the 1914–18 period. The immediate pressure of their subject-matter urged the early war novelists in the direction of documentation and witness. It was a pressure that left only limited room for conscious craftsmanship. Most writers were forced, by the requirements of authentic testimony, into an indeterminate area on the borders of autobiography and fiction. A measure of generic definition was lost, but there were gains in terms of human conviction and a sense of actuality. However, while the experience of fighting on the Western Front provided immediate and dramatic material for some established and many aspiring writers, not all were anxious to appear in print while the holocaust was still taking place. A few even regarded their experiences as inappropriate material for literary treatment and kept silence. Those who did write fall into two main categories. We saw in chapter 2 that some, like Dorgelès, were reluctant to 'exploit' their sufferings and those of their comrades.[2] They published their work when the war ended. Dorgelès's *Les Croix de bois* and Léon Werth's *Clavel soldat* both appeared in 1919. On the other hand there were writers who, for equally honourable reasons, sought publication as soon as possible in order to tell the truth to those at home and, in some cases, to counteract war propaganda.[3] Barbusse's *Le Feu* was published in 1916 and Duhamel's *Vie des martyrs* in 1917. None of these writers attempted to belittle the nightmare of the battlefield and each succeeded, in considerable measure, in the task of true testimony. The only writers who really emerge as failures are those who, through a lack of moral imagination or for propagandist reasons, used a discredited heroic rhetoric to minimize the horror and disguise the folly. It is only right to add that this type of novel, exemplified by René Benjamin's *Gaspard* (1915), was mainly a product of the early months of the fighting. This was a period when, even for many honest witnesses, the true nature and the significance of the war were still very unclear.

On the face of it the novel seems the most suitable literary form in which to give expression to the facts and conditions of war. As Holger Klein puts it: '. . . prose narrative, taking over in part the tradition of the great epics, is especially suited to the full re-creation of historical events and states of society. Moreover, as prose is the most frequently read genre of the modern era, this is the medium in which the war had its widest impact on the reading public.'[4] Nevertheless, these early war novels differed in emphasis from ordinary fiction in terms of their subject-matter and their aims. The more closely they dealt with the nature of the fighting in the trenches the more they used what might be called ready-made material. The major facts were witnessed, not invented. They resembled the traditionally heavily autobiographical 'first novel' of other writers and were in fact first novels in a number of cases. Again, their subject was a public and historical experience shared by thousands, and eventually millions, of their compatriots. Therefore the more the war became central to these works the more authenticity and actuality became required major aims. In other words there were limits, more strictly marked than in ordinary novels, to which truth could be modified or changed in the interests of art.

Two consequences affecting the form of these novels follow. One, resulting from the distinctive nature of their subject, is the repetition of certain incidents and scenes from novel to novel. Such set pieces as the baptism of fire, the infantry attack, the artillery barrage, or withdrawal from the front line recur on a number of occasions. These set pieces, in their turn, are given a common background of mud, rain, lice, barbed-wire, exhausted men, flooded trenches, and ruined villages. Such repetition, if not aesthetically exciting, may be some guarantee of truth. Again, a more significant feature, and one which must affect our critical approach, is the complex mixture of fact and fiction. It has already been pointed out that these books possess characteristics of both the war memoir and the novel (particularly when a first-person narrator is employed). It would therefore be pointless, even irrelevant, to follow the example of some commentators and apply to these works, in a rigidly normative way, those critical expectations which we bring to the analysis of ordinary novels. In fact, it is part of the interest of these narratives that they respond with what may be called generic flexibility to their subject-matter and their authors' purpose. They offer considerable justification of the present-day critical view that works should be appraised as 'texts' and not in terms of strict fidelity to a particular genre. At the level of form, therefore, a strictly genre-based approach is inappropriate. At the same time, this is not a disguised plea for a fully structuralist analysis. The case against a structuralist treatment of these texts is put clearly and firmly by Maurice Rieuneau:

. . . au risque de paraître rétrograde ou attardé, nous affirmons les plus expresses réserves vis-à-vis des théories qui veulent réduire un récit romanesque à une aventure du langage. Ceux qui ont écrit sur la guerre avaient une tout autre aventure à raconter et s'il est artificiel de distinguer une forme et un fond, il n'en est pas moins vrai que l'expérience a précédé l'écriture et l'a determinée dans sa réalité verbale et idéologique. C'est ce qui en fait, à nos yeux, l'intérêt, en dépit d'évidentes faiblesses.[5]

There is perhaps a danger or an injustice in insisting too heavily on the artistic limitations of the early war novels. It is well to remember that *Le Feu* and *Les Croix de bois,* for instance, were highly praised by many writers and both have continued to be bought and read more than sixty years after their original publication. It may be that one clue to their persistent appeal lies in their successful use of the repetitive element mentioned above. In novel after novel we find a three-part sequence consisting of anticipation of battle, experience of battle, withdrawal from battle. This cycle of anticipation, action, withdrawal — a variation on departure, quest, return — is met many times and we know that it is deeply imprinted on the human spirit. At a formal level, then, a number of war novels contain a mythic structure which has pervaded Western literature in a multitude of versions from the travels of Odysseus and quest of Orpheus to Dante's *Divine Comedy* and Bunyan's *Pilgrim's Progress*. Making a rather similar point in connection with English writing about the Great War, Paul Fussell uses one of the many valuable insights to be found in Northrop Frye's *Anatomy of Criticism:*

As Frye reminds us, a standard 'quest' has three stages: first, 'the stage of the perilous journey and the preliminary minor adventures'; second, 'the crucial struggle, usually some kind of battle in which either the hero or his foe, or both, must die'; and third, 'the exaltation of the hero, who has clearly proved himself to be a hero even if he does not survive the conflict'. It is impossible not to be struck by the similarity between this conventional 'romance' pattern and the standard experience re-enacted and formalized in memoirs of the war.[6]

There is much truth in Fussell's comment. But it is important to note that the best of the early war novelists modified this 'romance pattern' in markedly unromantic ways. Barbusse and Léon Werth probably took this tendency furthest. They transformed the crusade pursued by the hero into the chaos experienced by the victim – experienced in the mud and rain of the Western Front. But whether the tone is patriotic or pacifist, complaisant or debunking, there exists a structure to which we appear to make an instinctive response.

The presence of mythic patterns in a work should not be taken as necessary evidence of literary sophistication. Indeed, in the case of these particular novels, the basic nature of the material – individual or collective experience of modern warfare – imposed a mythic structure independently of authorial intention. There is little evidence that they consciously exploited the cycle of anticipation, action, withdrawal. We are dealing, in general, with aesthetically innocent narratives. This is a further reason why so many of them have remained out of print. They appear naïve to readers of a more knowing age whose sensibilities are attuned to ironic and oblique modes of writing. Their episodic, anecdotal style seems crude and unformed in comparison with later techniques of cross-cutting, counterpointing and general narrative control.[7] And yet it may be argued, with some justification, that the relatively simple narrative techniques of a Bertrand or a Dorgelès, a Barbusse or a Werth, convey most accurately the pre-ordained existence of the front-line soldier with its regular rhythm of fear, danger and boredom, set against a background of death and destruction.

As regards the subject-matter of these narratives, it is of course obvious that war, in common with love and death, has been a literary theme from the earliest times. Like love and death, too, it often served as a background or narrative framework against which other concerns were primarily explored. However, as Stanley Cooperman was one of the first to point out clearly, the early war novel broke with tradition under the pressure of a war which itself destroyed many precedents. With the spectacle of mass mechanized slaughter war ceased to be a narrative device and became a totally invasive narrative subject. Cooperman says: 'No longer one subordinate element among many contributing to a total aesthetic structure, environment – the war itself – became the chief protagonist; when this happened readers were left floundering in a situation where the traditional critical implements simply could not be applied.'[8] This shift of war to a position as central subject, together with its presentation as a form of mass martyrdom, demanded a moral response.

While these novels, then, are aesthetically innocent narratives, most of them also belong firmly to the literature of moral persuasion. The degree of persuasion naturally varies, but whether they are novels of honest witness and high traditionalist ideals, like Bertrand's *L'Appel du sol,* or novels of honest outrage and left-wing values, like Barbusse's *Le Feu,* they call for an ethical response. They work through direct emotional impact, not through subtle artistic effects. This is not to say that they are propagandist works, though no doubt Barbusse's book does come into this category. But it means, given the subject, that the moral stand they take will be judged, to a large extent, in terms of fidelity to the facts. The assumption is easily and naturally made that the moral message will derive its status and its strength from the fundamental truthfulness of the narrative.

Inevitably, then, these novels have given rise to a critical approach which has been broadly ethical. Their subject, particularly while the fighting continued, seemed to demand it; the authors themselves appeared to encourage it. Nevertheless, critical practice has proved neither clear nor simple. It is notoriously difficult to obtain agreement on moral criteria and these war narratives have not proved an exception. The convictions of critics and those of authors have clashed in a variety of ways. In general, the criteria in question have been the truthfulness of what is said and the passion with which it is expressed. Ideally, the truth and the passion should coincide, but in practice they often sort ill together. In the case of the early war novels – documents about the war and frequently denunciations of it – two forms of response arose.

Some critics, concerned above all with documentary accuracy, admired only those novels which avoided shrillness, were not unsympathetic to the traditional virtues of the battlefield, and presented war as a natural, if cruel, phenomenon. Other critics, chiefly sensitive to military mismanagement and the appalling sacrifice of human life, regarded novels of protest as alone worthy of attention, judging them according to the intensity of their denunciations. If the first group appeared to require a moderate account of unexampled violence, the second seemed to accept passion and unbalance as morally and artistically self-justifying.

While these contrasting critical approaches existed in some degree from the early days of the war, they became more clearly defined in the late 1920's and early 1930's. As the war began slowly to recede, and as technology and violence became seemingly inevitable features of modern society, there were those who experienced a measure of reconciliation with the fact of mechanized killing. Others, in the wake of a victory obtained at such enormous cost, contributed to a growing mood of pacifism and war repugnance. Critics seeking balance and restraint profited from the first of these attitudes. Those seeking an uncompromising denunciation of war profited from the second. The argument between these two sets of critics found what is perhaps its fullest and most precise form in the debate in America between Archibald MacLeish and Malcolm Cowley. The subject was *The First World War*, edited by Laurence Stallings, and it appeared in the *New Republic* during September and October 1933.[9] MacLeish complained of the partiality and lack of balance in many war novels (he had in mind post-war as well as wartime novels). Too many, he asserted, concentrated on the futility and the slaughter to the exclusion of the courage, the comradeship, the long periods of inactivity which also formed an integral part of the war experience. MacLeish's position implied that the role of literature is to explore and exhibit, not to preach and persuade. And it is true that the great works of art – *Hamlet* or *The Brothers Karamazov* – contain the woven texture of human contradiction and complexity rather than the single thread of partisanship.

Cowley, in reply, defended partisanship in terms of the special, even unprecedented, nature of the Great War. A balanced, exploratory approach would have betrayed its character and placed it falsely in the continuing perspective of traditional warfare. Selectiveness and passionate commitment were necessary to convey the exceptional horror of trench warfare and mechanized killing. Cowley, and the novelists who felt like him, saw the war as absurdly pointless slaughter;

MacLeish believed that the truth still demanded a recognition of heroism and generous sacrifice. This aspect of the debate was at least as much about terms as about facts.

While the writing of a novel of protest can be reconciled, at least in theory, with respect for the facts, some critics have been particularly sensitive to the distortions of fact, in the interests of propaganda or of art, which occur in novels of protest – and are by no means totally absent from 'traditionalist' narratives. As recently as 1968 C. E. Carrington wrote of his own lengthy experience of the Great War: '. . . I never came across a glorification of war; I heard no bloodthirsty sermons by militant clergy; I remember no invocations of the joys of battle . . . We were deadly serious about our assignment, without finding a necessity of often saying so, and there seemed no reason why we should not have fun when off duty, since we expected to die tomorrow.'[10] This is some way from the war as Barbusse or Werth describe it. No doubt it is a very anglo-saxon approach, phlegmatic and down to earth. But it also reminds us that if a writer were to confine himself to what he had actually experienced and seen with his own eyes, his account of the war might appear very limited and even positively unbalanced. The overall view of the individual was necessarily severely restricted. Referring to the sheer physical dimensions of the front, in terms of trenches and salients, Fussell writes of 'a series of multiple parallel excavations running for 400 miles down through Belgium and France'. He adds:

From the North Sea coast of Belgium the line wandered southward, bulging out to contain Ypres, then dropping down to protect Béthune, Arras, and Albert. It continued south in front of Montidier, Compiègne, Soissons, Reims, Verdun, St. Mihiel, and Nancy, and finally attached its southernmost end to the Swiss Border at Beurnevisin, in Alsace. The top forty miles – the part north of Ypres – was held by the Belgians; the next ninety miles, down to the river Ancre, were British; the French held the rest, to the south.[11]

This was a setting of such physical extent that the different types of terrain alone gave rise to a variety of war experiences. Also, it was so extensive that a total picture could not be obtained by a single individual. Rieuneau writes:

Une bataille de Napoléon pouvait être suivie, comprise et décrite dans son ensemble, par un observateur judicieusement placé. Ainsi fit Hugo pour Waterloo, et Stendhal dut fausser les données, restreindre le champ de vision de Fabrice pour créer son fameux épisode de *La Chartreuse de Parme*. En 1914 ou en 1916, point n'était besoin d'artifices de cet ordre pour donner l'impression de désordre, de décousu, de chaos. Aucun observateur, fût-il le

Général en chef, ne pouvait décrire la bataille dans son ensemble. Guerre de millions d'hommes, se jouant sur des centaines de kilomètres, et mettant en œuvre les ressources des nations européennes jusqu'en leurs arrières lointains, elle échappait totalement, par son échelle, au pouvoir de connaissance d'un personnage.[12]

For writers such as Barbusse, and indeed Dorgelès, [13] the attempt to create an overall picture of the war necessarily meant an element of 'invention' and an account of episodes which they themselves had not witnessed. In an apparently paradoxical way – one no doubt peculiar to art – the pursuit of a fuller 'truth' meant the creation of 'fictional' elements. This is something which J. Norton Cru criticized severely in 1930. Displaying a resolutely non-literary approach which demanded documentary realism and rejected the imaginative apprehension which art can provide, he complained of novelists who show their failure to understand war and their betrayal of it 'en la découpant en chapitres de roman feuilleton'. He even hints at an unworthy playing to the gallery when he adds: 'Cette trahison a d'autant plus de succès que le public y retrouve ses épisodes favoris.'[14] Cru's uncompromisingly documentary stand means that the war novel apparently favoured by MacLeish proves guilty of 'L'erreur traditionaliste: l'héroïsme' while that defended by Cowley betrays 'l'erreur pacifiste: la brute san-guinaire'.

This division into traditionalist and pacifist fiction, although too categorical, makes general sense if we turn to specific novels. Also, a brief consideration of two novels in particular – Adrien Bertrand's *L'Appel du sol* and Henri Barbusse's *Le Feu* – helps us to put into clearer focus the question of moral impact raised above. *L'Appel du sol,* representing the more traditionalist view of war, is not widely known, and copies are hard to come by. *Le Feu,* an uncompromising denunciation of war, was greatly admired by Wilfred Owen and Siegfried Sassoon when they read it in 1917 in translation. It sold extremely well and is the most famous novel of the 1914–18 period.[15]

  Although the differences between them remain fundamental, Bertrand and Barbusse share some broad characteristics as war novelists. Both are preoccupied by the horror of trench warfare. Both are natural preachers and proselytisers pursuing a positive emotional effect. Their fictional characters (mostly officers in the case of Bertrand and other ranks in that of Barbusse) are immensely talkative. The conversations which result are a major means of conveying their 'message' to their readers. Their descriptions of human suffering are vivid and harrowing, but the narrative element is fairly fragmentary. Rather than tell a story with a strong and distinctive linear form, they work with a series of scenes and episodes – almost set-pieces – which create something like a mosaic. However, in spite of such similarities, they have very different attitudes to the presentation of war and place their common experience in contrasting moral perspectives. Bertrand wrote from a humane and traditionalist position, showing a sympathetic – but certainly not uncritical – understanding of the classical military virtues of duty, discipline, honour, courage. Barbusse wrote from outside the military tradition as a civilian of strongly left-wing persuasion caught up in the horror of modern war. Bertrand opens a debate on war and the military experience whereas Barbusse insists on a single and exclusive interpretation of these events. Bertrand's novel is two-dimensional and seeks a measure of exploration. Barbusse's novel is one-dimensional and is concerned with demonstration and proof.

Bertrand, although the balance of his attitude is towards a conservative outlook, understands and articulates opposing viewpoints. He argues a case for military discipline and patriotism. His novel ends with the words: 'Mais la France continue. . . .' But several of his characters also express a sceptical attitude towards military ideals. Acceptance and protest are juxtaposed to convey a sense of the moral complexity inherent in the Great War. On the side of acceptance we must place Bertrand's use, noted earlier, of the traditional rhetoric of patriotism and war. Within the first six chapters we meet many predictable terms and phrases: 'grandeur morale', 'acceptation résignée', 'obéissance passive', 'grand sacrifice', 'abnégation', 'mission rédemptrice', 'mourir pour son pays', 'ce que la Patrie attend', 'appel autoritaire du sol de France', etc. Within the general tone created by this type of vocabulary the main characters (some of them regular soldiers) take a high moral view of both patriotic duty and military discipline. Several passages recall Vigny's *Servitude et grandeur militaires* not only in terms of the vocabulary used – as pointed out in Chapter 2 – but also in terms of moral emphasis and a general approach both to army life at large and the experience of war in particular. The following is part of a long Vigny-like speech by Nicolaï, a captain in the *chasseurs alpins*:

Vous verrez, dit-il, que l'obéissance passive, la servitude sont les vertus de la campagne. L'enthousiasme s'en va. L'abnégation demeure. Ce qui fait notre force en temps de paix le fera plus encore en temps de guerre. Il ne s'agira d'être crâne un jour en courant à l'assaut. Il s'agira d'obéir, d'attendre, d'oser, d'entreprendre, de persévérer . . . Il s'agira de se faire tuer pour des gens inconnus, à l'arrière, là-bas, qui ne se soucient pas de nous, qui s'ingénient à ne point grossir nos rangs, qui édifient des fortunes scandaleuses sur nos cadavres.

Voilà, mon enfant, ce que la Patrie attend de vous. Voilà la nature du grand sacrifice: sacrifice morne, triste, simple et patient.[17]

In passages such as this Bertrand is aware of those evils of exploitation which Barbusse denounces. But he conceives of a duty which overrides them and of an honour which can only be served by stoical acceptance. War is accepted clear-sightedly; it is not glorified. Stoicism is the attitude of other characters such as Vaissette, *ancien normalien* and *agrégé de philosophie,* who speaks of his 'soumission aux lois mystérieuses du destin et de la raison' (p. 259).

At the same time, Bertrand recognizes weaknesses in this position. Patriotism does not prevent him from showing the French army in a state of considerable confusion and disarray due to a lack of intelligent and responsible leadership. Vaissette, although a patriot, is used to counter Nicolaï's ideas when he sees the wounded and dying in a field hospital:

Vaissette n'avait point découvert de beauté morale dans ces souffrances, ni de grandeur dans ces agonies. Il n'avait pas entendu les phrases impérissables qu'il attendait confusément. Il n'avait pas éprouvé, au sein du cet asile de détresses, l'ivresse sacrée du combat. Nulle part il n'avait trouvé l'acceptation du martyre qui endure, avec une foi passionnée, un supplice pour une cause sainte. (p. 219)

One of the ordinary soldiers, Rousset, puts the anti-war case succinctly when he exclaims: '. . . c'est pas la guerre, c'est la boucherie' (p. 158). This view is confirmed by the terrible deaths and maimings described. And in the course of the novel the main characters – Nicolaï, Vaissette, Fabre, de Quéré – are all killed, while Angielli loses his reason. The final moral impression is one of extreme confusion and tragedy. There is much that is horrific; there is much that compels admiration.

If Bertrand is ready to encourage discussion and debate, Barbusse is determined to carry conviction. This determination is reflected in his use of first-person narrative which allows direct contact with the reader. Frequent authorial interventions serve a similar purpose and leave the reader in no doubt as to how events must be interpreted. Indeed, there are moments when the final chapter reads like a *Pravda* editorial. Not least, by forsaking the dynamic relationships of linear plot for something approaching the cumulative, static, patterning of a mosaic, Barbusse (and Bertrand also to some extent) is able to repeat, and therefore emphasize, the moral points he wishes to make.

The first of these points is the outrageous horror of war as experienced by soldiers the majority of whom are 'des civils déracinés'. [18] The following passage, describing the kind of wound that was not at all uncommon at this time, is typical of Barbusse's direct assault on the reader's sensibility by means of painful realism:

C'est un homme qui n'a plus de pieds. Il porte aux jambes des pansements terribles, avec des garrots pour refréner l'hémorragie. Ses moignons ont saigné dans les bandelettes de toile et il semble avoir des culottes rouges. Il a une figure de diable, luisante et sombre, et il délire. On pèse sur ses épaules et ses genoux: cet homme qui a les pieds coupés veut sauter hors du brancard pour s'en aller. (pp. 288–9)

Barbusse also preaches, through his fictional characters, an explicit anti-militarism. One of the soldiers (named Bertrand, as it happens) cries: 'Honte à la gloire militaire, honte aux armées, honte au métier de soldat, qui change les hommes tour à tour en stupides victimes et en ignobles bourreaux. Oui, honte: c'est vrai, mais c'est trop vrai, c'est vrai dans l'éternité, pas encore pour nous' (p. 159).

Towards the end of the novel the moral tone takes on an increasingly political character. War is interpreted as a particularly dramatic form of a continuing exploitation of the poor by the rich: '. .. les peuples entiers vont à la boucherie, rangés en troupeaux d'armées, pour qu'une caste galonnée d'or écrive ses noms de princes dans l'histoire, pour que des gens dorés aussi, qui font partie de la même gradaille, brassent plus d'affaires' (p. 342). Finally, Barbusse sees the war as preparing revolution – 'cette guerre, c'est comme la Révolution Française qui continue' (p. 340) – and looks forward to 'l'entente des démocraties, l'entente des immensités, la levée du peuple du monde, la foi brutalement simple' (p. 348).

It seems appropriate to end this chapter with a brief analysis of the effects likely to be achieved by these two very different presentations of war. One's first reaction is probably to say that *Le Feu* makes the greater impact because of its anti-war militancy. Barbusse does not run the risk of confusing the reader with antithetical arguments or of undermining his desired effect by presenting a 'human' picture of the slaughter. He works with such concepts as exploitation and class conflict. He interprets modern warfare as an intensification of capitalist evils. Nevertheless, history since 1918 has not confirmed Barbusse's message. It now seems naïve compared with that of Bertrand. Furthermore, the methods Barbusse uses to convey his message to the reader are open to considerable criticism. Kenneth Burke, in the course of his comments on the MacLeish/Cowley debate mentioned earlier, argues that militant pacifism, fed by unrelievedly horrifying details of war, may prove an aesthetic basis for essentially warlike and violent reactions. He maintains that horror, repugnance, and hatred can provide 'the firmest basis upon which the "heroism" of a new war could be erected'.[19] If Bertrand's approach is less positive, its subtle balance of opposites does not run the risk of creating a counter-violence. Barbusse's method, by contrast, with its fundamentally conflictual view of society, risks encouraging a counter-violence at variance with its anti-militaristic message. As Burke puts it: 'Sunday-school texts have ever been considered by sophisticated moralists the essential stimulus to "sin" – and I see no reason why the same fact should not apply to a Sunday-school simplification in dealing with the problems of war.'[20] The single thread of partisanship can all too easily prove self-defeating.

Finally, Burke argues that readers would have to respond in the direct and automatic manner of machines for the kind of persuasion used by Barbusse to have its intended effect. Fortunately, the widely canvassed machine model of human beings can be shown to be an illusion. Human stimulus and response, not least in the field of literature, are more complicated, more wayward, less predictable. In fact, *Le Feu* has been frequently admired for its dramatic rendering of war. It has been much more rarely praised as a stimulus to pacifism. If it is true that *'contradictoriness of response* is basic to human psychology',[21] *L'Appel du sol* may turn out, a trifle ironically, to be the more potent pacifist document.

CHAPTER 4

Maintaining Decorum
Benjamin, Bertrand, and Franconi

The term 'decorum' as used here is not a popular twentieth-century concept. One associates it, in various forms, with the eighteenth and nineteenth centuries. It implies a sense of moral, social, and artistic propriety. It involves ideas of decency, harmony, and proportion. It presupposes the enduring reality of philosophical and ethical values which it would be improper to question and barbarous to deny. This was the frame of mind in which most people, and the majority of writers, approached the war in 1914. They accepted a canon of decorum which included ideas of heroism, loyalty, duty, service. Few had any inkling of the totally new experiences, extending well beyond the limits of decorum, which awaited them at the front. In 1914, in Europe, war was still widely conceived of in terms of eighteenth-century rules designed to restrict the use of violence and force. In short, war was still regarded as operating within certain decorous limits. Writers, in particular, worked with a moral vocabulary which emphasized absolutes and was designed to express ideas of order, stability, progress. In the event, these are precisely the values which the Great War was to throw into disarray. In England Wilfred Owen was sharply conscious of the conflict between the Latin tag of Horace and the realities of this war:

> If you could hear, at every jolt, the blood
> Come gargling from the froth-corrupted lungs,
> Obscene as cancer, bitter as the end
> Of vile, incurable sores on innocent tongues –
> My friend, you would not tell with such high zest
> To children ardent for some desperate glory,
> The old Lie: Dulce et decorum est
> Pro Patria mori.

The pressure of events quickly forced a certain number of writers to realize that they faced a situation totally at variance with their moral assumptions as well as their expectations. They underwent various forms of anguished readjustment to the new realities and in the process they expressed outrage and protest. There were some, however, who either could not or would not accept that total war had permanently overturned the assumptions of decorum. They approached unprecedented experiences with a fundamental reliance on traditionalist ideas and forms of analysis. They tried to force the unfamiliar into familiar categories. They attempted to maintain decorum in the face of devastation.

For those who come later – particularly those, like ourselves, who have lived in a world of intense violence and moral confusion during the last fifty years – this is bound to be an unsatisfactory, and indeed a mistaken, attitude. But it is certainly not an uninteresting one. At the historical level it documents a genuine attitude widely held in 1914. At the artistic level it gives rise to a sometimes fascinating tension between violent subject-matter and restrained expression. For our immediate purpose here, this maintenance of decorum represents one end of a possible classification of war novels ranging from the optimism and would-be normalization of war in Benjamin, through the stoicism of Bertrand and patriotism of Franconi, to the humanity of Dorgelès or Duhamel and the more passionate and more political protests of Barbusse and the pacifism of Werth.

René Benjamin's *Gaspard* was published in 1915 and awarded the Prix Goncourt for that year. Initially it enjoyed great popularity with its passages of colourful popular speech and its amusing portrayal of Gaspard, a Parisian *marchand d'escargots* and a real 'card', who sees action at the front. Nowadays critics treat it very dismissively, finding its humour misplaced and its presentation of war irresponsibly cheerful. The following caustic summary of the novel may be taken as typical of this antagonistic critical reaction: 'The hero is intended to represent the unqualified devotion of the French working-class to the national struggle. He is cheerful, unsophisticated, picturesque in speech, droll in manner, fearless in action and true as steel at all times. He skips into battle, is wounded twice, decorated and returns home to sire future heroes. The moral of the story is clear; the nation is one and indivisible, and war little more than an uncomfortable excursion during which, if one should have the great misfortune to get wounded, one's sense of humour remains intact'.[1] This is a precise account of one way in which decorum is maintained. While it is easy to see why Benjamin's novel has given such, partly ideological, offence, it is certainly not totally devoid of insights into the nature of human reactions to war. Nor is it true that war is presented as a pure frolic. Nevertheless, *Gaspard* is dominated by a conventional attitude[2] which must strike us as inadequate in face of the reality and significance of its subject. Benjamin maintains decorum in the sense that he promotes certain set ideas of chivalry and courage, reducing the barbarity of war to a minimum. He emphasizes the comic side of war, something which irritates a certain type of reader, and uses comedy for purposes of false reassurance. Nevertheless we find Dorgelès, whose reaction to the war was very different, admitting later: 'Mais oui, on s'amuse à la guerre, et quand les mouches des mauser viennent nous siffler: "fini de rire", le drame garde malgré tout son côté comique.'[3] One must keep a sense of proportion in judging *Gaspard,* remembering that many men clearly enjoy the comradeship of war and seem to fulfil themselves in battle. Reaction to Benjamin's novel has often been a matter of individual temperament and ideological choice. This is no doubt inevitable, given Benjamin's own outlook, but it does mean that 'objective' moral or literary standards of judgement have been more frequently claimed than employed.

Much of Gaspard's humour and heroism are unconscious. He lacks the sensitivity or imagination to be either a truly heroic figure or a deeply tragic one. But these very limitations are the key to his survival. He has his moments of despair or anger, but the essence of his character is a cheerful capacity to absorb horror and adapt to unfamiliar circumstances. He is a natural survivor. This capacity to adapt and endure is seen by Benjamin as a general human trait. He uses it as one method of reducing the frightening or shocking aspects of war. He writes: 'Mais l'homme est étrangement souple. Aux pires aventures il s'habitue et s'accommode avec une prestesse qui d'abord déroute et qui, en fin de compte, est admirable.'[4] This is the principle of reassurance which is applied, for example, just after Gaspard has a leg amputated. Benjamin says of man in general: 'Vous le tuez à demi: il jouit de son reste . . . Il s'adapte, s'arrange, il vit! Vivre, c'est l'essentiel' (p. 287). This is Benjamin's general attitude throughout *Gaspard.* He is the incorrigible optimist – committed to 'life' and convinced that human beings can always adjust to catastrophe and in this sense overcome it. To some extent, of course, he is right. No picture of human beings would be true or complete if it ignored their capacity for endurance and their adaptability. But Benjamin leaves the matter there. He does not ask whether it is right that people should be put into this kind of situation. He does not challenge the suffering and destruction that war brings about. He does not protest that circumstances must be changed but implies that they should be cheerfully endured. He suggests that attitudes, not situations, must be transformed. He therefore also implies that the individual has basic control of his own life even in war – a pre-1914 assumption which the experience of the Great War effectively destroyed.

It would not be fair to say that Benjamin gives no indication of the horrifying aspects of war. He is even aware, at least in part, of the new character of some of the horror. He rightly refers, for example, to the 'lutte affreusement inégale contre l'artillerie prussienne' (p. 119) during the early stages of the war. There are also realistic enough scenes of refugees thronging the roads or wounded soldiers returning from the front for a rest period: 'Un foullis d'hommes blessés, fourbus, boitant, se traînant, dont on apercevait les linges tachés de sang autour des membres ou bien des fronts' (pp. 97–8). The result is that he cannot be accused, strictly speaking, of failing to note the horror. What he does do, however, is employ various devices to reduce its impact.

One method is to describe suffering in generalized and abstract terms. In a scene describing a number of wounded soldiers lying on the floor of a church in Lorraine the use of abstraction is clear; 'C'était le gémissement naturel de la Terre à Dieu; la souffrance sous le Ciel, allongée sur des dalles . . .' (p. 144). Here we see suffering as a concept, rather than individual sufferers, stretched out on the church floor. Acceptance of the scene is also encouraged by the expression 'gémissement *naturel* de la Terre' and it is further normalized and generalized by the comment: '. . . c'est l'image la plus simple et la plus émouvante de la misère humaine' (p. 145). The suffering of war is fitted into a human continuum. Finally, there is an attempt to make the experience of these men more acceptable by means of a concluding sentence which is both tasteless and meaningless in the comfort it vaguely suggests: 'La chair tout entaillée geint et crie sur la paille, et les pierres de l'église qui l'abritent un instant ont l'air de dire: "Nous, nous savions tout cela . . . et nous vous attendions" ' (p. 145).

A second device used by Benjamin is the contrast which he sometimes sets up between a fundamentally horrifying scene and the heroic attitude of one individual observing it. One or two clinching sentences are used at the end to lessen or to alter the impact:

Mais l'ennemi, maintenant, étendait son tir. Du haut d'un bois où il embrassait la plaine, il venait sans doute de découvrir tous ces blessés qui, comme Gaspard, s'en allaient derrière les lignes françaises, clopin-clopant, seuls, à deux, misérables et gémissants, et pressant le pas, soutenant leurs plaies jusqu'à l'ambulance qu'ils cherchaient de loin d'un œil hagard. Il décida cruellement de les achever. Et alors, ce fut une nouvelle pluie d'obus, plus épouvantable que les autres, car tous ces hommes atteints n'avaient plus ni la souplesse ni l'énergie de se coucher vite, de cacher leur tête, et beaucoup étaient atteints de nouveau, deux, trois fois; et ils repartaient toujours, hurlant plus fort, affolés, tout saignants, des loques de chair, sur qui les canons allemands s'acharnaient.

Gaspard, lui, n'était pas effaré. Il était sublime, simplement. Il allait son pas, suant et soufflant, et il disait:

– Tant pis! . . . J'm'en fous! Au p'tit bonheur! . . . Si on est crevés ensemble, on s'ra crevés ensemble! (p. 127)

Here Gaspard's tough and fearless determination is used to give an altered perspective to the scene. It is implied that a higher truth is to be found in the bold and spirited individual as against the suffering mass. Once again personal attitude is presented as superior to public circumstance.

Not the least important of Benjamin's devices to normalize war is his cautious treatment of the fact of death. It is noticeable in *Gaspard* that to be wounded – something which entails the devotion of nurses and brings a life of relative ease and tranquillity – is a much more common experience than to be killed. Indeed, Benjamin explicitly presents fatigue and hunger as more to be feared by the soldier than death. He writes: '. . . la mort, parfois, tue d'un coup, sans souffrance, tandis que la faim vous talonne une armée pendant des jours et des jours' (p. 59). The idea of 'la mort . . . sans souffrance' is dishonest and unacceptable. Benjamin deliberately draws a veil over the grotesque deaths, the terrible woundings and maimings, which were a particular characteristic of the new mechanized slaughter of 1914–18. It is clear that the stark finality of death encourages this kind of distortion if Benjamin is to maintain his decorous and unalarming picture of war. But the quality of his novel suffers in consequence. The most one can say is that its general outlook reflects one attitude which was common at that period and it therefore possesses some documentary interest. In doing so it reminds us of the very large gap in sensibility between 1914 and the present. In another episode involving death a young soldier, dying of his wounds, tells his mother of his experiences: 'C'était . . . c'était pas épouvantable: on s'y fait' (p. 193). This is far removed from a modern intellectual reaction to the same circumstances yet there is no doubt that it was a common enough response during the Great War. Benjamin's fictional characters certainly had their real life counterparts.

These, then, are some of the devices used by Benjamin to encourage an acceptance of the near normality of war. The experience of war is presented not as a scandal and outrage but as part of the continuing process of living. It is seen as something which can be related to familiar generalizations about human nature and the human lot. It can be described and accounted for within the limits of decorum. Chapter 2 above has made it clear, however, that these ideas are false and that Benjamin was fundamentally mistaken in his attitude. *Gaspard* remains an inadequate and misleading rendering of the unique reality of the Great War. No doubt patriotism was Benjamin's main motive. It is also not at all clear that he genuinely understood the special nature of events between 1914 and 1918. But in the end, one expects a writer to prove equal to his chosen subject. While it has to be admitted that Benjamin's picture of the war reflects faithfully enough the attitude of many French citizens, particularly during the early months of the war, this is simply another way of saying that his novel is an imaginative and moral failure. It has a certain documentary value, but it documents inadequacy rather than insight. It portrays some undeniable qualities of human beings, but fails to convey the specific characteristics of a war which actually rendered many of these qualities irrelevant. This failure to match the war with adequate moral and imaginative judge-ment receives concentrated expression in the final lines of the novel. Gaspard, meditating on the future that awaits his son's generation, says to himself: 'Eux, ils hériteront, ils s'engraisseront, ils boufferont que d'la dinde truffée, mais les Boches . . . ben les Boches, c'est toujours nous qui leur aura tanné la peau!' (p. 319).

In the previous chapter we looked briefly at the form of moral impact made by Bertrand's *L'Appel du sol.* It must now be examined further, less as an exercise in persuasion than as an expression of decorum. We have just seen that René Benjamin maintained decorum largely by his psychological approach: war is really not so terrible; human beings can adapt to most situations; one leg should still be regarded as better than none, etc. Bertrand's use of decorum, by contrast, operates at a much more philosophical level. He believes firmly in absolute values. The *chasseurs alpins* of his novel are 'les soldats de l'Idée' (p. 146). They may not always be conscious of the precise values which they are defending, but a unique moral beauty is claimed for this 'martyre inconscient pour une idée qui nous dépasse' (p. 16). Although his view of war is less optimistic, and much less superficial, than that of Benjamin, he sees it as a challenge to maintain moral values rather than as an infraction of all ethics. Nicolaï, for example, is confident that 'ce qui fait notre force en temps de paix la fera plus encore en temps de guerre' (p. 33). War is a proving ground in which the moral imperatives of peacetime – loyalty, duty, honesty, service, courage – confirm their enduring status by their continuing relevance. Bertrand also maintains decorum when he goes on to claim, on several occasions, that the conditions of war serve to bring out the most noble qualities of human beings. Such views not only place Bertrand, despite many differences, in the same general category as Benjamin. They emphasize his distance from the novelists of protest who were concerned to deny or disprove precisely such ideas. A novelist like Barbusse attacked traditional values in the light of his experience at the front and pointed up the brutalizing and corrupting aspects of war. What is striking about Bertrand's approach, and what makes it superior to that of Benjamin, is the way in which he maintains his views against a background of horrifying and discordant facts which he does not seek to minimize or normalize. He discusses his ideas, with commendable honesty, in the context of events which appear to deny them. He does not necessarily compel assent, but he undoubtedly deserves a hearing. His concern is not to underplay the slaughter and the suffering, and yet to preach a doctrine of stoical acceptance and, when necessary, of patriotic self-sacrifice.

One cannot fail to be struck by the high seriousness and intellectual austerity of this novel. From the earliest chapters the tone is one appropriate to reflection and patient understanding rather than to protest and outrage. *L'Appel du sol* is also quintessentially a war novel. It deals, in a spirit of the most serious enquiry, with the related issues of war, death, and patriotism. It pursues this enquiry by means of a dialectic of action and thought. There are vivid and painful scenes of fighting and killing: an artillery barrage, a bayonet charge, trench warfare, etc. Such action then prompts speculation and analysis on the part of Bertrand's intellectual characters during periods of relative inactivity. They seem very French in the nature and intensity of their philosophical debates.

The fighting described takes place in the early weeks of the war.[5] It is accompanied by a lively sense of the unprecedented nature of this particular war: the use of heavy artillery against virtually unprotected troops; the frequent confusion and lack of any clear chain of command; the reduction of human beings to the status of cogs in a blind and blundering military machine; the cruelly high proportion of casualties. These and similar points are in Vaissette's mind when he exclaims: 'Cette lutte de toute l'Europe . . . est le bouleversement le plus formidable de l'histoire. Qu'est-ce désormais que Cannes ou que

Marignan?' (p. 130). One also has the impression that Bertrand mainly writes of what he has actually seen: German spotter aircraft; an aerial bombardment; trees shredded by shells; cyclist messengers riding through fields because the roads are raked by machine-gun fire; the different sounds made by bullets as they hit tins, sacks, and human flesh. The details are often convincing by their very unexpectedness.

Not the least important aspect of Bertrand's realism is his awareness that there are those who profit by war, who ensure their personal safety in civilian jobs, or who indulge in irresponsible and chauvinistic propaganda on behalf of a cause to which they themselves make no significant sacrifice. Of the latter – particularly the journalists among them – he writes through the comments of one of his characters:

Et le monde se fait un concept de la guerre d'après leurs articles, qui correspondent à l'idée vague qu'ils s'en faisaient pour avoir lu l'*Iliade* et les divers traités d'histoire qui sont en honneur dans nos lycées et dans nos écoles primaires. Pour eux, ils sont bien tranquilles derrière leur bureau de travail. Nous, nous avons vécu depuis quelques jours les heures que vous connaissez. Vous verrez que c'est eux qui auront raison. Quand nous reviendrons, après nous avoir fêté pour nos exploits ou nos blessures, on ne croira point que la guerre est telle que nous la décrivons: car elle apparaîtrait comme trop dure et trop simple, comme sans panache et toute soumise aux lois du destin. (p. 78)

Bertrand obviously has a sharp sense of the way in which this particular war of 1914, with its efficient and increasingly mechanized techniques of killing, was idealized and misrepresented as part of a literary tradition going back to Homer. He points to a very different interpretation, far removed from chivalry and romance, when he uses Vaissette to refer to those 'nécessités économiques qui déterminent toutes les guerres'. Nevertheless, he still finds scope for a high-minded but honest reading of the situation which Vaissette puts as follows:

. . . les réalités du monde matériel et physique poussent à ces crises du domaine matériel et physique. Mais une guerre n'a pas de grandeur que si l'idée s'en mêle, si elle est dominée par les réalités du monde psychique et moral.
   Ainsi, je crois que nous luttons pour assurer la domination des penseurs, des philosophes et des artistes, sur les fournisseurs des armées et sur les fabricants de canons. Sans doute c'est grâce à ces derniers que nous vaincrons et non point grâce aux écrivains qui épanchent leurs enthousiasmes dans le *Bulletin des Armées*: mais c'est parce que chez nous les penseurs sont les maîtres. Cette suprématie intellectuelle est la source de toute force . . . et nous aurons la victoire parce que l'élite de notre race a compris Racine et aimé Ronsard. (pp. 146–7)

This is the essence of Bertrand's idea of decorum. It involves a belief in the supremacy of ideas over material facts. It implies that certain ideas express an unchanging and ultimately irresistible truth. It sees the Great War as an occasion to identify and proclaim this truth. Bertrand stands at the opposite end of the scale from Henry James who, as early as August 1914, described the war as 'this unspeakable giveaway of the whole fool's paradise of our past'.[6]

Despite Bertrand's sense of decorum and feeling for tradition, his attitude is not to be identified with that belief in the 'Great Crusade' which was derided by many commentators in the 1920s and 1930s.[7] He is not afraid to show in his novel the collapse of various illusions as the war progresses. For example, the early confidence that all would be over by Christmas ('la guerre sera finie avant trois mois') or the idea, reminiscent of Benjamin, that perhaps the fighting would not prove so terrible after all. In the same way de Quéré, who has strong Christian beliefs, admits his quick disillusionment with the idea of a crusade:

Je vais vous faire une confidence. J'ai confondu jusqu'ici mon amour pour la France et mon culte de Dieu. Mon patriotisme et ma foi se mêlaient dans le même enthousiasme d'action. Cette guerre était une croisade. A présent, ce n'est plus tout à fait la même chose. Quelques semaines de campagne et la tragédie des heures d'hier m'ont apporté un peu de clarté. Oui: je crois et j'aime mon pays. Mais ces deux passions sont devenues des choses distinctes . . . Si je meurs, je serai mort en bon chrétien, mais je ne serai pas mort pour le christianisme: je serai mort pour mon pays. (p. 193)

The agnostic humanist Vaissette adopts a similar attitude. He began, he says, by identifying his 'religion of man' with his patriotism. But the actual experience of war has changed his outlook. He can no longer regard his patriotism as an expression of humanist confidence and aspiration. His patriotism has become purely instinctive. If de Quéré is not fighting for Christianity, Vaissette is not fighting for humanism. Both are fighting for France, but derive a certain comfort and strength from Christianity and humanism respectively.

The cumulative effect of their war experiences on the views of these two characters is used later in the novel to build up a Christianity/humanism debate in the reader's mind. Vaissette comments on the increasing horror of weapons of war and adds: 'Il y a longtemps que mon âme voltairienne doute de Dieu. Cette guerre en est la négation définitive' (p. 250). De Quéré, by contrast, says of Vaissette's humanist assumptions: 'Cette guerre est la faillite de la raison! Ce sont vos stoïciens qui prétendent . . . que l'homme est mené par la raison. . . . A quoi sert la science et où est la raison?' (p. 251). A few lines later Vaissette adds: 'Admirez . . . comme nous pouvons accommoder la réalité du monde sensible au goût de nos théories. Rien ne prouve ni ne réfute rien.' This is the point at which Bertrand characteristically invites the reader to decide for himself whether the Great War testifies to the death of God, or the death of man, or to neither, or to both.

Returning to the subject of patriotism, it is clear that this is not a simple concept in *L'Appel du sol* despite the implication of this title. It does, of course, have the nationalist connotations of territorial loyalty and love of the French soil. Bertrand, commenting on his characters, sees them as moved – consciously or unconsciously – by 'l'appel autoritaire du sol de France, de ses collines et de ses brouillards, de ses plaines, de ses bois, de ses fleuves et de ses montagnes . . .' etc. (p. 126). But the following discussion among a group of other ranks suggests that patriotism can be a powerful motive without being a particularly clear or uniform one:

– Pourquoi te bats-tu, Diribarne? fit-il.
Diribarne eut un geste vague. Il ne pouvait expliquer. Il savait bien pourtant. Rousset intervint.
– Puisqu'on nous a attaqués . . . , dit-il.
– Sans doute, répondit le sergent. Mais ce n'est pas tout. Pourquoi ce pays attaqué veut-il se défendre jusqu'à la mort?
– Pour la fin des guerres, déclara Angielli.
Diribarne avait trouvé:
– Oui, pour qu'ils ne nous embêtent plus, et qu'on soit les maîtres chez nous.
Le caporal Gros eut un mot sublime de simplicité, de candeur, de vérité:
– Il faut bien se battre, coquin de sort, pour être les plus forts et qu'on ne soit plus un peuple de vaincus.
– Moi, je me suis engagé pour reprendre l'Alsace, assura Pluchard. (pp. 115–16)

For officers such as Vaissette, Fabre, and de Quéré, patriotism is an intellectual concept which has relatively little to do with territorial integrity. Their discussions recall in particular the debates which took place in France, especially on the subject of education, in the twenty years prior to 1914. All of them see the war in terms of a fundamental cultural conflict between France and Germany, though their interpretations differ in emphasis.

De Quéré, the Christian traditionalist, admires German discipline and order up to a point. He says that France possessed these qualities in the seventeenth century but subsequently yielded to 'liberté, désordre, anarchie'. He insists that 'il n'y a de permanent que ce qui est mesuré' and continues: 'Les Allemands ont accepté cette contrainte. Ils ont été des organisateurs merveilleux. . . . Grâce à la méthode de leurs universités, de leur commerce, de leur armée, ils ont pu déferler jusqu'à ces collines françaises . . .' (p. 143). Nevertheless, patriotism and a sense of certain enduring spiritual values temper his enthusiasm for Germany's achievements. He concludes that even organization and efficiency, if devoid of cultural depth, must ultimately fail. It is this depth that the Germans lack; the conclusion de Quéré draws is that they will be defeated in the end because 'l'idée ne les a pas suffisamment façonnés'.

Vaissette accepts that Prussian scholars 'connaissent mieux que personne la philologie et la chimie' and also speaks of the fascination which the Latin south has exercised over the German mind. His argument is that the Germans, despite their great interest in Latin civilization, do not properly understand its essence. He refers to German tourists, Baedeker in hand, visiting the great monuments of Graeco-Roman culture, and says: 'ils en comptent les pierres et en dénombrent les vestiges sans en saisir l'âme sacrée' (p. 145). They respond to quantity and miss quality. Towards the end of the novel de Quéré expresses the view, shared by Vaissette, that the Germans are using their formidable gifts and organizational powers in the service of force rather than 'la beauté morale' (p. 270).

On balance, and despite the title of Bertrand's novel, patriotism is conceived of more as loyalty to certain moral and intellectual values traditionally associated with France than as territorial fidelity. It is not a militant sentiment, and it is less easy to sustain the more terrible the slaughter becomes. Vaissette and de Quéré, in particular, become increasingly disillusioned. At no point is their patriotism in any doubt, but both are led towards some reassessment of their fundamental beliefs. The humanist Vaissette exclaims: 'L'homme n'a jamais été aussi dur pour l'homme. Je ne peux plus croire au progrès humain' (p. 285). And de Quéré, originally presented as a well-armed Jesuit (intellectually and militarily), comes to the desperate conclusion that 'toutes les choses de l'esprit sont stériles, les choses du cœur seules ont une réalité féconde' (p. 286).

Inevitably, these discussions of war and patriotism also involve facing up to the fact of death. Unlike Benjamin, Bertrand emphasizes the simple truth that war means death. Commenting on the enormous number of casualties he says: 'Mais cela, c'était le sort de la guerre. On était là pour mourir, pour voir mourir les autres' (p. 187). Among the various characters in the novel Fabre at least realizes that the kind of war they are fighting gives little scope for the traditional heroic death. Under the conditions of mechanized killing death is more often a matter of chance than of choice: 'Avec les engins modernes on n'est plus exposé quand on se découvre que quand on se terre. C'est une question de chance' (p. 73). Vaissette too, although his patriotism is never seriously in doubt, has a moment when he views the war almost objectively. His humanist instincts encourage him to say:

Que doit-on penser de nous dans Sirius, puisque nous nous rassemblons ici à seule fin de tuer méthodiquement le plus de nos semblables pour cette raison qu'ils ont un casque gris au lieu d'un béret bleu ou d'un képi rouge, que très souvent leur nez supporte des lunettes d'or et non, comme le mien, un binocle, et qu'ils hurlent 'Vorwaerts' au lieu de crier 'En avant'? (pp. 119–20)

In general, however, it is a more traditionalist view of death in battle which seems to pervade the novel. Fabre, for instance, despite his awareness of the totally arbitrary occurrence of death in a modern war, insists that men are ennobled by this fact. They are ennobled less by the act of dying than by having to live with the continual possibility of being killed. In a statement which is reminiscent of Vigny he says:

la grandeur morale de la guerre . . . consiste à nous faire vivre avec l'idée de la mort. Il se joue ainsi dans l'âme de chacun de nous un drame autrement profond que le drame extérieur de la bataille. La guerre est la honte de l'humanité si on la considère en elle-même; elle en est la sanctification si on la voit dans le cœur de ceux qui la font. (pp. 83–4)

War, death, and patriotism take on a special significance and value for Bertrand in the sense that they combine to teach men how to sacrifice themselves for an idea. To die for a cause, to die for a belief, to die for one's convictions is to die nobly. Man is the only living creature capable of renouncing his physical existence in this way.

Un Tel de l'armée française, by Gabriel-Tristan Franconi, was first published in book form in 1918. It is less fully realized, in strictly novelistic terms, than *Gaspard* or even *L'Appel du sol.* It is an interesting example of the way in which the variety and pressure of war experiences can push as competent a writer as Franconi beyond the strict limits of generic purity. One feels that the mixture of styles and concerns is the result of deliberate choice rather than artistic inadequacy. The forty-three mostly short chapters vary in nature from narrative or character analysis to documentation and socio-cultural speculation. Chapters such as 'En Ligne' or 'Patrouille' amount to straightforward war narrative. A series of colourful characters at the front explain such chapter headings as 'Lulusse de Charonne' and 'Le Pote'. The need to provide factual information for civilian readers emerges in 'Exégèse de certaines phrases militaires' or 'La Relève'. Finally, chapters on social and cultural ideas include 'Une chaumière, un cœur et l'indépendance'. Such chapters add up to what is described in the novel as 'une mosaïque faite de tous ces souvenirs, petites pierres boueuses, chatoyantes, ensanglantées . . .'.[8]

The hero, referred to throughout simply as 'Un Tel', is clearly meant to have ideal universal status. He is a kind of Everyman and the reader is invited to admire – possibly even to emulate – his courage, leadership, and ideas. It remains true, however, that he possesses a distinctive character and the biographical details attributed to him are mostly taken directly from Franconi's own life. It is worth adding that Franconi, who was killed in July 1918, had quite the most distinguished military career of the Great War novelists in France. His outstanding bravery was referred to on all sides. He was mentioned in dispatches eight times and received the *médaille militaire,* the *croix de guerre,* and – posthumously – the *croix de la légion d'honneur.*

Franconi maintains decorum, in the general sense outlined at the beginning of this chapter, as firmly as either Benjamin or Bertrand. His vocabulary contains familiar and automatically accepted expressions such as 'espérance française', 'adversaire implacable', 'verser un sang vigoureux', etc. This is also the language of patriotism and France is described as 'le plus beau pays du monde occidental'. Nevertheless, Franconi makes no attempt to analyse patriotism as Bertrand did. He simply refers to that sense of common purpose which, in wartime, unites all decent people, however their ideas or backgrounds may vary, in a determination to defend their families and homes. Significantly, he distinguishes patriotism from what he describes as the 'vaines et pompeuses formules de l'union sacrée' (p. 42).[9] In fact, Franconi's decorum has little to do with absolute values although his novel, through the person of Un Tel, contains a strong defence of traditionalism. His concern is with practical realities rather than with what he terms 'le grotesque des idées absolues' (p. 17). Where Benjamin tends to be evasive and Bertrand indulges in somewhat abstract idealism, Franconi remains matter-of-fact.

If there is one value which Un Tel is shown to prize above others it is personal freedom. But he interprets this value in practical terms. Although he is described as the typical representative of a generation in love with ideas, his sense of personal freedom quickly leads him to reject anarchism. After a brief period of theoretical approval of anarchism, he finds that in practice it amounts to nothing more than 'une tyrannie stupide' (p. 18). It is this same love of freedom, combined with a natural courage and daring, that later makes him impatient with 'cette discipline qu'il importe d'observer en présence des réalités sévères de la guerre moderne' (p. 91). In general he opposes intellectual structures which he finds are without roots in reality. He is also against the abstraction, as he sees it, of modern 'isms'. He is a poet who, as we shall see later, scorns modern experiments in literature and art. He rejects the tyranny of the modern and identifies personal freedom with a vague traditionalism. As Franconi puts it, 'Un Tel entend gronder en lui les échos attardés d'anciennes clameurs' (p. 9).

As a novel about war *Un Tel de l'armée française* presents its subject in a generally favourable light. Although there is neither the patent attempt to normalize war which characterized *Gaspard,* nor any particular emphasis on war as a moral proving ground as in *L'Appel du sol,* the comradeship and the excitement are both stressed. Un Tel is a natural soldier. He describes not only his battle experiences but the many colourful characters whom he met in the trenches and whom he grew to admire and trust. He appears largely indifferent to both discomfort and danger. Early in the novel we read: 'Les gourbis sont étroits, encombrés de munitions; l'eau y coule les jours de pluie, des claies pourries y recouvrent le sol, les rats y foisonnent, mais on y goûte un bonheur réel' (p. 35). This is typical of the clear-eyed acceptance of circumstances which marks Franconi's view of the war. The following short passage, too, is significant less for what it says about Un Tel than for the distinction which it implies between writers who make epic heroism out of war and those, like Franconi, who view it on a much more practical level: 'Quels êtres particulièrement doués, solidement bâtis, animés de passions divines et surgis d'une antique épopée sont donc les combattants de cette grande guerre? Un Tel cherche des dieux, autour de lui, et ne voit que des hommes' (p. 36). Franconi's novel makes it clear that the only alternative to protest against war is not simply an unrealistic idealization of it. He does not denounce war, but neither does he approach it as a kind of noble sport played by supermen. On the contrary he has a clearer sense than most writers within the tradition of decorum that the soldier is at least as much a victim as a victor: '. . . le combattant, couvert de vermine et de vase, est une pauvre chose perdue en la tempête, un être dont la chair, cinglée des vents, est offerte, nuit et jour, aux coups du destin' (p. 104). It is against such a background, and to the accompaniment of occasionally horrifying details, that Franconi's generally matter-of-fact and low-key approach makes its full impact.

The effect of war service on the individual, particularly on an individual 'd'une race sportive et spirituelle' such as Un Tel, is of considerable interest to Franconi. We have already seen that the admitted need for discipline irks the lively and individualistic Un Tel. He is very much the type of impulsive and positive person in whom war brings out strong qualities of leadership and daring. He responds instinctively to danger and is persuaded that he bears a charmed life. Not least, he derives comfort and support from the thought of the wife and child whom he loves. At a more general level, Franconi writes at some length about the way in which war gives rise to a sense of the supernatural. He notes this phenomenon as a fact, but remains sceptical about its value, describing it as 'un désir d'irréel'. He also refers to simple-minded soldiers who claimed to see 'un drapeau qui flottait dans une étoile' in the sky above the Belgian town of Dixmude. In connection with what he calls 'un mysticisme . . . . né de la guerre' Franconi raises a question which anticipates some later passages in the novel: 'Cette foi, qui ne se relie, à l'heure actuelle, à aucune confession déterminée, reportera-t-elle, vers des buts humains, une force, une passion à de meilleures fins réservées?' (p. 80).

It is said that *Un Tel de l'armée française* was intended as a reply to Barbusse's *Le Feu*. Whether or not this is strictly true, it will be clear that neither pacifism nor protest have much part in Franconi's response to the events of 1914–18. Nothing could be more contrary to Barbusse's attitude than Franconi's bald statement: 'La guerre est une impérieuse nécessité' (p. 144). And he adds a comment which emphasizes Un Tel's role as an exemplar of decorum: 'Un Tel, convaincu de l'efficacité de ses actes, assuré de défendre ses intérêts et ses affections, n'écoutait pas les paroles désabusées de quelques camarades' (p. 144). Above all, Franconi accepts war, with something more positive than resignation, as being inherent in human nature:

> . . . instinctivement, l'homme sera toujours poussé, de siècle en siècle, par cet éternel désir d'errer sur les routes et de se battre, besoin instinctif qui heurte les races et les fait s'entr'égorger, éternel dédain du mâle envers la mort, orgueil d'être fort et jeune qu'une gouape héroïque, en son parler d'arsouille, exprimait ainsi:
> – Cette guerre! C'est pour montrer que nous avions du sang dans les veines. (p. 129)

Here again Franconi faces facts as he sees them. The terms 'gouape héroïque' and 'parler d'arsouille' suggest that he might have wished things to be different. But such wishes do not prevent him from stating firmly what he believes to be the truth.

As in most war novels, whether of decorum or of protest, *Un Tel de l'armée française* expresses contempt for 'le muflisme du civil'. Nevertheless, Franconi's matter-of-factness results in a distinction made by relatively few writers. He points to the essential and sometimes courageous work of those who supply the front-line troops. As he says, 'il est bien que chaque veilleur posté au créneau soit doublé à l'arrière d'un auxiliaire dévoué qui lui prépare sa vie et lui recharge ses armes' (p. 69). When hc turns to those who work further behind the front in what he calls 'un extrême arrière démoralisant où fleurit l'amateurisme de la guerre', he is severe yet fair in his judgement and avoids the caricature in which so many writers indulged:

Stratèges incohérents penchés sur des cartes dérisoires, généraux de plume et combien peu d'épée, maniant à la fois les sophismes les plus contradictoires et les armées, ancien insurgé déguisé en bon berger, tels furent nos amateurs de la guerre. Ils la firent dans les salles de rédaction, les salons académiques et les brasseries littéraires, alors que toute la jeunesse de France agonisait sur les nouveaux champs catalauniques.

Pourtant, malgré l'infamie de ces amateurs, Un Tel n'ignore pas que certains, dont l'exemple ne fut pas suivi, poussèrent leur amour de la guerre jusqu'à la faire eux-mêmes. Ils se battirent, courageusement comme les autres, et moururent. (p. 71)

The reference to academic salons and literary bars is significant. Franconi had published some verse before the war and regarded himself as a poet and man of letters. He took a keen interest in artistic ideas being developed during the war. In particular, he was strongly opposed to the theories of the avant-garde. This was in keeping with his general suspicion of modern 'isms' (the third chapter of his novel has the title 'Ismes et crates'). Fernand Divoire, in his essay on Franconi, describes the latter's pre-war poetry as 'l'expression ordonnée et puissante des sentiments dans la forme traditionnelle de la race'.[10] This formulation confirms Franconi's practice of decorum in literary expression as well as in other ways.

From one point of view the attacks on modern art which occur at various points in the novel do not have much obvious and direct relevance to the war. On the other hand, they are integrated into the overall pattern of the book as part of the broad picture of the *arrière*. It is sometimes suggested that anti-modernism at this period was proto-fascist, but obviously this is not necessarily so. The leaders of the Soviet Union, and indeed of many left-wing governments, have hardly been well disposed towards aesthetic experimentalism. Franconi can be amusing, as in his account of a sculptor, Mortné, who argues that sculpture should be 'une géométrie inexplicable où les troncs de cône chevaucheront des parallélépipèdes' (p. 105) or of another aesthete who wishes that 'la compensation de l'objectif et du subjectif lui permît de réaliser le vrai bloc plastique' (p. 117). And there may be a reference to Apollinaire in a remark about 'ultra-modern' poets who overturn traditional syntax and topography for lack of any more fundamental originality. Nevertheless, some of Franconi's attacks do leave an unpleasant taste in the mouth, more particularly because of their occasional racist overtones and general xenophobia. An irrational attitude identifying modernism with left-wing politics and corrupting foreign and Jewish influences comes out clearly when Un Tel, on leave in Paris, visits a café frequented by avant-garde intellectuals:

Des juives aux cheveux taillés comme de vieux Bretons, à la croupe large, férues d'esthétique et des questions sociales, âpres à soutenir leur race errante, trônaient en des poses martiales, condamnant sans douceur nos institutions et nos œuvres. Leurs époux, frêles adolescents venus des Carpathes lointaines, approuvaient, sans y rien comprendre, les discours de ces viragos.

Autour des petites tables chargées de soucoupes, les métèques audacieux qui prétendent imposer leurs maladies mentales et leurs tares à la pensée française se donnaient rendez-vous. . . . Un Tel exècre cette foule. (pp. 113–14)

Passages such as this do not occur in the novels of either Benjamin or Bertrand. Franconi's attitude is the most overtly ideological of the three and its political aspects emerge more clearly in his speculations on the kind of society which should exist in France once the war has ended. He writes about war itself in a matter-of-fact way. Once he turns to a consideration of peacetime values he displays a form of right-wing romanticism which Holger Klein calls, with some justification, 'idealist pre-fascism'.[11]

The corruption and sterility of French party politics prior to 1914 was a commonplace of intellectual debate on the eve of the war. The Great War itself was regarded by many, however, as an opportunity to make a new political start once peace had returned. Some argued that the party political system could be reformed. Others, more disillusioned, looked for an alternative to the party system. Franconi appears to have belonged to this latter group which attracted the more extreme adherents of both left and right. At several points in the novel Un Tel's rejection of the party system is emphasized. For example: 'Les partis politiques et leurs bas intérêts ne séduisirent point Un Tel, dont la nature indépendante rêvait de se dévouer et de combattre' (pp. 18–19). The danger of Un Tel's dream was, of course, that it led him in the direction of a rejection of parliamentary democracy in favour of an ill-defined movement based on certain military virtues and composed of associations of *anciens combattants*.

This rejection of democracy, as outlined in the novel, has to do not only with an evident lack of idealism in party politics but with Un Tel's early experience of utopian egalitarianism. In the period before the war, when he flirted with anarchism,[12] he was disillusioned by the spectacle of a communist-inspired community which was quickly destroyed by internal strife. The narrator says of Un Tel:

Au reste, l'échec d'une colonie communiste où des ouvriers, des professeurs et un vacher s'arrachèrent, durant quelques semaines, les cheveux, sous l'œil irrité de saint Bakounine, suffit à lui prouver qu'il importait de rejeter à jamais, comme utopique et néfaste, le désir de faire vivre en commun, sur un même plan social, les diversités d'hommes. (p. 18)

Although Un Tel is no egalitarian he does not favour one of the usual forms of social or intellectual élitism. He finds his particular élite among his fellow-combatants who will form 'l'aristocratie de demain'. He makes the very doubtful assumption that his companions at the front, deeply imbued with a sense of fraternity and of public-spirited devotion to duty, will be able to impose their will on the powers that be if they organize properly. It seems rash to deduce from Franconi's novel that he favoured a military take-over. Indeed, he specifically says that the groups of ex-combatants which he has in mind will be unarmed. But Un Tel does intend to set up groups which, in ways not specified, and outside the existing parliamentary framework, will influence public opinion in the direction of justice – not least of justice for the *anciens combattants*.

This latter point appears to be the main motive. It arises from an understandable concern, shown also by Barbusse and other left-wing writers, that the war should not have been fought in vain and that its lessons, learned in blood and death, should not be forgotten. Franconi dismisses the view that once the war is over those who have seen active service will only be concerned to enjoy themselves and compensate for four years of suffering. In a passage that is obviously more naïve than menacing he writes:

Le droit nouveau, né dans la tranchée, s'oppose absolument à cette conception basse de la vie future des soldats victorieux.
Un Tel a décidé de faire suivre, chez les citoyens, l'esprit de fraternité et de dévouement qui anime les soldats. Il défendra, au nom de ceux qui se sont battus, au nom des morts, le droit des combattants au bien-être, à la vie équilibrée.

Grouper les soldats de la guerre, ceux qui vraiment l'ont faite; être une force raisonnable et puissante et imposer aux pouvoirs publics la volonté des hommes qui firent la France victorieuse, telle est l'intention d'Un Tel.

Son programme social est simple. Il veut secourir les victimes de la guerre en mettant à contribution les fortunes des munitionnaires, commerçants enrichis au cours de la tourmente, qui se doivent de faire vivre les enfants et les veuves des héros. Il faut à tout prix, une révolution fût-elle nécessaire, extérieurement à toute idée politique ou confessionnelle, exiger qu'une place honorable soit accordée aux combattants dont les sacrifices et les efforts surent assurer la continuation de notre vie nationale. (pp. 170–1)

However, in a later passage, Franconi shows that he has in mind something much more active than an opinion-forming body and that he is ready to work outside and even against constitutionally elected groups:

Certes, cet esprit de corps est redoutable pour l'avenir; il a déplacé l'organisation des partis et des classes, et nulle puissance humaine ne pourrait, maintenant, lutter contre. Les bandes sont constituées; elles ont des chefs, puissants parce qu'ils sont aimés de ceux qui les suivent; redoutables, car ils ont triomphé des pires dangers, vaincu la mort en d'innombrables combats. Ces bandes militaires déséquipées, revenues à la vie sociale, garderont leur esprit communiste, leur amour du danger, leur besoin d'être fortes; elles auront, peut-être, un peu moins d'apparente brutalité. Envers elles, les États n'exerceront aucun moyen répressif. Elles se différencieront des groupes, sans honneur, qui régnaient avant la guerre sur la République: financiers véreux, démagogues assoiffés, rhéteurs ventrus qui pillaient leurs compatriotes, en ce qu'elles auront été créées, pour des buts nobles, dans l'épreuve et sans autre ambition que de partager des souffrances. En vérité, une nouvelle féodalité se lève sur le monde! (pp. 227–8)

It is also clear from several other references in the text that Franconi believes these ex-soldiers will possess inherent authority not only because they have suffered but because they are men of action. Action, according to his dangerous theory, is the immediate source and justification of political and social authority. Those who have power as men of action will show themselves 'indifférents aux systèmes politiques et sociaux'. They will exercise extra-parliamentary control over the nation's destiny.

This is an attitude which both right-wing and left-wing revolutionaries have in common. Indeed, political debate in the 1920s makes it clear that many individuals, whether they moved in a fascist or a communist direction, contemplated similar methods to achieve their ends and often began from a common criticism of bourgeois democracy. It is therefore not surprising that Franconi, in the final expression of his generally right-wing views, should attack capitalism (as Drieu la Rochelle, for example, was later to do):

Être l'esclave de l'or est bien le pire des asservissements. Indifférent à l'égard du capital, Un Tel ne toléra pas que se crée, néanmoins, contre lui ou sans lui, une aristocratie financière, injuste et méprisante; il se tiendra éloigné des partis et des sectes qui jugulent la pensée et lui imposent des modes inférieures ct communes; il revendiquera le principe absolu de la désunion sacrée, la liberté pour tous de penser ct d'exprimer des idées sans les faire entrer dans le cadre d'un parti, le droit de n'avoir d'autre lien que ses affections. (pp. 264–5)

These social and political ideas have taken us far beyond the fictional worlds of Benjamin and Bertrand. Franconi used his novel to say much more than they did about the post-war world to which he looked forward. This may be partly explained by the fact that *Un Tel de l'armée française* was published later than the other two novels, though it appeared in the periodical *L'Éveil* in 1917 before being published in book form in 1918. Concern with the post-war world also appears to be an aspect of Franconi's realism and matter-of-factness. His courage and patriotism are never in doubt, but he was understandably anxious that they should not have been exercised in vain. Hence he saw the war and the subsequent peace as two integral parts of one whole. Benjamin, in *Gaspard,* gave no serious consideration to the conditions of peace. Bertrand, in so far as he anticipated the future, saw it in broad moral and idealistic terms. Franconi saw the war primarily not as something which would naturally regenerate men but as an experience which had to be exploited in practical ways to ensure the type of post-war society which he desired. It is not without irony that Benjamin survived the armistice whereas both Bertrand and Franconi were dead by the time it was signed.

CHAPTER 5

Expressing Protest (I)
Barbusse and Duhamel

The term 'protest' is used here to describe the attitude expressed by most of the better-known novelists who wrote their work during the Great War and as a result of personal experience. 'Protest' is not the precise opposite of 'decorum'. Neither category is wholly uniform and the contrast between them is not total. Nevertheless, as against decorum, protest implies a different general perspective as well as different emphases. It includes reactions which range from humane shock at war's reality to positive pacifist and political propaganda. Often, though not always, it involves severe questioning – even outright rejection – of traditional ideas and official values. In the circumstances of the time it often began as a necessary corrective to war propaganda and as a reaction to civilian *naïveté* or ignorance. The novels of protest refuse to accept the chivalric-heroic ideal, emphasizing the butchery and general dehumanization of war. However the term 'protest' is not intended, any more than the term 'decorum', to indicate a distinct literary category. It is simply a somewhat rough-and-ready way of grouping together certain writers whose reactions to their experiences were broadly alike. To use a distinction made by Irving Howe in another connection, 'protest' is used here as a 'perspective of observation' rather than as a 'category of classification'.[1]

The novel, since its heyday in the nineteenth century, has tended to move in two essentially divergent directions: towards the detailed exploration of private sensibility or towards the expression of wide public concerns. On the second of these fronts, and in a manner which became particularly marked as a result of the Great War, the novel has advanced from an exposition of the *workings* of society to a scrutiny of the *idea* of society as a moral and political concept. Increasingly, novelists 'think in terms of supporting or opposing society as such;

they rally to one or another embattled segment of society; and they do so in the name of, and under prompting from, an ideology'.[2] This comment describes the tendency of several war novelists, and more particularly of certain novelists of protest. Either they already subscribed to an ideology which they applied to the situation (something which the novelists of decorum also did in their own way), or the spectacle of unparalleled human suffering and death brought about a rapid political education or encouraged ideological explanations. The novel, which was rapidly developing techniques for the expression of both private and public crises, proved a particularly appropriate vehicle, in France if not in Britain, for the expression of protest in the face of individual and national catastrophe. In fact the war novel proved a means of bringing together, at least temporarily, the two divergent directions of fiction mentioned above.

As already suggested, the best-known French novelists writing under the immediate impact of war are those who expressed moral and social protest. However, they were not always the most gifted writers among those who, in their various ways, responded to the situation. In some cases – and no doubt often in keeping with their own desires – they were admired as moral voices rather than as artists. In many ways this is right, though of course persuasive power and literary skill are always intimately related at some level. However, various writers of protest have been the objects of over-indulgent criticism either because their readers shared their political prejudices or because aesthetic objections seemed markedly out of place in the context of war's enormities. In fact, the criticism of protest literature involves many difficulties and not a few temptations. If the writers of decorum have often been dismissed – sometimes quite unfairly – as knaves or fools, the writers of protest have occasionally been too readily presented as saints or seers. Stanley Cooperman, who was certainly no friend of writers who maintained decorum before the horrors of war, is right to remind us that there are expressions of anti-war protest 'no less absurd than the pseudo-literature of the Crusade itself'.[3]

If the novel of protest creates difficulties for the critic, it also causes problems for the writer. Indeed, the novel of protest is probably more difficult to compose satisfactorily than the novel of decorum. The very passion that informs it can easily prove a source of moral, psychological, or artistic distortion. Nor is it easy to bring the concrete and the abstract, the details of war and the claims of ideology, into a satisfactory balance. It is obviously important that a novel which protests against war should nevertheless capture the quality of actual experience at the front. It must render human behaviour and individual feeling in a convincing manner. At the same time it must take strong moral exception to much that is most realistic and dramatic in its own content. The novelist of protest must, in short, practise the art of persuasion without falling into the trap of overt propaganda. His aim will be to make the relatively abstract element of protest grow naturally and inevitably out of the concrete events described. Abstraction has to be absorbed into experience, ideology into action, set views into diversity of motive and response. Only in this way can the moral order behind protest – and therefore protest itself – be adequately expressed.

A second problem follows. Like most successful political or religious novels which are something more than direct allegories, novels of protest must allow the interplay of contrasting yet inter-dependent ideas. We saw in the previous chapter that Bertrand went some way along this road in *L'Appel du sol,* though the debates between his characters take place within decorum rather than between the rival claims of decorum and protest. Only a confrontation between protest and those things against which it is directed, a confrontation allowing argumentative power to both sides, can escape the restrictiveness of propaganda. It is the function of literature, including the literature of persuasion, and as against mere propaganda, to work with contrasting viewpoints and to face those awkward facts which tend to undermine or destroy ideological neatness. The novelist of protest will even gain status, and ultimately prove more persuasive, by writing at times against his own convictions and predispositions. The best literature convinces by open discussion rather than by closed assertion.

A third problem can arise, more particularly in any novel of protest which takes war as its specific theme. Since fighting armies – not least in the Great War – are characterized essentially by discipline and obedience, it is not at all easy to make protest an integral part of the action, as distinct from characterizing the writer's own response to his subject matter. Furthermore, most men seem to possess an instinctive psychological mechanism which enables them to live with horror, however much they protest inwardly against it, by occupying themselves with immediate practical concerns. As both Dorgelès and Barbusse, among others, were to point out, the business of mere survival, the need to eat and sleep, to kill fleas or to dry one's sodden uniform, absorbed attention, encouraged acceptance of one's lot, and left little time or energy for protest. Barbusse describes this self-protective mechanism clearly in *Le Feu*:

On se détache du tragique événement pressenti. Est-ce impossibilité de le comprendre tout entier, découragement de chercher à démêler des arrêts qui sont lettre close pour nous, insouciance résignée, croyance vivace qu'on passera à côté du danger cette fois encore? Toujours est-il que, malgré les signes précurseurs, et la voix des prophéties qui semblent se réaliser, on tombe machinalement et on se cantonne dans les préoccupations immédiates: la faim, la soif, les poux dont l'écrasement ensanglante tous les ongles, et la grande fatigue par laquelle nous sommes tous minés.[4]

This strikes one as a true picture. But it means that Barbusse must often rely on authorial intervention, or must put lengthy intellectual statements into the mouths of his very unsophisticated characters, in order to convey a major part of the novel's protest. One is moved and convinced when a soldier, gazing at rotting corpses in a landscape of mud and water, simply exclaims: 'Voilà la guerre'.[5] One is much less convinced, and certainly not moved, when the narrator delivers a lengthy homily on the practical nature of equality while discussing freedom and fraternity as mere abstract concepts.[6]

There is one further general comment which ought to be made before turning to some individual novels of protest written during the 1914–18 war. This is the first war which gave rise – and in an overwhelming way – to a literature of protest. Indeed, it is not an exaggeration to see it as a historical turning-point in the evolution of the European moral sensibility. It has already been pointed out in Chapter 2 that the concepts and vocabulary generally available to writers on war in 1914 were primarily heroic and proclamatory. The virtues of war – courage, patriotism, discipline, comradeship, fighting skills, etc. – were identified with the profession of arms. But the reaction of a civilian army (whether volunteers or conscripts), together with the scale of the slaughter (often for no tangible gains and sometimes in the service of tactical folly), led to a fundamental change of attitude among intellectuals. So much so, indeed, that to find any virtue in the experience of war was to risk the severest moral or political criticism. This was the reaction, for example, to both Montherlant and Drieu la Rochelle who expressed nostalgia for the 'virile fraternity' of the front in contrast to what they interpreted as the decadence of the post-war world. It is not well known, however, that Montherlant, looking back on the war in 1924, both saw its historical significance in the sense just indicated and regarded the shift in the balance from acceptance to protest as a 'résultat heureux'. Having pointed again to the way in which the experience of war teaches love and admiration of one's comrades, he nevertheless continues:

Mais ce fait admis – cette création d'un bien par la guerre – toute la question est: vaut-il le sang versé?

Le passé a répondu: oui. Songeant que les hommes autrefois étaient plus durs, alors que les guerres l'étaient moins, ne les jugeons pas.

Le présent ne peut pas faire cette réponse. L'hypertrophie monstrueuse où tend la guerre moderne a eu au moins ce résultat heureux de faire chavirer la balance, le mal créé par la guerre l'emportant assez sur le bien pour que cette proportion nouvelle frappe les esprits d'attention et d'alarme.[7]

We shall now examine the work of several writers for whom the evils of war greatly outweighed its virtues and who therefore felt compelled to protest vigorously in the name of humanity, fulfilling the intellectual's traditional role as the 'conscience malheureuse' of society.

The most famous novel of protest published in France during the Great War is undoubtedly *Le Feu*. Henri Barbusse experienced the front-line fighting at various times between December 1914 and early 1916 when he was invalided out of the army. He had already published poetry and fiction well before the outbreak of war (he was forty-one in 1914) and *Le Feu* was partly written in the trenches and completed in hospital. It was serialized in the periodical, *L'Œuvre,* from 3 August 1916 and published late in the same year. It sold extremely well,[8] made a deep impression on the public, gave rise to a good deal of controversy, and certainly influenced the writings of other war novelists. The final page is dated December 1915 and one is struck by the fact that such a thoroughgoing work of protest should have appeared so relatively early and passed through the censor's net. In this last respect the work seems to have encountered fewer difficulties than Dorgelès's *Les Croix de bois* published over two years later.

As its sub-title, 'Journal d'une escouade', implies, *Le Feu* is narrated by a member of a squad of seventeen infantry soldiers. Many of them are killed – some in particularly horrifying circumstances – before the end of the book. This is not, however, a novel with a plot which develops and unfolds through successive chapters. The amount of action is limited and a relatively small proportion of its pages is given over to the description of actual fighting. A great deal of it consists of conversations among the men forming the squad, together with further passages of moral and political protest by the narrator himself. Various scenes, themes, and conversations follow one another in quick succession. They coalesce into an increasingly weighty denunciation of the war and of the society which has allowed it to happen. This is partly why many of the chapter-headings read like a glossary of military terms: 'Le Barda', 'La Sape', 'Bombardement', 'Le Feu', 'La Poste de Secours', 'La Corvée', etc. These various headings and settings allow Barbusse to repeat, and therefore to underline heavily, a number of his criticisms and protests. They also contribute to the fact that *Le Feu* covers most of the issues dealt with in wartime fiction: the devastation of the landscape and the destruction of whole villages; the mud, water, lice, and rats associated with trench warfare; the horrifying killing; the alleged easier and safer life of the officers; the baptism of fire; the profits made out of the war by civilian *entrepreneurs*; the contrast between the battlefield and the home front; the fact of propaganda and the folly of each set of combatants invoking the support of a 'nationalistic' God; the prospects of the post-war world, etc. *Le Feu* is a comprehensive, as well as an energetic, document of protest. The fact that to write it required considerable courage is implied in the brief thirteenth chapter. This is placed at the centre of the book and when a member of the squad learns that the narrator intends to publish a truthful account of his experiences he exclaims: 'Quoique je ne m'y connais pas en livres: c'est courageux, ça, parce que ça s'fait pas, et ce sera très chic si tu l'oses . . .' (p. 169).[9]

Although he is mainly concerned with the need to protest, Barbusse is not unaware of the ideals and values to which the writers of decorum subscribed. He does not deny the facts of courage and devotion and allows his narrator to observe briefly: '. . . on a une vague notion de la grandeur de ces morts. Ils ont tout donné; ils ont tout donné, petit à petit, toute leur force, puis, finalement, ils se sont donnés, en bloc. Ils ont dépassé la vie; leur effort a quelque chose de surhumain et de parfait' (p. 268). A statement of this kind, even though it plays no very prominent part in the novel, is a necessary contrast to the overall atmosphere of protest. Unrelieved protest, particularly in the context of war and human suffering, can ultimately appear to lack discrimination and seem to be heartless. The fact that men can suffer and die for a cause compels respect and invites admiration. There is also the fact that many men look back on their war experiences with a measure of nostalgia, even with some sense of pleasure in achievement and a tendency to underplay the horrifying aspects. In short, the intelligent practice of protest must make some allowance for the deep instinct of many, including ex-combatants, to accept the fact of war and absorb it into their general comprehension of life. It is true that in *Le Feu* Barbusse expresses moral outrage at the wickedness of stupid generals and unscrupulous profiteers, but his position is one which many of the common soldiers, whom he seeks to celebrate, would have rejected out of hand. Hence a certain sense of unease throughout the book.[10]

There are several levels of protest in *Le Feu,* ranging from the instinctively moral to the consciously intellectual. It is the first of these levels which is most easily conveyed and makes the greatest impact. In effect, Barbusse allows the facts to speak for themselves, horrifying his readers with details of human suffering and mutilation. There are many such passages of which the following is a typical example: 'Le petit Godefroy, tu le connais? le milieu du corps emporté, il s'est vidé de sang sur place, en un instant, comme un baquet qu'on renverse: petit comme il était, c'était extraordinaire tout le sang qu'il avait; il a fait un ruisseau d'au moins cinquante mètres dans la tranchée' (p. 48). Such passages as these build up to a severe denunciation of modern war as an exercise in butchery rather than the pursuit of glory. A strong and repeated effort is made to deprive war of all its glamour. One is reminded of Wilfred Owen's 'those who die as cattle' by the comments of one of the soldiers on the idealization of war by civilians: 'C'est tout à fait comme si une vache disait: "Ça doit être beau à voir, à la Villette, ces multitudes de bœufs qu'on pousse en avant!" ' (p. 330). The men in the squad regard themselves as potential slaughterhouse material, but they also see themselves as butchers, not heroes (p. 347). Not least they express concern, a concern presumably shared by Barbusse, that the horror of war is too great to be believed and grasped: '. . . comment, sans y avoir été, s'imaginerait-on ça – l'faudrait être fou! dit le chasseur' (p. 331). A desperate determination that the unsayable should be said, the unthinkable thought, the unbelievable believed, intensifies Barbusse's protest throughout the novel.

The fact that, at worst, the men regard themselves as butchers and, at best, are unsure whether they are behaving like Cornelian heroes or vicious killers, leads to a second level of protest. Not only does war kill or physically mutilate those who must be regarded as its innocent victims. It also leaves terrible moral scars on both the dead and the living, the casualties and the survivors. War is described as being 'aussi hideuse au moral qu'au physique' and one character comments on its brutalizing effect: ' – Tout de même, qu'est-ce que nous sommes depuis deux ans? De pauvres malheureux incroyables, mais aussi des sauvages, des brutes, des bandits, des salauds' (p. 335). Again, the traditionally glorious aspects of war are denied. A few army leaders may achieve what is conventionally termed 'la gloire militaire' but the thousands of ordinary soldiers are being required to leap into 'un effroyable néant de gloire' (p. 347).

Apart from the physical and moral destruction of human beings, the kind of warfare which first appeared in 1914 also devastated the countryside and transformed the natural world into a terrifying nightmare. Before they were approached by troops, landscapes were annihilated and villages reduced to rubble by long-range artillery. There is a regular recurrence in *Le Feu* of such phrases as 'la vaste plaine stérilisćc, cautérisée (p. 150), 'ce paysage de sabbat' (p. 225), 'des champs écorchés et martyrisés' (p. 348), etc. The phenomenon of concentrated violence is shown in all its intensity and the impression is given that it is fundamentally unnatural because it destroys natural objects. The scale of protest is widened as it takes in not only the extinction of human life but of the physical world which supports it. Only protest on such a scale, dealing as it does with the fundamental features of human existence, is at all likely to carry conviction, to change attitudes, to make it clear that war in the modern world is no longer a great crusade or a stepping-stone to glory.

These various forms of protest, essentially moral, humane, and instinctive, are what one might expect of any man of goodwill. They suggest the shock which the facts of the front-line fighting induced in most participants, and they represent the level at which most war protest was carried out. Barbusse goes much further than this, however. Although he protests sincerely at this level, the degree of spontaneity is limited by the fact that he already approached the war, before having experience of the front, in a strong anti-war spirit. As early as 9 August 1914 he had written to the editor of *'L'Humanité*: 'Voulez-vous me compter parmi les socialistes antimilitaristes qui s'engagent volontaire-ment pour la présente guerre?'[11] This makes his position clear enough and throws light on the more intellectual and political level of protest on which the novel ends. In fact, from this early date, he conceived of the war as a means by which to hasten the political changes which he sought. Therefore he observes in the same letter: 'Cette guerre est une guerre sociale qui fera faire un grand pas – peut-être le pas définitif – à notre cause.' This explains the element of contradiction in Barbusse's more intellectual forms of protest. War is to be condemned, but also to be exploited for socio-political ends. War profiteers and battle-intoxicated generals may in fact be unconscious architects of the socialist utopia. Hence a phrase on the very last page of *Le Feu* which appears to undermine the main emotional burden of the preceding 348 pages: 'Si la guerre actuelle a fait avancer le progrès d'un pas, ses malheurs et ses tueries compteront pour peu.' This suggests a moral revaluation and a relationship between ends and means which, however familiar in the more violent manifestations of left-wing ideology, dismisses with astonishing insouciance the kind of protest which we have so far examined.

The transition from moral protest to intellectual attack is facilitated
by various critical references to pro-war propaganda. The 'establish-
ment' is first denounced in terms of the way in which the State and the
Church support the war-effort. Barbusse equates the war as patriotic
crusade with the 'lies and sterility' to be found in the pious pamphlets,
cards, pictures, and other scraps of debased propaganda found
scattered from the pockets and packs of a group of dead German
soldiers (p. 271). There are also several references to the folly of French
and German troops, dug in less than 100 yards from one another,
invoking the same God, celebrating the same mass, yet under orders to
destroy each other. Associated with these ideas is the view that war is a
dramatic demonstration of God's non-existence. Such human suffering
is incompatible with the concept of a God of love. The atheism of the
soldiers is given repeated expression and their attitude is summed up
by one of their number who says: 'Pour croire en Dieu, il faudrait
qu'il n'y ait rien de c'qu'ya' (p. 287). One should add, however, that
Barbusse does not make this kind of criticism in his own name or
through his narrator. He maintained elsewhere, on more than one
occasion, that few priests were genuinely exposed to danger.[12] But a
few pages after the remark just quoted above he allows his narrator to
comment as follows on the death of an army chaplain whose ideas and
beliefs he none the less found thoroughly alien:

Je regarde cette énorme masse immobilisée, et je songe que cet homme était
bon. Il avait un cœur pur et sensible. Et combien je me reproche de l'avoir
quelquefois malmené à propos de l'étroitesse naïve de ses idées et d'une
certaine indiscrétion ecclésiastique qu'il apportait en tout! . . . Je me rappelle
la fois où il m'a tant exaspéré avec son explication sur la Sainte-Vierge et la
France. Il me paraissait impossible qu'il émît sincèrement ces idées-là.
Pourquoi n'aurait-il pas été sincère? *Est-ce qu'il n'était pas bien réellement
tué aujourd'hui?* Je me rappelle aussi certains traits de dévouement, de
patience obligeante de ce gros homme dépaysé dans la guerre comme dans la
vie – et le reste n'est que détails. (p. 294)

It is in the final chapter of *Le Feu* that Barbusse makes his main
intellectual protest with its social and political assumptions. He uses
the comments of the soldiers in the squad to attack militarism (identified with Germany) and nationalism (identified especially with a
younger generation than his own). In common with many socialists of
the period, whose descendants now acclaim Third World nationalism,
he held internationalism as an ideal and regarded nationalism as little
more than a way of making crimes seem like virtues. He argues that
economists, historians, and others are quite wrong to regard

antagonism and conflict between national groupings as justified and natural. He asserts – sensibly, at a theoretical level – that nationhood is based on very arbitrary facts of geography and that, in any case, national purity is a myth. One of the soldiers expresses his anti-nationalism in much more direct and pithy terms when he exclaims: 'Les chauvins, c'est d'la vermine' (p. 337).

At a more complex level of argument Barbusse justifies his position on the grounds that it is not enough to win the war, to defeat the enemy. War itself must be defeated and this can only be achieved, paradoxically, by continuing the war in peacetime. The paradox here is to be explained by the fact that he regards the conditions of warfare, and the experience of war by the common soldier, as a microcosm of the peacetime capitalist macrocosm. This seems to be what he meant in 1914 when he described the war as a 'social' war. In other words – and clearly begging several important questions in the process – he sees war as an especially concentrated and dramatic form of that sacrifice of the 'people' by the 'bosses' which, in his view, characterizes western society. The argument is not a notably logical one. Put in its least paradoxical terms it suggests that the ordinary soldiers, having defeated the German enemy, must then turn to attack the leaders of peacetime society whose wartime counterparts are the privileged generals and the dishonourable profiteers. The experience of war will have greatly sharpened their political awareness and given a cutting edge to their sense of injustice and oppression. It will have shown them how to extend, and bring to a more effective and practical conclusion, the French Revolution of 1789 ('C'est la Révolution Française qui recommence', p. 3). It is no doubt with the Revolution in mind that Barbusse introduced into the closing pages of *Le Feu* a discussion of the three ideals of liberty, equality, fraternity. It is significant that he regards equality as the only reality among these ideals and, in the person of the narrator, dismisses fraternity and liberty:

Je leur dis que la fraternité est un rêve, un sentiment nuageux, inconsistant; qu'il est contraire à l'homme de haïr un inconnu, mais qu'il lui est également contraire de l'aimer. On ne peut rien baser sur la fraternité. Sur la liberté non plus: elle est trop relative dans une société où toutes les présences se morcellent forcément l'une l'autre. (p. 341)

It is not a large step from this position to the hard-line communism adopted by Barbusse in the 1920s and 1930s, ending with a eulogistic biography of Stalin.[13] Holding firmly to the view that society must be ordered by 'scientific' laws, and asserting that the end justifies the means, he rejected anything which he regards as sentimental moralism, argued the need for violence, opposed liberal concepts of freedom, and accepted an essentially conflictual, class-based view of human relationships. These ideas were to emerge clearly in the post-war argument between Barbusse and Romain Rolland when the latter declined to join the editorial board of *Clarté*.[14]

The final pages of *Le Feu* make an unfortunate end to the novel. For one thing, most of the assumptions behind them have been denied by the subsequent history of Europe. Also, the absence of genuine argument or discussion in these pages creates an impression of dogmatism and propaganda. This is both disturbing and irritating, particularly after the many striking details and vivid descriptions which enriched the protest of the earlier pages.

What we have followed, in this account of Barbusse's novel of protest against the war and against the social structure which, in his view, brought it about, is his movement from precise realistic detail to general prophetic vision. Much of the novel remains memorable because of its documentary value and the sense it conveys of lived experience, but it ends with such vague invocations of futurity as: 'L'entente des démocraties, l'entente des immensités, la levée du peuple du monde, la foi brutalement simple . . . Tout le reste, tout le reste, dans le passé, le présent et l'avenir, est absolument indifférent' (pp. 348–9). It would be difficult to give clear meaning to such a statement. However, coming as it does after the earlier sections of *Le Feu,* it serves to remind us that this novel brings together in a striking way elements of the epic, the documentary and the visionary. It begins with the picture of a symbolic storm raging round Mont Blanc, it goes on to an account of the sufferings and deaths of individual soldiers, and it ends with some hope for the future suggested by a ray of light glimpsed between two black storm clouds. All three literary modes – allegory, mimesis, prophecy – contribute in their different ways, and with varying degrees of success, to that sense of uncompromising protest which characterizes Barbusse's novel.

War protest generally, including a sense of outrage at the butchery of the trenches, is essentially a point of departure in Barbusse's work. For Georges Duhamel, however, horror at the killing and wounding of ordinary men is something much more like a total position. Duhamel's war writings are characterized by a complete commitment to humanitarian goals and a concern to convey the full emotional impact of what he has witnessed. His reaction, and the appeal which he addresses to his readers, are both associated with the high ideals of traditional humanism. In many ways he shares the assumptions of those writers who sought to maintain decorum. Unlike them, however, he saw the war not as a theatre for the exercise of traditional virtues but as the graveyard of many of the most important moral values.

In the years before 1914 Duhamel had produced a number of fairly modest literary works and was a leading figure, with other young writers and artists, in the idealistic Abbaye de Créteil community. He also possessed medical qualifications and after the outbreak of war he worked as an army surgeon behind the front line. He was rightly described by Dorgelès as one of the 'écrivains-soldats de ma génération'.[15] In view of his particular role during the war, his two main works of this period, *Vie des martyrs 1914–1916* and *Civilisation 1914–1917,* are not wide-ranging protests against all aspects of the fighting. They concentrate in a major way on the phenomenon of torn and mutilated human flesh. After the war Duhamel and Barbusse were fairly loosely associated for some time in the *Clarté* movement, but whereas Barbusse argued the need for violent social revolution, Duhamel, as we shall see in Chapter 7 below, looked for salvation in a renewal of the traditional values of western liberal humanism.

Vie des martyrs was published in 1917 and *Civilisation* in 1918. The latter volume was awarded the Prix Goncourt for that year. Neither book is a novel in the strict sense of the term. Both are collections of scenes and sketches, mainly of the wounded and dying in various field hospitals and clearing stations at different times and places during the war. As in so much war writing, fiction and reportage are combined to produce *souvenirs romancés.* They include descriptions of conditions at Verdun and on the Somme, with the demand for medical services generally exceeding supplies. Gruesome details of wounding and mutilation are not concealed, though Duhamel somehow manages to describe these things more respectfully, as it were, than Barbusse. His intention to tell the truth to the world emerges clearly in *Vie des martyrs* as he addresses one of his own characters: '. . . je ne veux pas que toute ta souffrance se perde dans l'abîme. Et c'est pourquoi je la raconte très exactement' (p. 33).[16] He succeeded, and both books made a deep impression on their readers.

There is no doubt that Duhamel was concerned to explain clearly, and as a doctor, the technological assault on the human body experienced during the Great War.[17] This machine-perfected killing is referred to in *Vie des martyrs*:

Tous les médecins ont pu remarquer l'atroce succès remporté, en si peu de temps, par le perfectionnement des engins de dilacération. Et nous admirions amèrement que l'homme pût aventurer son fragile organisme à travers les déflagrations d'une chimie à peine disciplinée, qui atteint et dépasse en brutalité les puissances aveugles de la nature. Nous admirions surtout qu'une chair aussi délicate, pétrie d'harmonie, créatrice d'harmonie, supportât sans se désagréger aussitôt, de tels chocs et de tels délabrements. (p. 103)

At the same time, he also drew attention to the heroic manifestations of the human spirit and the often disconcerting reactions of individuals in the face of such suffering. In an earlier section of the same book, 'Mémorial de la vie des martyrs', he sketches brief portraits of more than twenty wounded or dying men which are by turns impressive, touching, or enigmatic. Duhamel writes of their 'vies précieuses', their 'pauvres âmes extraordinaires', and he sees to it that we respond not only to the damaged materiality of these human beings but also to their unquenchable spirituality. Here again Duhamel comes close to the writers of decorum. He has too exalted a view of men to accept that they can ever 'die as cattle'. And as he looks at a military cemetery 'd'hommes jeunes et forts' he imagines the hundreds of small wooden crosses saying: 'Il y a donc quelque chose de plus précieux que la vie, il y a donc quelque chose de plus nécessaire que la vie . . . puisque nous sommes ici' (p. 80).

This is clearly far removed from the language of total and irreducible protest. Suffering is not presented as being wholly negative. Nevertheless one could argue – and indeed this seems to be part of the burden of Duhamel's message – that the very qualities in men which suffering uncovers or releases make it all the more outrageous that human beings, possessing such potentiality, should be physically broken and crushed in this way. Protest can thus be strengthened precisely because it recognizes positive as well as negative elements in the object of its attack. And so, even when Barbusse and Duhamel are protesting against the same feature of war, their protests take on very different characteristics. The uncompromising and unilinear view of Barbusse reflects his dogmatic marxism; the more tentative and 'multiple' view of Duhamel reflects his much more open and flexible position. This is not necessarily to say that Duhamel's protest is the more impressive and convincing. In some ways it is inevitably less sharply defined than that of Barbusse and often tips over into sentimentality. It seems fair to say that both writers are more precise about what they attack than about what they advocate or defend. However, in reading Duhamel, one does not have that sense of being manipulated for only partly disclosed ends which one sometimes experiences in reading Barbusse.

The more one reads Duhamel, in fact, the more one is struck by the difference between his protest, both its form and its substance, and that of Barbusse. At the formal level Duhamel is a master of the economically sketched scene and an exponent, above all, of expressive understatement. Where Barbusse so often conveys horror by the heavy, cumulative methods associated with nineteenth-century realism, Duhamel achieves the same ends by means of an impressionistic brevity and suggestiveness. In *Civilisation,* for example, his account of Revaud who dies after having a leg amputated is moving in its discretion and restraint. The short account of Revaud's death is typical:

Revaud passa une nuit suffisamment bonne, et quand, le lendemain, Mme Baugan pénétra dans la chambre, il lui dit comme à l'ordinaire:
'Ben, madame Baugan! J'ai assez bien dormi!'
Il dit cela, puis il pencha la tête sur le côté, il ouvrit la bouche peu à peu, et il mourut, sans faire d'histoires.
Mme Bougan s'écria:
'Pauvre Revaud! Mais, il est mort . . .'
Elle l'embrassa sur le front et, tout de suite, elle commença la toilette funèbre, car la journée est longue et il ne faut pas perdre de temps.
Mme Baugan habillait Revaud et bougonnait avec bonté, parce que le cadavre ne se laissait pas habiller facilement.
Sandrap, Mery et Remusot ne disaient rien. La pluie ruisselait le long des vitres qui continuaient de trembler, à cause du canon. (pp. 19–20)

Such understated presentation will intensify most readers' response. It is simple, yet also sensitively and artistically managed, and it does not lack realism. No doubt this type of literary expression was regarded by Duhamel as being in keeping with his subject matter. He refers several times to the modesty and discretion of these suffering and dying men, as in this comment on one of them in *Vie des martyrs:* 'Il mourait avec une discrétion, une espèce de modestie, un oubli de soi-même qui rachetaient tout l'égoïsme du monde' (p. 177). In fact, Duhamel stands for classical *mesure* in his literary response to catastrophe whereas Barbusse is drawn towards the relative *outrance* of naturalism. Barbusse's naturalism goes with his social and political preoccupations while Duhamel's more classical restraint reflects a concern with ethical solutions. Barbusse identifies civilization with a society transformed by political revolution. Duhamel sees it as the outcome of a spiritual revolution characterized by a rejection of material values, a genuine concern for suffering individuals, and a set of arrangements which will bring to the surface the essential goodness of the human heart. It is noticeable that Duhamel does not speak of a 'social war' or suggest that this martyrdom of men will have been justified if it results in the dictatorship of the proletariat.

At the stage of *Vie des martyrs,* indeed, Duhamel is not prepared to discuss in any detail the future of society. He concentrates on the immediate relief of suffering and the expression of protest. As the narrator operates on a soldier, Grégoire, he breaks out: 'Vous tous, messieurs, qui vous réunissez pour parler des causes de la guerre, de la fin de la guerre, de l'usure des effectifs et des bases de la société future, excusez-moi de ne point vous donner mon opinion sur ces graves questions; je suis vraiment trop occupé par la plaie de ce malheureux Grégoire' (pp. 153–4). It is only a year later, in the closing pages of *Civilisation,* that the narrator, as he contemplates a new sterilizer, allows himself some brief comments on the nature of a civilized society:

On se trompe sur le bonheur et sur le bien. Les âmes les plus généreuses se trompent aussi, parce que le silence et la solitude leur sont trop souvent refusés. J'ai bien regardé l'autoclave monstrueux sur son trône. Je vous le dis, en vérité, la civilisation n'est pas dans cet objet, pas plus que dans les pinces brillantes dont se servait le chirurgien. La civilisation n'est pas dans toute cette pacotille terrible: et, si elle n'est pas dans le cœur de l'homme, eh bien, elle n'est nulle part. (p. 189)

The more he meditates on war, in fact, the more Duhamel sees it as a particularly intense and dramatic manifestation of the general fault of modern civilization. This fault – indeed this folly – is the application of science and technology without humanity. Men do not simply suffer from machine-made weapons of destruction. The rational and scientific attitude has reached a point where the medical treatment of these human victims is itself mechanical and detached, reducing men to abstract entities. Describing the latest type of field ambulance in *Civilisation* the narrator comments:

C'est le comble de la science, comme les canons de 400 sur voie ferrée; ça suit les armées avec moteurs, machines à vapeur, microscopes, laboratoires, tout un outillage d'hôpital moderne. C'est le premier grand atelier de réparation que l'homme blessé rencontre au sortir de l'atelier de trituration et de destruction qui fonctionne à l'extrême avant. On apporte là les pièces les plus endommagées de la machine militaire. Des ouvriers habiles se jettent dessus, les déboulonnent en vitesse et les examinent avec compétence, comme on ferait d'un frein hydropneumatique, d'une culasse ou d'un collimateur. Si la pièce est sérieusement avariée, on fait le nécessaire pour lui assurer une réforme convenable; mais si le 'matériel humain' n'est pas absolument hors

d'usage, on le rafistole avec soin pour le remettre en service à la première
occasion, et cela s'appelle 'la conservation des effectifs'. (p. 181)

Duhamel was to draw straightforward conclusions, and to express
them directly in his own voice, in *La Possession du monde* which was
published in 1919: 'La civilisation scientifique et industrielle, basée sur
l'intelligence, est condamnée . . . Son règne aboutit à un immense
échec. C'est vers les ressources du cœur que se tourne notre espoir.'[18]

These various quotations make it obvious enough that the humanism
underlying Duhamel's protest is more emotional than intellectual. It is
rooted in feeling rather than grounded in rational analysis. It places its
main emphasis on individual reformation rather than collectivist transformation. The humanist in Duhamel puts his confidence in 'le cœur
humain'. At this point, then, his protest can be prone to sentimentality.
His descriptions of human suffering in the dressing stations avoid
sentimentality by the low-key and understated presentation already
described. This is true both of the scenes of doctors working on
wounded men in *Vie des martyrs* and the panoramic descriptions of
the battlefield in *Civilisation*. But in the passages of reflection which
he adds to some of these scenes emotional assertion takes the place of
logically worked out argument. Words are in danger of becoming a
substitute for thought. Where Barbusse trailed off into intellectual
imprecision (as in the 'entente des immensités' passage quoted above),
Duhamel concludes his *Vie des martyrs* in sentimental vagueness:
'Union des cœurs purs pour l'épreuve! Union des cœurs purs pour que
notre pays se connaisse et s'admire! Union des cœurs purs pour la
rédemption du monde malheureux!' (p. 189). He shows little or no
capacity to solve the old and familiar dilemma that lies in wait for a
simple humanist faith. He does not face the implications of the fact
that the very evils to which men are subjected by war are evils created
by man.

Duhamel's humanism implies that the answer to the catastrophe of
war is to be found in arrangements which will somehow ensure that
the finest qualities of men dominate their tendencies to weakness and
evil. The problem of war is seen as an ethical one. It is an evil that
must be overcome by moral means. To this extent the Great War
seems to have been interpreted by Duhamel as a wrong turning, a
reversal of the right moral elements in man's development rather than
a radical crisis in western civilization. Ultimate confidence in the
fundamental workings of human nature was central to his whole
position. He faced the suffering and death caused by war, resisted any

temptation to ignore the human folly of which it was a manifestation, yet retained his humanistic optimism.

As regards the idea of a wrong turning taken by modern man, we have seen that Duhamel largely identified this with the attitude of scientific rationalism (which Barbusse, in contrast, interpreted as the only sound basis for human progress). He was dismayed by the increasing evidence of a society given over to materialism, abstraction, quantification, a society which looked for collectivist solutions to individual problems and which treated human beings as mere elements in a logistic exercise. All this was the peacetime equivalent of that 'civilisation scientifique et industrielle' which wrought such destructive havoc in the context of war. He appears to have maintained faith in the future, at least in part, by arguing that science, despite its manifest excesses, was also itself devising imaginative counter-measures against these very things. Thus, gazing at the latest medical equipment, he writes in *Civilisation*: 'C'était la réplique de la civilisation à elle-même, la correction qu'elle donnait à ses débordements destructeurs; il ne fallait pas moins de toute cette complexité pour annuler un peu du mal immense engendré par l'âge des machines' (p. 187). In fact, of course, there is little comfort to be found in this type of argument. It implies a continuous chain reaction in which the civilizing responses of science depend on repeated and prior outbreaks of technological barbarity.

The misapplication of scientific skill and rationalistic analysis are obviously the surface expression of deeper, underlying ills. At the end of *Civilisation* Duhamel touches on this fact, indicating that civilization has failed to live up to its own highest ideals. He identifies these ideals with art and religion:

La civilisation, la vraie, j'y pense souvent. C'est, dans mon esprit, comme un chœur de voix harmonieuses chantant un hymne, c'est une statue de marbre sur une colline desséchée, c'est un homme qui dirait: 'Aimez-vous les uns les autres!' ou: 'Rendez le bien pour le mal!' Mais il y a près de deux mille ans qu'on ne fait plus que répéter ces choses-là, et les princes des prêtres ont bien trop d'intérêts dans le siècle pour concevoir d'autres choses semblables. (p. 189)

The humanist in Duhamel defines civilization here in terms of its art – its music and sculpture. The abiding testimony of art brings a measure of comfort and hope. It is evidence of man's ability to understand and express spiritual truth. But Duhamel, although an agnostic humanist, also seeks his ideal in the teachings of Christ. He implies that civilization must be based on the Christian faith. He admits that a difficulty remains, however, since Christian ideals have been betrayed by men, and not least by Christians, for nearly two thousand years. Nevertheless, he gives little evidence of facing the consequences of this fact. He does not go significantly beyond the expression of solemn invocation. It is the achievements of the human spirit in adversity that move him most. His instinctive reaction is one of compassion for victims rather than of anger at perpetrators.

One has to conclude that Duhamel's expressions of protest were not based on a realization of the fundamental significance of the war – what Malraux was later to describe as the twentieth-century 'death of man' following on the nineteenth-century 'death of God'. Rather, he equates the Great War with a general tendency of man to fail to give practical expression to his own highest ideals. It is only fair to add, however, that very few participants in the war understood what it meant until time for further reflection and greater detachment had elapsed. And if we can hardly share Duhamel's suggestions about the meaning of the war, we must remain impressed by the tact and compassion with which he portrayed its horror.

CHAPTER 6

Expressing Protest (II)
Dorgelès and Werth

It is natural that one should seek to establish certain comparisons and contrasts between Barbusse's *Le Feu* and Dorgelès's *Les Croix de bois.* With the possible exception of *L'Appel du sol,* they are the two most impressive novels written in France under the immediate impact of war. They contain memorable, and often very similar, accounts of human experience – above all the experience of suffering and horror – on the Western Front. At the formal level, too, they treat their common subject matter in much the same way. A first-person narrator allows the reader to follow the fortunes of a squad of men drawn, in Dorgelès's case, from a wide variety of social backgrounds. The conversations of these soldiers are reported at considerable length and mainly in colloquial transcription. By the end of each novel many of them have been killed after passing through the familiar pattern of initiation into modern warfare and participation in a series of attacks interspersed with rest periods behind the lines. Neither novel has a plot in the conventional sense. There is no evolving intrigue culminating in a dénouement. The increasing familiarization of the men with horror and catastrophe creates some sense of development and forward movement, but the overall pattern is created more by separate juxtaposed scenes than by linear advance.

Since Dorgelès did not publish his novel until 1919, it is usually assumed that he benefited from the appearance of Barbusse's work in 1916. Nevertheless, he claimed in 1964 that he was uninfluenced by earlier war novels for the simple reason that he had not read them. But he does admit familiarity with some magazine extracts from Benjamin's *Gaspard,* Malherbe's *La Flamme au poing,* and *Le Feu.*[1] In fact, it would be difficult to deny some notable similarities between his fictional character Sulphart and Benjamin's Gaspard. At a more general level, his basic choice of material and methods reflects closely the earlier options adopted by Barbusse.

While they share a common intention to register protest, Dorgelès
and Barbusse express this protest in very different ways. We saw in the
previous chapter that Barbusse exploits his material as vigorously as
possible and intervenes in his novel in order to tell the reader how he
should react to various incidents. Dorgelès, on the contrary, is much
more inclined to allow the facts to speak for themselves without benefit
of authorial comment. Where Barbusse adds a dimension of moral
and ideological outrage and seeks to persuade the reader to share it,
Dorgelès relies on the effect of direct witness. He seems to have a confidence in the reader's response which Barbusse curiously lacks. The
fact is that Barbusse interpreted the Great War as a particularly striking
sympton of social and political evils which he wished to transform by
revolutionary means. This political and ideological dimension is
absent from *Les Croix de bois.* In fact, Dorgelès is perhaps closer to
Duhamel in the sense that he responded to his war experience in predominantly moral and psychological terms. Nevertheless, as against
the writings of either Duhamel or Barbusse, *Les Croix de bois* is both
more pragmatic and more restrained in attitude and tone. The general
approach is one of cool assessment, without any hint of moral or
political stridency. For Barbusse, in particular, protest means anger
and a direct assault on his readers' sensibility. For Dorgelès it means
careful documentation and trust in the instinctive moral response of
his audience.

In 1913 Roland Lecavelé was arrested for his part in an anti-military
protest outside the Gare de l'Est. By August of the following year,
although he had been exempted (like Barbusse) from military service,
he joined up as a volunteer. He fought on the Western Front and won
the *croix de guerre.* In 1916 he transferred to the Flying Corps and a
flying accident eventually brought his active service to an end in June
of that year. He remained in uniform, occupying various posts including
that of instructor at Longvic. On 1 April 1919, on the very day on
which he was demobilized, his novel *Les Croix de bois* appeared under
his literary name of Roland Dorgelès. From that time onwards the
name Dorgelès was associated first and foremost with his achievements
as a war novelist. In 1917, in collaboration with Régis Gignoux, he had
published a satire on arms manufacturers and the life of the *arrière* in
La Machine à finir la guerre. In 1919, in addition to *Les Croix de bois,*
he published a collection of short stories under the title *Le Cabaret de
la belle femme.* Both books of 1919 drew on the very large collection
of notes and sketches written by Dorgelès during more than four years

of war. Several later works returned to aspects of his wartime experiences. Dorgelès himself described *Le Réveil des morts* (1923) as a 'livre
d'après-guerre où la guerre saigne encore',[2] and other war writings
include *Souvenirs sur les Croix de bois* (1929) and *Bleu horizon* (1949).

On several occasions Dorgelès commented on the origin and nature
of *Les Croix de bois*. We have already seen that he attempted to minimize the influence on his work of other writers. In the same way, while
he admits that he made an enormous number of notes during his war
service, he claims that he later lost most of them.[3] His purpose here is
clear. As a professional writer, and although a sober witness of the
horrors of war, he is anxious that *Les Croix de bois* should be accepted
as an original novel, as a work of the artistic imagination, and not
interpreted as a lightly fictionalized memorandum. He claims for this
book the truth of art rather than the detailed accuracy of documentation. This is the emphasis contained in his assertion: '. . . j'ai
incorporé dans un récit imaginaire des éclats de vérite.'[4] At the same
time, although he underlines the artistic and imaginative qualities of
his work, he makes it clear that his novel was initially prompted and
shaped by his moral experiences and not by his story-telling instinct or
by technical considerations of plot. He suggests that the incidents of
the novel were invented with the purpose of creating an authentic
moral experience for the reader, a 'long enseignement de grandeur et
de misère, d'héroïsme et de férocité'.[5] The writer in Dorgelès was
originally attracted by the unique human experiences which war
offered, the total change of direction which it gave to his life, the
opportunity of examining human behaviour by recourse to what he
termed 'ce grand confessionnal que furent les tranchées'.[6] The need for
moral protest soon made itself clear, however, and he tells us:
'J'apprenais à souffrir, pour témoigner au nom de ceux qui ont tant
souffert.'[7] In fact, the motive behind *Les Croix de bois* is the creation of
an artistic monument to his companions in war. Given his subject matter
and the sufferings of his companions, such a monument also becomes an
expression of protest. But this protest is circumscribed – yet for many
readers also intensified – by the fidelity and scrupulousness which such
a monument requires.

This last point means that facts are never made subservient to the
demands of protest in *Les Croix de bois*. On the contrary, the degree
of protest is dependent on the details recorded in the course of creating a
fitting literary monument to the dead. Whereas Barbusse chooses details
that will fortify the reader's sense of outrage, Dorgelès creates or
remembers details that will renew the reality which he and his

companions experienced. Thus, on certain occasions, his soldiers sing. On others, they have a temporary sense of well-being.[8] And at least twice we are shown a soldier picking flowers on the battlefield. Such an activity is unthinkable in *Le Feu*. In a similar way, Dorgelès's less narrow focus allows him to report natural details which escape Barbusse's attention. Indeed, he possesses a more direct sense of the natural world being destroyed by the weapons of war. He repeatedly notices the birds that frequent the battlefield – a kestrel, carrion, crows, a lark, partridges, ducks, a chaffinch – and there is a memorable scene of rabbits, their fur alight, running past a burning farmhouse set on fire by an artillery bombardment (p. 49). Barbusse's landscapes are often visionary and hallucinatory in quality. Those of Dorgelès remain closer to everyday life as he notes birds and animals, people moving in a farmyard, an abandoned reaping machine on the edge of the battlefield. But the destruction and distortion of nature (e.g. '. . . quelques pieux qui avaient été des arbres', p. 205) never quite conveys the sense of primordial chaos suggested by Barbusse.

The fact that Dorgelès's protest is laconic and non-ideological, by comparison with that of Barbusse, can be seen in various other ways. For example, as noted in the previous chapter, there is a passage towards the end of *Le Feu* in which the concept of equality is discussed in political terms and in a context in which liberty and fraternity are dismissed on practical grounds. The concept of equality also occurs briefly in *Les Croix de bois* but here there is no political discussion. Gilbert Demachy, a law student in civilian life, expresses doubt when Sulphart, a Parisian factory worker, links equality with republicanism. Sulphart's definition of equality, if it lacks finesse, appears more realistic and more in character than would an abstract and high-sounding political formulation:

> – Puisqu'on est en République on devrait tous être égal.
> Gilbert, qui n'est pas démocrate, hausse les épaules et fait sa petite moue de guenon déçue.
> – L'égalité, c'est un mot, l'égalité . . . Qu'est-ce que c'est, l'égalité?
> Sulphart réfléchit un instant. Puis il répond sans vouloir rire:
> – L'égalité, c'est de pouvoir dire m. . . . à tout le monde. (p. 158)

One has no sense here that Dorgelès is using this conversation to press on his readers a particular political viewpoint. Once the material has been placed before the reader he is free to interpret it or respond to it as he will. Dorgelès consistently respects his readers' autonomy.

It was pointed out in Chapter 3 that most war novels written between 1914 and 1919 contain a three-part pattern which may be roughly described as anticipation of battle, experience of battle, withdrawal from battle. *Les Croix de bois* is no exception. The first third of the book takes its tone and interest from the impending menace of battle experience and possible death or disfigurement for the small group of soldiers whom we meet in the first chapter. The sense of foreboding and the opportunities for irony are handled by Dorgelès in a way that also contributes to the protest against war which the novel quietly articulates. Foreboding is pre-eminent as a battalion of reinforcements leaves for the front, its rifles decorated with flowers. It is described as being 'fleuri comme un grand cimetière' (p. 5) and watched by women 'qui attendaient, sur le môle des gares, le retour improbable de leurs maris partis' (p. 6). Later, as the newly arrived soldiers pass a military cemetery, the narrator says of the dead buried there: '. . . l'on eût dit que leurs croix se penchaient, pour choisir dans nos rangs ceux qui, demain, les rejoindraient' (pp. 47–8). Yet irony takes over at this point in the sense that, for Gilbert Demachy and others, including the narrator, their first sight of battle is disappointing. It leaves them unmoved and unexcited. It seems unreal. The narrator says of Demachy:

C'était pour lui une déception, cette première vision de la guerre. Il aurait voulu être ému, éprouver quelque chose, et il regardait obstinément vers les tranchées, pour se donner une émotion, pour frissonner un peu.

Mais il se répétait: 'C'est la guerre . . . Je vois la guerre' sans parvenir à s'émouvoir. Il ne ressentait rien, qu'un peu de surprise. Cela lui semblait tout drôle et déplacé, cette féeric électrique au milieu des champs muets. Les quelques coups de fusil que claquaient avaient un air inoffensif. Même ce village dévasté ne le troublait pas: cela ressemblait trop à un décor. C'était trop ce qu'on pouvait imaginer. Il eût fallu des cris, du tumulte, une fusillade, pour animer tout cela, donner une âme aux choses: mais cette nuit, ce grand silence, ce n'était pas la guerre . . .

Et c'était bien elle pourtant: une rude et triste veille plutôt qu'une bataille. (p. 51)

On the face of it, this passage does not persuade the reader of the need for protest. But it does suggest honest witness. War in Belgium and France was by no means a matter of constant fighting and sustained dramas. At a later point in the novel the narrator even characterizes war as waiting for something to happen – waiting for the arrival of relief troops, waiting for letters, waiting for food, waiting for day-break, waiting for death.[9] By not plunging us immediately into the horrors of war, Dorgelès uses a literary device which gives the impression that the facts are being allowed to speak for themselves, without distortion. Also, by delaying his direct account of the nature and experience of war, he makes the impact of the full facts the more devastating when it comes. In other words, he secures the confidence of the reader and then builds up protest on the firm basis of this confidence. Such apparently dispassionate and realistically secured protest gives to *Les Croix de bois* a tone and a quality often lacking in *Le Feu*.

The transition from anticipation to experience of war is made in a scene in which the small group of men whose fortunes we follow in the novel – and who are due to go into battle within forty-eight hours – gazes at the dead soldiers lying in no-man's-land. The inevitable and lethal effects of technological war begin to make themselves very clear. War certainly means boredom and inaction. But it also means fearful maiming and killing. This is followed by several scenes as horrifying as any to be found in Barbusse. The details are so terrible that they constitute a protest which needs no authorial gloss.[10] As in so many war novels, the stench of death and rotting corpses is emphasized. Also, sheer practical considerations – even considerations of survival – mean that the living occasionally tramp over piles of dead comrades in a trench or build them into a rampart behind which to shelter from the enemy's fire.[11] A shortage of stretchers, together with the enormous number of dead, also means that the latter are inevitably treated with scant respect in other ways: 'Alors, on traînait par les pieds, tous les morts glanés dans les champs, on les tirait avec une corde, comme les chevaux étripés des corridas . . .' (p. 363). Dead Germans are sometimes treated with even less consideration: '. . . des morceaux d'hommes émergeaient du mur. A un pied clouté qui dépassait, Sulphart avait accroché ses musettes et les mitrailleurs avaient posé leur pièce sur le ventre gonflé d'un Allemand dont un bras pendait et que cachait à peine une gangue friable . . .' (p. 366). Once again, in passages of this kind, authorial comment is avoided and the reader is left to react as he will. Dorgelès has confidence that the reaction will be one of horror and outrage needing no further prompting or guidance by the author.

The other brief incidents in *Les Croix de bois* should be noted for the part they play in the general strategy of protest. The most notable occurs in the brief Chapter 9, ironically entitled 'Mourir pour la patrie', which describes the death of a soldier executed by firing-squad for insubordination. This is an incident which Dorgelès exploits to the full and which recalls, incidentally, the execution of a deserter in Chapter 10 of *Le Feu*. For once, the details are carefully and consciously chosen and arranged to call forth a maximum response from the reader: the fear and horror of the victim; the fact that he has two children ('Deux gosses; grands comme son poteau . . .', p. 232); the charade of his trial; the way in which he has to be dragged to his execution; the feelings of the firing-party and of the men obliged to file past his corpse ('C'est un soldat, ce tas bleu?', p. 230). The scene was included in the original 1919 edition – no doubt because the armistice intervened between the initial objections of the military censorship and the submission of the completed manuscript to Albin Michel. It is one of the main reasons for Dorgelès's early conviction that his work would be regarded as unacceptably subversive.[12]

The second incident involves a reference to what was also the potentially subversive subject of the 1917 mutinies. In this case however, despite an allusion to the famous 'baa-ing' of some troops as they moved up to the front line like lambs to the slaughter, the presentation is brief and factual in manner: 'Penchés à l'arrière des camions, des soldats aux cils blancs [de poussière] s'amusaient à crier: "Bée! bée! . . ." et le convoi ferraillant emportait dans le bruit leur plainte de moutons. D'autres chantaient' (p. 353). Obviously, the choice of the verb 's'amusaient' and of the phrase 'd'autres chantaient' is a calculated one. The phrasing is deliberately designed to reduce the significance of this incident to a minimum. Honest witness no doubt requires its retention, but Dorgelès chose not to exploit it as part of his protest against the savagery of war and the image of the abattoir which this savagery prompted in the minds of some of its human victims.

Both Barbusse and Dorgelès describe several occasions when the troops withdraw from battle for a temporary rest period behind the front line. However, given that he published his novel in 1916, Barbusse could not describe the final return from the war in the detail provided by Dorgelès. What Barbusse does is to look forward, theoretically, to the end of the war. He writes with passion of a post-war world which will have learned the political lessons of war and which will have eradicated exploitation and enthroned equality. In *Les Croix de bois,* on the contrary, there is no political theorizing. At the level of everyday events, however, Sulphart is wounded and discharged shortly before the end of the war and meets a series of disillusioning experiences summed up in the sentence: 'Tous ces civils qui osaient parler de la guerre le mettaient hors de lui, mais il ne détestait pas moins ceux qui n'en parlaient pas, et qu'il accusait d'égoïsme' (p. 428). The obvious inconsistency attributed to Sulphart in this sentence, an inconsistency which is another example of Dorgelès's honest witness, in no way lessens the gap between war experience and civilian incomprehension. It is a short step from this position to the narrator's view, conveyed on a more abstract, generalized level, that the sufferings and lessons of the war will soon be forgotten:

La vie va reprendre son cours heureux. Les souvenirs atroces qui nous tourmentent encore s'apaiseront, on oubliera, et le temps viendra peut-être où, confondant la guerre et notre jeunesse passée, nous aurons un soupir de regret en pensant à ces années-là. . . . Et nous dirons avec un sourire: 'C'était le bon temps!' (pp. 433–4)

In these closing pages the phrases 'C'était le bon temps' and 'on oubliera' are repeated several times in what is clearly more sorrow than anger. For all the expressions of protest which it contains, *Les Croix de bois* is not an angry book. But the genuineness of protest prevents it from falling into cynicism. Resignation rather than cynicism prompts the narrator's earlier remark: 'Allons, il y aura toujours des guerres, toujours, toujours . . .' (p. 304). This is, of course, a far cry from Barbusse's vision of 'l'entente des immensités' and 'la levée du peuple du monde'. For good or ill, it has also proved to be a more accurate prophecy.

It is clear, however, that what Dorgelès's characters will forget is the moral significance of the war, not its detailed surface features. Indeed, more than once in *Les Croix de bois,* the narrator speaks of sights and smells that will stay with him throughout his life (the appearance and stench of rotting corpses, for example). Elsewhere he declares: 'Je ne pourrai plus jamais regarder un bel arbre sans supputer le poids du rondin, un coteau sans imaginer la tranchée à contre-pente, un champ inculte sans chercher les cadavres' (pp. 132–3). External appearances and visual details will remain imprinted on the mind. But their moral significance will be forgotten.

This last point is one aspect of the human response to the phenomenon of war, a subject which appears to interest Dorgelès a great deal. He gives the impression of being relatively uninterested in the political implications of events, but he notes on many occasions the various ways in which men react to the pressure of war. In the early chapters, before the more lethal realities of the fighting have been experienced, he reports the cheerfulness and sense of humour shown by the men. He also refers to the various stratagems to which they resort in order to make life more bearable or more comfortable – what he calls 'les premiers principes d'astuce et de mauvaise foi nécessaires à un militaire en campagne' (p. 38). It is also prior to their first major experience of battle that the men discuss what they would willingly do, or willingly renounce, if it meant bringing the war to an end. Once they have been in action, however, and suffered serious casualties, the points of psychological interest change for the narrator. The actual fighting brings out qualities of courage and self-sacrifice, but it also reveals in the majority of men what is no doubt a necessary hardness of attitude. The local peasants are greedy and selfish in their economic exploitation of the troops. But these troops themselves are just as selfish and unprincipled in their own sphere. The narrator, echoing the pessimism of La Rochefoucauld, exclaims at one point: 'Comme l'homme est dur, malgré ses cris de pitié, comme la douleur des autres lui semble légère, quand la sienne n'y est pas mêlée!' (p. 135).

To grow a protective skin of indifference towards others is an understandable reaction and a natural attempt at self-preservation. It has little effect, however, when one faces directly the threat of sudden death or permanent maiming. The abrupt withdrawal of all physical security puts the past into a new perspective: 'Il a fallu la guerre pour nous apprendre que nous étions heureux' (p. 171). Similarly, the likelihood of physical annihilation makes continued existence, on almost any terms, totally desirable:

Nous acceptons tout: les relèves sous la pluie, les nuits dans la boue, les jours sans pain, la fatigue surhumaine qui nous fait plus brutes que les bêtes; nous acceptons toutes les souffrances, mais laissez-nous vivre, rien que cela: vivre . . . Ou seulement croire jusqu'au bout, espérer toujours, espérer quand même. Maintenant et à l'heure de notre mort, ainsi soit-il . . . (pp. 240–1)

This hope, in order to become genuinely effective, is somehow developed further into a firm and stubborn conviction that one will not be killed. The reaction may be a curiously illogical one, but Dorgelès insists upon its reality. It appears to be the outcome of a psychological mechanism that enables men to face the worst. There is no question of mere fatalism, of believing that one will not be killed provided a particular shell does not carry one's 'number'. This is a more positive conviction of personal invulnerability, and Dorgelès paraphrases one form of its expression:

Mourir! Allons donc! Lui mourra peut-être, et le voisin et encore d'autres, mais soi, on ne peut pas mourir, soi . . . Cela ne peut pas se perdre d'un coup, cette jeunesse, cette joie, cette force dont on déborde. On en a vu mourir dix, on en verra toucher cent, mais que son tour puisse venir, d'être un tas bleu dans les champs, on n'y croit pas. Malgré la mort qui nous suit et prend quand elle veut ceux qu'elle veut, une confiance insensée nous reste. Ce n'est pas vrai, on ne meurt pas! (p. 169)

Despite Dorgelès's insistence here, one has to admit that this attitude is far from being apparent in several scenes in *Les Croix de bois*. It sorts ill with the anxiety and tension of the men as they wait to go into an attack. It is undoubtedly an attitude which a few individuals adopted, but one has difficulty in believing that it was a widespread reaction to the dangerous experiences of the Western Front.

One other form of confidence is again presented by Dorgelès as a general phenomenon, yet seems more likely to have been a minority reaction: 'Toutes les sapes, toutes les trancheés étaient pleines, et de se sentir ainsi pressés, reins à reins, par centaines, par milliers, on éprouvait une confiance brutale. Hardi ou résigné, on n'était plus qu'un grain dans cette masse humaine. L'armée, ce matin-là, avait une âme de victoire' (p. 264). Contrary to the sense conveyed by many writers of being a small unit blindly manipulated by a huge and impersonal machine,[13] Dorgelès emphasizes the confidence which collectivism inspires rather than the loss of individual identity with which it is more usually associated. He chooses to underline a sense of group identity rather than a feeling of isolation and alienation. One suspects that many individuals actually experienced group loyalty, comradeship, and 'une âme de victoire'. The opposite sense of individuality being eliminated by the group is possibly more the outcome of intellectual reflection on these experiences than an immediate effect of living through them.

In general, then, although Dorgelès's subject-matter in *Les Croix de bois* is commonplace enough in terms of war literature, the human reactions which he describes are often distinctive and individual. There is a sense in which, despite his claims to the contrary, he is conveying the experiences of *his* war rather then *the* war. Indeed, it seems inevitable that he should do so, in common with so many others who wrote under the immediate impact of the fighting. The aim of creating an overall sense of *the* war is only attainable – if at all – by those such as Jules Romains who wrote considerably later and from a more distant and detached viewpoint.

Personal witness and measured protest are combined in *Les Croix de bois* with a degree of artistic manipulation which again gives the novel some distinctive features. Repeatedly, in the course of reading the novel, one is aware that Dorgelès possesses the writer's eye for visual detail and the writer's ear for natural speech rhythms. The more consciously 'literary' effects are not always well judged, however, and the writing is sometimes forced or inappropriate in tone. Self-conscious artificiality is apparent in a simile such as: 'Je suis resté une minute interloqué, mon sourire oublié sur mes lèvres comme un drapeau du 14 juillet qu'on n'aurait pas pensé à décrocher' (p. 108). There is something equally false and coquettish in an image of early morning: 'Il n'y a pas longtemps que le jour a fini sa toilette . . . . Et le ciel sort des brassées de nuages blancs qu'il met à sécher, comme du linge' (p. 83). Nevertheless, such lapses are rare and do not seriously detract from the impression of a genuine craftsman at work. Thus, although the nature of the subject, and Dorgelès's closeness to it, do not lend themselves to an overall 'architecture' of the novel, *Les Croix de bois* contains several examples of a skilful handling of the material. Much of Chapter 6, for instance, is taken up with the narrator's suspicions of the Monpoix family with whom his squad is temporarily billeted on its withdrawal from the front line. A series of small incidents occur suggesting that père Monpoix, and possibly his daughter, may be in league with the Germans and guilty of spying on the French. In fact, the suspicions of the narrator are never resolved, and Monpoix goes into a curious decline and dies in his sleep. Throughout the chapter the reader shares the tension and uncertainty experienced by the narrator, his 'doute hésitant', 'échafaudage de soupçons', 'trouble inexplicable', 'crainte vague', etc. The whole episode is carefully built up on a rising scale of doubt and suspicion. It remains in the mind all the more readily because no totally conclusive evidence is finally forthcoming. Also, it serves to add an intriguing dimension to the soldiers' lives as they rest behind the front. The reader's interest and curiosity are effectively aroused and sustained during one of the less dramatic phases of the novel.

Dorgelès's skill as a story-teller and his ability to convey anxiety and tension are also apparent in Chapter 8. Half-way through this chapter the sound of underground tapping is heard. A feeling of acute anxiety, and in some cases of real panic, spreads among the men as they gradually realise that the Germans are tunnelling under their lines in order to place a mine beneath them and blow them sky-high. Pages of prolonged tension follow as the 'coups de pioche' can be heard day after day and the soldiers have learned that the whole operation should take the Germans about a week or eight days:

Toc . . . Toc . . . Toc . . . Elle creusait toujours . . . Toc, toc . . . Puis elle s'arrêtait. Nous écoutions alors, plus angoissés. Non. Toc . . . Toc . . . Toc . . . Cela dura deux jours encore, et une nuit. Quarante heures que l'on comptait, qu'on arrachait, par lambeaux de minutes. Deux jours et une nuit à écouter, la bouche sèche de fièvre. (p. 225)

In the end the tension is broken for this particular squad as they are relieved by fresh troops before the mine explodes. The horror is not broken, however. As they enter the village – and safety – they hear a tremendous explosion in the area which they have recently left and realize that the fourteen men who replaced them have almost certainly all been blown to bits.

Other chapters in this novel show different aspects of Dorgelès's narrative skill. For example, in Chapter 9, to which reference was made earlier, the execution of a soldier in front of a firing squad combines drama and pathos in a memorable way and sketches the central issue of military discipline with concentration and economy. Chapter 13 offers another form of macabre tragedy as a group of soldiers, on leave behind the front, mistake the significance of a bouquet of white flowers on the door of a house with closed shutters. Only after they have hammered on the door and forced the woman of the house to open it do they realize that the flowers and the shutters indicate not a brothel but a home in which a young child lies dead. Such scenes, and those mentioned earlier, continue to give *Les Croix de bois* a remarkable range of mood and tone. The experience of war, in its direct and indirect forms, is given a variety of expression which convinces while it entertains. Witness is not subordinated to protest nor is protest to witness. Laughter and anger, confidence and fear, triumph and tragedy, survival and death, combine to create the material both of Dorgelès's witness and of his protest.

If pacifism is the ultimate expression of protest against war, it would seem that Léon Werth's novel, *Clavel soldat,* formulates the ultimate rejection of those values which were used to justify and sustain the fighting between 1914 and 1918. Indeed, it is the most unswervingly pacifist novel written under the immediate pressure of these events. Werth himself saw twelve months of service at the front before being invalided out of the army in August 1915. His novel is a piece of lightly fictionalized autobiography.

The few critics who have commented on *Clavel soldat* have tended to link Werth with Barbusse.[14] There is certainly a sense in which *Le Feu* established a new tradition of angry protest against war from which a number of later writers, including Werth, drew considerable inspiration. However, Werth's anger in *Clavel soldat,* though less so in its sequel *Clavel chez les majors,* is much more contained than that of Barbusse, without in any way lessening the impact of his protest. Also, while Barbusse entertained vast hopes of a post-war future based on the rise of the masses, Werth wrote a pessimistic work in the course of which his hero loses much of his faith in the capacity of ordinary people to bring about an era of international peace and social justice.[15] And although links have been suggested between *Clavel soldat* and the pacifist elements in Barbusse's novel *Clarté,* the latter work was published a bare three months before the former and does not appear to have exercised a direct influence.

There is, in the end, a fundamental difference between the protest of Barbusse and that of Werth. In an earlier chapter we saw the danger, formulated by Kenneth Burke and confirmed by much of Barbusse's post-war thought, that a certain kind of protest literature will encourage violent reactions even though it is protesting against violence.[16] Barbusse appears to set one violence (which he holds to be justified) against another violence (which he regards as indefensible). The distinction recalls that made thirty years later by Merleau-Ponty between 'progressive' and 'reactionary' violence.[17] Werth's pacifism, on the other hand, prevents him from indulging in this type of left-wing, latter-day scholasticism. At the same time, his strong and unsentimental rejection of war, particularly in terms of the effect it has on men's minds, ensures that he does not fall into the logical trap of producing a protest literature which offers no more than a new violence in place of the violence which it repudiates.

Léon Werth's novel, though not published until May 1919, was mainly written in 1916 and 1917. The narrative content refers to events between mid-1914 and mid-1915. Although it contains a number of 'set-piece' episodes, *Clavel soldat* is predominantly a reflective essay on the impact which war and military life have on human beings. It is, if anything, less fully 'realized' as a novel than either *Le Feu* or *Les Croix de bois.* Meditation, interior monologue and direct comment by the author provide the dominant literary modes, together with a thin narrative thread. We follow the experiences of André Clavel, an employee of the French Ministry of Agriculture, from the pre-mobilization summer of 1914 to his departure on leave from the front more than a year later. Nevertheless, the novel lacks firm narrative shape. It provides a series of incisions into Clavel's experience rather than a rounded and structured fiction with a clear beginning, middle and end. In fact, it is a good example of that absence of generic definition which characterizes so many early war novels.[18]

If a steady commitment to pacifism frees Werth from the charge of provoking warlike sentiments by the nature of his protest against war, this does not solve all problems of presentation or remove all potential contradictions. For example, it does not seem wholly appropriate or logically acceptable that the pacifist hero should not only witness war directly but participate very fully in it. If he is a pacifist, why is he fighting at the front? If he is fighting at the front, how can he be a genuine pacifist? Werth could conceivably have solved this problem by making his pacifist hero a stretcher-bearer or an auxiliary in a field hospital. He could then have used this main character to denounce war without involving him in a marked contradiction. The main drawback might have been, however, that such a figure would be denouncing war at one remove, as it were – in an essentially ancillary role and not as a directly involved participant. The stretcher-bearers arrive after the *baptême du feu;* they do not have immediate experience of it.

It is to Werth's credit that he allows the contradictions in Clavel's position to remain. But he enables the reader to understand them better – possibly even to accept them – by giving his work the form of a *Bildungsroman*. It is a novel in which we follow the development of Clavel's ideas under the pressure of events. We see him change from a collectivist and revolutionary form of pacifism to a private and anarchistic one. By following his war 'education' in some detail we understand better than would otherwise be the case his negative, pessimistic and inconclusive final position.

It remains true, of course, that Clavel's position remains contradictory to the end. Although he expresses a hatred of war with increasing vigour, he does not rigorously confront his deeds with his convictions. Occasional short-lived thoughts of desertion do not prevent him from fulfilling all his duties as a soldier at the front. It may be argued, however, that the contradiction between Clavel's ideas and his actions accurately reflects a difficulty lying at the heart of much pacifist theory. Pacifism only becomes a practical possibility in a world in which public attitudes, as shaped by current educational practice and as encouraged by church and state, have been totally transformed. This is why Clavel repeatedly criticizes modern society and his fellow-combatants. They represent an outmoded yet tenacious set of values which make pacifism appear at best eccentric and at worst morally despicable.

The practical problems surrounding pacifist ideals are touched on early in the novel. In the opening pages André Clavel is presented as an essentially humane man, regarded as an anarchist by his friends yet held to be 'très gentil quand même'.[19] He associates war very specifically with commercial interests and with the distorted imaginings of the elderly, the irresponsible, and small-minded shopkeepers:

Il y a bien cette petite mercière de ma rue, de votre rue, qui dit:
– Les affaires ne vont pas, il faudrait une bonne guerre.
Il y a aussi M. Barrès, qui, chaque matin, en se levant, répète:
– Je suis Jeanne d'Arc . . . Je suis Jeanne d'Arc . . .
Mais il y a aussi, dans les asiles, quelques vieux délirants, qui disent:
– Je suis Napoléon.
Est-ce que ça compte? (p. 12)

Clavel's reply, at this stage, to his own question is to say that these ideas are of little or no importance. Such attitudes will be rejected by the sound instincts of the working class once these are given proper expression. Clavel says of the common people: 'La vérité est en lui . . . Il est la grande nébuleuse d'où le monde naîtra' (p. 13). War represents an outdated way of thought, common enough among governments and heads of state – and sexagenarian shopkeepers. But the workers will have none of it once they see it for what it is – part of a set of old-fashioned ideas which encourage a necessarily anachronistic view of the world. Clavel is against war on principle, though not against patriotism, because war is a means of shoring up a collapsing and outmoded social order. At this stage, then, he appears to hold a revolutionary pacifism which is not too far removed from the position of Barbusse.

Inevitably, these ideas were quickly shattered by the general response to mobilization. Clavel witnesses an undeniable enthusiasm for war in the streets. The right and left appear to be at one in their military and patriotic fervour. Clavel's own response is initially a divided one – dramatically divided in the sense that he immediately obeys the call to arms and yet, on the train from Bordeaux to Paris, has a day-dream in which he imagines himself being shot by a firing-squad for evading the call-up. In this confusion between his theoretical pacifism and actual military service, Clavel seeks advice from his friend Barrias who holds revolutionary views and writes for anarchist publications. To Barrias he puts the crucial question: 'Pourquoi va-t-on se battre?' and receives the reply from his left-wing friend: 'C'est la guerre de la civilisation . . . C'est la dernière guerre . . .' At this point, when war is still not a reality for him and when he has not actually experienced its horror, Clavel is prepared to accept Barrias's answer without further explanation since 'l'homme qui incarnait pour lui une manière de religion avait parlé.' Werth adds: 'Clavel ne se demanda pas comment Barrias avait acquis cette certitude. Il entendait ces mots magiques pour la première fois. Où Barrias les avait-il pris? Qui les lui avait donnés comme un talisman, ainsi qu'il les donnait à Clavel?' (p. 31).

If Clavel accepts this 'talisman' so readily, he does so not only because of confidence in his friend but thanks to those ancient virtues, embedded in his middle-class upbringing, which rise to the surface, despite his political views, at a moment of national crisis. Werth is careful to tell us early on that Clavel is 'de souche et de formation bourgeoise' (p. 10). His school and his family had successfully inculcated the necessity of facing up to tests and fulfilling one's duty. Furthermore, the reality of duty was demonstrated to him. It was linked with family and country and during his final years at school he was a member of the 'Union patriotique' of his region. It is hardly surprising, then, that he should experience a certain satisfaction, despite his ideological opposition to war, in doing his duty and volunteering for active service. When he takes a horse-drawn cab to his apartment in Paris and explains that he is joining up, the old cabbie expresses his approval of 'l'homme qui va faire son devoir'. Clavel gets deep satisfaction from this response. Similarly, a neighbour on his staircase makes her approbation clear when she learns of his intention. Werth comments: 'Ah! ce besoin qui est en nous d'être approuvé. Par n'importe qui. Ce besoin de penser et de sentir comme les autres. La peur d'être un monstre . . . Il est l'homme qui n'a rien à craindre du jugement des hommes. Quel repos . . .' (p. 25). It thus seems as though, under pressure, Clavel reacts and behaves little differently from non-pacifists. Despite the fact that he tries to link theory and practice by calling himself by the paradoxical term of 'guerrïer pacifiste', he accepts it as his duty to share in the killing of German soldiers since the latter are attacking his country and attacking the ideal of peace for which he stands. Above all, 'il entre dans la guerre, il consent à la guerre, puisqu'on ne lui a laissé que ce moyen de sauver la paix' (p. 50). He lives out the moral and intellectual confusions and contradictions of the revolutionary pacifist position in 1914. The concrete experience of war, however, does not allow him to maintain this position for long. As we shall see, he moves steadily towards a much more negative and pessimistic form of private, anarchistic pacifism.

In his account of trench warfare Werth inevitably repeats some of the familiar details found in Dorgelès, Barbusse or Bertrand. These items include the reactions of men under shellfire (p. 121), the frequent boredom (pp. 151–2), the view that officers are excessively privileged over other ranks (pp. 190–1, 410, 413), a bitter portrait of an army medical officer (p. 98), the horrifying wounds (p. 189), two executions by firing-squad (pp. 361–2, 367–8). However authentic such details may be, their ubiquitous presence in the novels of the period eventually and inevitably blunts their impact. Although through no fault of these writers (since the typical experiences öf the Great War are their common subject), these repeated experiences and attitudes tend to become literary commonplaces. In these circumstances it is refreshing to find that Werth does not rely exclusively on such details. There are elements in *Clavel soldat* which both bear the stamp of individual observation and distinguish it, in terms of atmosphere and perspective, from *Les Croix de bois* or *Le Feu*.

One such feature is the way in which Werth sometimes removes the glamour of war, not by emphasizing the horror (which can itself create a form of glamour) but by conveying the unromantic ordinariness of a scene. He notes, for example, the banal litter of the battlefield: 'Le sol des routes, le sol des champs, le sol des bois est jonché de conserves, parfois de bouteilles vides' (p. 76). This is hardly a backdrop to glory. At another level, too, glory is undermined by various laconic references to the number of soldiers killed or wounded in error by their own side. A surgeon claims that he has extracted more French than German bullets from the bodies of wounded French soldiers (p. 323), other soldiers are mowed down by their own artillery (e.g. p. 323), while a French major is shot at night and in error by one of his own sentries (p. 117).

Perhaps the most distinctive feature of the war as recounted in *Clavel soldat* is the reference, on a number of occasions, to desertion and deserters. At one point, Clavel is briefly tempted to escape from war by surrendering to the Germans (p. 284). Shortly afterwards he speculates, if not very seriously, on the possibility of desertion and escape to Switzerland (pp. 288–9). Towards the end of the novel he says explicitly: 'Si je vais en permission je déserterai' (p. 394). At several points German deserters are picked up by the French (e.g. pp. 301, 341) and later there is a reference to desertions from both sides (p. 421). This marked preoccupation with desertion, theoretical rather than practical in Clavel's case, is an obvious enough element in his dilemma as a pacifist caught in the toils of war.

In fact, desertion through pacifist conviction was a rare phenomenon during the Great War. Indeed, pacifism of any kind was difficult to sustain precisely because of the enormous obstacles placed in its path by traditional education, by newspaper and government propaganda, and by a general campaign of pressure and sometimes of misrepresentation. It is this widespread bias against pacifism, and in favour of war, which explains why *Clavel soldat* denounces more sharply than most war novels of the period all efforts to exact obedience and allegiance from soldiers and civilians alike. Not only do newspapers publish 'abject lies' but soldiers themselves see their own experiences in terms of set propaganda categories and not as they really are. As Werth observes: '. . . la convention des choses est plus forte que les choses' (p. 129). Those who lack clarity of vision in peacetime will equally lack clarity of vision when faced by war. They see what they have been taught to expect and not what is actually in front of them. This is why soldiers are described on several occasions as *automates*. It also explains the fact that 'ils voudraient n'être pas à la guerre. Mais ils consentent à la guerre' (p. 148). Were they to be in any danger of seeing things more clearly, army discipline would ensure that they did not act in accordance with this clarity. These various points, made several times in the novel, are brought together in one particular passage:

Le journal de la petite ville où est le dépôt du régiment circule dans la section. Un lieutenant qui fut blessé le 27 septembre, puis évacué, y raconte la bataille, cette marche sous les obus, cette marche en bon ordre, cette marche sans autre incident militaire que les morts et les blessures, et où la compagnie la plus avancée vit l'ennemi à quatre cents mètres. Un général, qui regardait la bataille avec une jumelle, a, dit-on, pleuré d'admiration en contemplant ce bel alignement. Mais Clavel regardait sans jumelle . . . Le général n'y était pas . . . Clavel y était . . . La plupart des hommes allaient en avant, parce qu'ils savent qu'il faut marcher, parce qu'on leur a dit que les fuyards sont des lâches et passent au peloton d'exécution. Double argument qui joint la contrainte à la persuasion. (pp. 128–9)

In other words Werth, as a volunteer soldier, scorns that *obéissance passive* which Bertrand admired and which Psichari, the professional army man, regarded as a crowning glory of the military life.[20]

In various other passages Werth emphasizes the extent to which men react to those military ideals inculcated in them during childhood. At the moment of facing or mounting an attack they automatically return to the tenets of their military 'faith' in the same way as some people, faced by the approach of death, reach out instinctively towards the values of a youthful religious upbringing. Such reversionary automatism rouses Clavel's bitter scorn. It shows itself most despicably, in his view, when a firing-squad, consisting of ordinary soldiers, obeys the order to execute a fellow-soldier who has refused to go into the trenches. One such execution is described briefly and factually. Subsequently, a group of men discuss whether or not they would have agreed to join the firing-squad. The passage continues:

– Salauds . . . dit Clavel. Ce sont des salauds . . . Leur obéissance stupide
quand il faut rester là ou aller à l'ennemi . . . Passe. J'ai accepté ça . . . J'ai
été dupe comme eux, au départ. Mais qu'ils obéissent à l'ordre de tuer un
camarade, qu'alors il n'y ait en eux qu'un vague apitoiement mêlé à leur
éternelle résignation, que tout n'éclate pas en eux, qu'une grande lumière ne
soit pas créée, que la discipline qui pèse sur eux ne crève pas d'un coup . . .
non . . . non . . . je ne peux plus aimer la foule. (p. 362)

On this occasion, as on several others, Clavel's anger is directed not so
much against the 'warlords' of the home front as against the ordinary
soldiers in the trenches. He insists that these latter submit too readily,
fail to assert their humanity, become the unresisting instruments of a
set of antiquated myths. It is clear, indeed, that Clavel experiences
considerable difficulty in judging his fellow-soldiers with any degree of
generosity. He attempts to distinguish at one stage between pity for the
individual *poilu* and hatred of the ideas which the same *poilu* thought-
lessly or passively accepts and furthers. But again he is brought up
against a paradox in the pacifist position. Evidence strongly suggests
that the soldier's effective qualities as a soldier are closely linked to the
ideas he holds. Can one, for instance, be an effective fighting man
without adopting the starkly simple and resolutely anti-pacifist position
of his friend Declerq: '. . . les Allemands sont des cochons. Il faut les
tuer' (p. 72)? Practical logic seems to conclude that if one admires
military ideals one cannot totally condemn those who embody them
effectively, while if one condemns military ideals one cannot like and
admire those who apply them uncritically and determinedly. With
something much closer to desperation than logic, Clavel intensifies the
paradox when he decides that he, the pacifist, must meet the problem
by volunteering for the most dangerous missions just as the men
whom he criticizes seek an answer in automatic obedience to the
commands they receive. He moves further and further towards moral
self-isolation and what he terms 'le dur mépris qui se tait' (p. 414).

It might still be argued that Werth is not so much criticizing ordinary
men as showing how the conditions of war distort their common
humanity. One can interpret in the same way various incidents in *Clavel
soldat* which are somewhat unusual in war novels of the period: the
patrol which deliberately returns without approaching the German
positions claiming it could not make contact with the enemy (p. 79);
the theft of Clavel's new rifle and its anonymous replacement by a
dangerously jammed weapon (p. 86); the looting of French villages by
French soldiers (p. 133). All these things are part of what is regularly
presented by official propaganda as something noble and splendid,

'l'ordre de la guerre'. Clavel refuses to accept this order. And precisely because he opposes 'l'ordre de la guerre' he does not adopt a revolutionary pacifism which would be committed to using the lessons and even the methods of war to overthrow a society in which war is endemic. Rather, he turns to a pacifism which seeks personal rather than corporate solutions. He has come to lack sufficient confidence in the common man to believe that things can be radically altered. He seeks consolation in the abstract formulations of Spinoza's *Ethics,* takes a bitterly pessimistic view of man, emphasizes the folly and horror of war whatever the cause it may ostensibly serve.[21] War has demonstrated that twentieth-century man is incapable of resisting collective pressures. Moral courage, as against the physical courage demanded by war, is markedly lacking. Clavel exclaims: 'Hommes d'obéissance, esclaves sans amour et sans haine, je ne puis plus vous aimer' (pp. 229–30). It seems as though Clavel's original love and pity for human beings has been effectively destroyed by the experience of war.

It is perhaps only right, in the sense of being authentically human, that Clavel should not be totally consistent. Although he makes a sweeping condemnation of those who fail to resist the basic ideology of war, he appears to accept – with some irony, but certainly without anger or explicit censure – a young reserve officer, Lieutenant de Machard-Pasquier, 'connu pour ses opinions réactionnaires'. The faintly ironic tone of his portrait should not conceal the extent to which he accepts the implications of ideas which, in theory, he should totally reject:

De Machard-Pasquier respira les notions de son milieu: tradition, religion, supériorité de l'ancien régime. Dans cette famille provinciale, traditionaliste par tradition et non par mode, les notions ne s'assemblaient pas en système de combat. Elles ne circulaient guère dans la conversation et n'étaient que la formule de la vie, telle que l'argent permettait de la vivre, et la religion de la concevoir. Pour que cet honnête garçon, d'esprit mou, fût troublé, il eût fallu un conflit entre ses actes et ses principes, un amour ou d'impérieux désirs. Or, il ne couchait pas avec ses bonnes. La guerre, pour lui, prolongeait la caserne et ne posait aucun problème. Le sacrifice à la patrie est prêché partout. Jadis, il se fût sacrifié au roi. Et il était plus que jamais, par la guerre, dans l'obéissance vieille comme le monde, confirmée aussi bien par les doctrines de son milieu que par le consentement universel. Et, si l'on meurt, Dieu vous accueille, Dieu qui est une sorte de colonel définitif. (pp. 96–7)

The explanation of this passage may be in part that de Machard-Pasquier is wholly consistent and exactly as Clavel expects him to be whereas the ordinary soldiers, of whom he had initially expected so much (the sound instincts and regenerative potential of the working-classes, etc) let him down badly by their ready surrender to the demands of war and of military life. In a sense, too, de Machard-Pasquier compels respect because of the heroic folly (or selfless dedication) with which he leads his men over the top 'accomplissant le rite commandé, en homme bien élevé, comme il fût monté sur les marches de l'autel le jour de son mariage' (pp. 159–60). The simile here emphasizes the mad inappropriateness, in Clavel's eyes, of everything the young lieutenant stands for. But the succeeding sentence, which points out that de Machard-Pasquier's body was never found, carries an authentic emotional charge.

Léon Werth cannot be accused of simplifying the dilemmas of a war-time pacifist in *Clavel soldat*. He allows his hero to fall into various kinds of contradiction, and the novel offers no simple or positive conclusion as Clavel goes on leave to encounter the ignorance or indifference of the civilian population. But Werth does sustain a thorough detestation of war at a time when so many pre-1914 pacifists had renounced their ideals and rapidly adopted the conventional attitudes and vocabulary of bellicism.[22] This is an honest book, honest both in its anger and its moral/intellectual confusion. It was followed in the same year of 1919 by a sequel, *Clavel chez les majors,* which contained more anger (directed more particularly against the *arrière*) but offered no new solution to the paradoxes of pacifism. Scorn and disgust are expressed against all who collaborate, consciously or unconsciously, with the 'official' conception of the war. Protest reaches a climax of bitterness and contempt.

PART THREE

The Response to Catastrophe

CHAPTER 7

The Emotional Response
Duhamel and Faure

It is a relatively short step from the narration of war to an evaluation of its significance. It may even be said that each of these activities implies the other. We have seen that most war novelists, in the course of describing their own experiences or those of their fictional characters, conveyed clearly enough some form of meaning or value in the events which they recounted. From an early stage in the fighting, indeed, writers of all kinds (and not merely novelists) began to meditate on the importance of what they were witnessing. Their various responses to the Great War, their interpretations of it, continued well into the 1920s. Although this was a natural development in one sense, in another it required courage and determination. Jacques Rivière was only one of many who regarded the war as an unparalleled horror and an unparalleled absurdity which seemed to defy understanding. He therefore felt obliged to ask the question: if war is the absurdity which it appears to be, how do men come to fight so readily in war in apparent defiance of reason? In other words, war must have some meaning despite its surface meaninglessness. It is essential to discover this meaning. And Rivière adds: 'Ayons donc le courage de le chercher.'[1] The aim of the chapters which follow is to investigate some of the forms which this courage took and some of the very different responses to war published during or shortly after the events of 1914–18. Faure and Alain attempted to answer Rivière's question directly, to explain the function and nature of war in human affairs. Duhamel and Valéry found more oblique meanings in war which led them to reconsider the nature of civilisation. But while Alain and Valéry exercised a sharply analytical and rational approach, Duhamel and Faure expressed their different ideas in more emotional terms and through the use of more lyrical language.

For a few writers, of course, the war was scarcely problematical at

117

all. They continued to see it in 'official' terms which provided a ready-made framework and left little room for moral or intellectual problems. Henri Massis, for example, despite his direct experience of the front, saw the Great War as the necessary and heroic sacrifice of a generation on behalf of the greatness of France and the freedom of mankind.[2] Victor Giraud saw it as the life or death struggle of French moral and religious culture against the barbarity of German 'scientisme'.[3] In similar terms Ernest Psichari, just before his death on active service in the early weeks of the war, regarded it as a crusade, as a 'grande et magnifique aventure' which, as we saw in Chapter 1 above, he held to be 'nécessaire à l'honneur et à la grandeur de la France'.[4] Most intellectuals who experienced the fighting, however, found a militaristic and nationalistic response to the war inadequate, if not positively immoral, given its horrifying human cost and its implications for many intellectual and ethical assumptions of the pre-war era.

We saw in an earlier chapter that Georges Duhamel (1884–1966) produced some of the most harrowing accounts of human suffering written during the war years. His liberal beliefs were shocked by the spectacle of a technological war in which the resources of science seemed to be concentrated on the destruction of human life. Nevertheless, in both *Vie des martyrs* and *Civilisation* he also expressed a deep and tender admiration for the courage and capacity for sacrifice which men displayed under the conditions of warfare. In an apparently paradoxical way the Great War both invalidated and confirmed his humanist convictions. In *Civilisation,* however, he indicated what might be regarded as a solution of the seeming paradox. He drew a clear distinction between the new, rationalist, scientific, and quantitative culture which, he claimed, was responsible for the war and the traditional, humane, qualitative culture which was being destroyed in the process. He saw the war, in fact, not as direct evidence of the failure of humanism but as the outcome of a foolhardy and conscious rejection of humanist values. The restoration of these values became one of his major preoccupations from the later years of the war onwards. It is a central theme of *La Possession du monde* (1919) and is taken up again in such works as *Entretiens dans le tumulte* (1919), *Scènes de la vie future* (1930) and *Querelles de famille* (1932). What Duhamel offered, in these and other writings, is what P. H. Simon was later to describe as 'l'invitation de destituer la civilisation scientifique du rang d'idole à celui de servante'.[5]

As early as 1917, while the war was still in progress and its outcome quite uncertain, Duhamel was turning his thoughts positively towards the future and considering the lessons to be learned from war. *La Possession du monde* was completed in 1918, prior to the armistice, and published in the spring of 1919. It was very much an act of faith, all the more impressive because of the difficult and discouraging conditions under which it was conceived and written. He describes its composition as having proved 'une véritable école de solitude, de patience et d'application'.[6] The tone is emotional, lyrical, poetic. Duhamel does not so much argue a case as issue an appeal on behalf of certain traditional and humane values. There is little of the incisiveness to be found in an Alain or a Valéry. Also, others are left to analyse the war and its consequences in political, historical, and economic terms. Duhamel directly addresses men of goodwill whom he hopes to move emotionally rather than convince intellectually. Indeed he claims that there is little point in seeking to arouse the intellectual qualities of men since these are still totally absorbed by the immediate practical demands of war. He is addressing the inner moral sense of his readers, what he calls 'le cœur'[7], for this is the element in man which, as the war has shown, persists through all vicissitudes and remains proof against external events however catastrophic. His aim is to intervene in that dialogue with the inner self which, he claims, the great majority of men maintain despite the demands made on so much of their energy and attention by war and suffering.[8]

Although critical of Christianity, Duhamel draws heavily in *La Possession du monde* on a mixture of religious and idealistic concepts and terms. He implies an essential and intimate connection between what he calls man's 'soul' and something like a platonic world of Ideas, a 'monde presque purement idéal' (p. 19), which is the only source of truth. The vital link between the two is continually broken by the intrusive claims of that relativist and positivist emphasis which characterizes modern society. Man is less and less conceived of as a spiritual being and the consequences for human behaviour are deplorable. The treatment of human beings as numbers or as war 'material' is simply the logical outcome of earlier nineteenth-century developments. Duhamel insists that the post-war world must be built by and for men on the basis of a proper evaluation of human value. His first injunction is positive:

Ne point ignorer son âme d'abord!
Songer à l'âme, y songer une fois au moins dans le désordre de chaque tourbillonnante journée, c'est bien le commencement du salut.
Songer à l'âme avec persévérance et respect, l'enrichir sans cesse, cela sera notre sainteté. (p. 16)

His attitude to the future therefore follows logically enough: 'L'avenir qu'on nous laisse entrevoir semble la négation même du bonheur et la perte de l'âme. Il faut, en ce cas, l'examiner avec bonne foi et le refuser ensuite de toutes nos forces' (pp. 19–20).

The formulation of the phrases just quoted – and of a number to be quoted later – may serve to remind us that Duhamel's expression of his ideas tends to reflect their vague or impressionistic character. He uses terms lyrically rather than analytically; he implies definitions but rarely makes them explicit; he often apostrophizes the reader or makes liberal use of repetitions, rhetorical questions, exclamation marks, etc. This type of writing proved attractve to many readers, particularly in the immediate post-war period. The infectious idealism of this 'tendre poète', as Faure called him,[9] was undoubtedly appealing. Nevertheless, his book was also criticized on these very grounds. It was rightly regarded as unacceptably vague, generalized, and emotional. As the years passed it became increasingly unreadable and many of those who turn to it today are likely to treat it with amused scorn. Those who criticized it on its appearance were quick to sense its superficiality and *naïveté*. One hardly needs to share the social and political presuppositions of Massis to understand his claim that *La Possession du monde* combined facile optimism with a vague and suspect religiosity.[10]

In a sense, of course, Duhamel might reply that the content and manner of his writing were determined in part at least by the audience which he was addressing. He was conscious, like most of his contemporaries, of the accelerated decline in religious certainties (at least in the population generally, if not in the small intellectual and artistic élite already mentioned in Chapter 1) which occurred during the second half of the nineteenth century. As he saw it, then, he was mainly speaking to men and women who, deprived of a positive Christian faith and subject to the impact of the Great War, were likely to be disorientated and disillusioned. The best he could do, consciously or unconsciously, was to try to revive and appeal to the secularized vestiges of an earlier Christian culture. That he was actually conscious of this problem, at least in some measure, is suggested by his own comment:

Voici qu'une génération d'hommes est venue qui n'a plus confiance en les félicités surnaturelles de la vie future et qui semble n'avoir plus rien à espérer d'un monde consumé de haine et livré, quoi qu'il arrive, pour de longues années, à l'incohérence, au dénuement, aux passions égoïstes.

En vérité, les programmes des factions sociales ne nous sont d'aucune consolation; rien n'y parle de l'amour et des vrais biens; tous ces monuments d'éloquence ramènent à la haine et au déchirement. (pp. 30–1)

He even goes so far as to quote the unequivocal analysis of Maeterlinck: 'Jusqu'à présent, les hommes sortaient d'une religion pour entrer dans une autre; au lieu que nous abandonnons la nôtre pour aller nulle part. Voilà le phénomène nouveau, aux conséquences inconnues, dans lequel nous vivons' (p. 31). At this point, however, Duhamel draws back – perhaps for fear of being thought too 'religious' in sympathy. He makes it clear that he does not consider the war to be a consequence of the breakdown of Christianity and goes on to emphasize the contribution made by this religion, despite the teachings of its founder, to warfare and killing.

The situation which Maeterlinck describes, and to which Duhamel seeks to respond, is one way among many of formulating the contrast between pre-war confidence and wartime disarray which characterized the first two decades of this century in western Europe. Duhamel emphasizes the sharp difference between the widespread assumption, before 1914, of continuing human progress and the apparent regression of humanity, after 1914, into elaborately organized and ingeniously sustained barbarity. As a direct physical outcome of this retreat from reason whole areas of France have come to resemble enormous graveyards. Duhamel speaks of countrysides 'où il y a maintenant plus de charniers que de villages' (p. 174). Such dramatic contrasts and consequences demand an explanation and this is part of what Duhamel offers in *La Possession du monde*. What has happened, he says, is that European civilization has taken a wrong turning, that men are violating the natural world for technological and materialistic ends and that they are suffereing an inevitable nemesis. He is not simply thinking here of that destruction of the natural landscape to which several novelists, notably Barbusse and Dorgelès, also referred. He is concerned as well at the way in which natural materials – wood, stone, metal, etc. – are no longer the objects of that almost mystical respect and veneration which is their due but have been torn from the earth and subjected to human distortion for unnatural purposes. A brief reminiscence clarifies his point of view:

Je me rappelle avoir vu des collines éventrées par le bombardement et qui étaient semées de longs éclats de fer torturés; le culot d'un obus monstrueux m'apparut, un jour, dans ces conditions, et je trouvai véritablement inhumain ce produit du travail des hommes: le noble métal avec lequel on eût pu faire tant de choses belles et bonnes, prenait une figure odieuse. L'homme avait réalisé ce triste miracle de dénaturer la nature, de la rendre ignoble et criminelle. (p. 99)

For Duhamel, then, the war notably focused and dramatized the worst potentialities of technological advance and material prosperity.

It pointed out clearly what he held to be the fundamental character of industrial and scientific civilization. He interpreted the war as a warning to mankind to change direction, not by going into reverse but by altering its emphasis and by rescuing certain fundamental moral values. Nowadays, no doubt, Duhamel's attitude would be criticized as 'luddite' by some and praised as responsibly 'environmentalist' by others. Much the same division of opinion greeted his ideas when they first appeared in 1919. It was Duhamel's profound conviction, however, born of a deep emotional anxiety in response to the war, that scientific civilisation was developing not alongside, but at the expense of, moral progress. The war, he says, 'nous a permis de mesurer toute l'humiliation de la civilisation morale devant l'autre, la civilisation scientifique et industrielle . . .' (p. 136).[11] In his view, then, the response which war demands is a reassessment of human priorities and a rediscovery of truly humane values. Once such values are identified and pursued we shall learn not to exploit and destroy the world of man and natural objects but to possess the world in all its potential richness and diversity.

This response means that, for much of *La Possession du monde,* Duhamel leaves the immediate question of war and turns to the lessons which the spectacle of war is teaching him. He proposes a lyrical and idealistic philosophy of life which is not our main concern here but which must be described briefly. He begins with the assumption that happiness is the major goal of human life. This view would appear to be an understandable psychological response to the misery and danger of war, but Duhamel denies that his choice of happiness as the central value of human life has any direct link with experience of the trenches. He recognizes, of course, that suffering and happiness are related, that birth and pain are inseparable, and indeed that suffering can educate and prepare for happiness. He also takes the traditional view that great art feeds, at least in part, on suffering. But he also accepts that 'toutes les douleurs ne nous grandissent pas, ne nous augmentent pas. Il y en a de stériles, de desséchantes, d'inavouables' (p. 163). No doubt many of the sufferings of war, both physical and mental, come into this latter category and Duhamel insists that a sense of the importance of happiness is a deep and abiding instinct impressed on the individual by his own inner voice.[12] Happiness is particularly important because it is the one profound, stable and persistent good in a world of crumbling values.

Having established and characterized the central importance of happiness in this way, Duhamel conveys his message by a direct address to this instinct for happiness in his readers. And because he is addressing a deep instinctual element in man he is able, on these very grounds, to justify further his predominantly emotional approach to 'men of goodwill'. It is his conviction that purely intellectual arguments would miss the mark. His purpose is to stir hearts and rouse souls – to use what, as he reminds us, Pascal termed 'les connaissances du cœur et de l'instinct'.[13] His appeal is to the sensibility rather than the intellect of his audience.

It has already been pointed out that Duhamel offers few precise definitions. This is true of happiness, the term 'bonheur' which he uses so frequently. He does, however, distinguish between 'bonheur' and 'jouissance', making it clear that by happiness he does not mean selfish or egotistical pleasure. He appears, rather, to conceive of happiness as a form of knowledge and love which has to do with a total and sympathetic openness to the diversity of human experience. This idea of openness is also present in the term 'possession' in his title. On the subject of possessing the world he writes: 'Il ne faut rien refuser; il faut tout accepter, tout évaluer, tout mettre en réserve' (p. 63). This is his formula for happiness and he applies it to the world of men, to the world of nature, to the world of art.

As regards the world of men, Duhamel advocates greater acceptance of other human beings and greater commerce with them as a source of happiness. It is a mistake to assume, of any individual, that he is boring or uninteresting simply because he initially annoys us or fills us with indifference. We must learn to 'possess', in Duhamel's special sense of the word, the world of men: 'En vérité, l'immense peuple des hommes est à vous. Prenez et mangez, vous ne sauriez trouver plus belle nourriture' (p. 91). This is the advice of a convinced humanist who states on a later page: '. . . il faut que l'homme ait foi en sa divinité!' (p. 224). The attitude to the world of natural objects should be similarly all-embracing since Duhamel holds as an article of faith the sweeping claim that 'il n'est pas un objet au monde qui ne soit pas une source de bonheur' (p. 95). He has much to say about the intricate marvels and simple beauties of nature and writes from the devastated battlefield:

Quand la paix sera de retour, si vous venez me voir au mois de mai, je vous conduirai sous le grand sycomore qui verdoie dans le fond du pré. Et là, écoutant voler, vibrer, aimer et vivre les millions de bêtes qui peuplent la frondaison fraîche, nous ferons ensemble un si curieux voyage que vous laisserez en route le plus lourd de votre tristesse. (pp. 119–20)

Finally, on the subject of the arts, he sees them as another element which will minister to the individual's spiritual needs. Like man and nature, music, literature or painting can bring him a deep and lasting happiness which will also be a form of knowledge and understanding. In particular, because art is not simply a narrow question of technique but a complete way of life, it permits – even requires – the artist to 'possess' the world. Duhamel contrasts the spiritual richness of Lucretius, Shakespeare, Rembrandt or Goethe with the mere accumulation of material wealth associated with Croesus. This possession of the world at these three levels – the human, the natural, the artistic – will enable men to live 'en état de grâce' (p. 214), and Duhamel adds: 'Toute richesse morale semble s'accroître d'être possédée en commun' (p. 228).

The general thrust of the argument in *La Possession du monde* is away from present reality and towards future possibility. This is a natural emphasis in a book which seeks to draw lessons from the war. It is of some wider interest to note, however, that in a chapter entitled 'Les Refuges' Duhamel appears to ignore the present in the course of claiming that memory and anticipation, 'le souvenir' and 'l'avenir', provide men with their two legitimate means of consolation and confidence. There is no doubt considerable psychological significance in the fact that, in the middle of war itself, Duhamel should appear to skirt round the present and ask his readers to concentrate on the past or the future.[14] At a formal level this position prefigures his very traditional humanism. He establishes a close connection between past and future, arguing that the future can only be secured by a revival of past values. He foresees a darkly threatening and possibly catastrophic future looming ahead unless certain pre-industrial or anti-materialistic attitudes are revived and allowed to shape future policy. To this extent Duhamel continues the pre-war analysis and prognostications of Péguy and, in some measure, of Bloy and Sorel. Like them he is convinced that man has taken a seriously wrong turning. The war which they predicted is the war which he is experiencing. It offers at once dramatic and bloody confirmation of this fearful lapse of civilization.

In the final pages of *La Possession du monde* Duhamel again responds directly to the war and looks at the prospects for humanity. He believes that whatever the eventual outcome of the war its devastating effects, both material and spiritual, will last for a considerable time. Characteristically, he pays most attention to the spiritual consequences and anticipates Valéry's famous conclusion when he writes: 'Entre tous nos sujets de déception, s'il en est un qui nous demeure pénible, c'est l'espèce de faillite dont voici convaincue notre civilisation' (p. 252). On the same page he formulates the question insistently posed by the war and repeated in anguish by so many people after 1914. This question asks 'comment "un siècle aussi avancé dans la civilisation" a pu engendrer cette démoralisante catastrophe.' Another of Valéry's comments is anticipated when Duhamel points out that some of man's best qualities and gifts have actually contributed to the disaster. In these final pages, and in answer to the questions and problems raised by the war, Duhamel returns to an indictment of scientific rationalism which includes the following characteristic passages:

. . . jamais la barbarie n'avait atteint dans la brutalité et la destruction des résultats aussi monstrueux que ceux dont notre civilisation industrielle et scientifique est désormais capable. Celle-ci ne serait-elle donc qu'une forme à peine travestie de la barbarie? . . . .

Avec son cortège d'inventions ingénieuses et de complications savantes, l'intelligence fait figure d'irresponsable ou de criminelle dans le grand désordre du monde. Elle paraît non seulement incapable de donner le bonheur aux hommes, mais encore fort propre à les égarer, à les corrompre, à les servir dans leurs querelles. Elle a su armer les conflits; elle n'a pu ni les conjurer ni les résoudre.

La civilisation scientifique et industrielle, basée sur l'intelligence, est condamnée. Elle a, depuis de longues années, accaparé et affolé toutes les énergies humaines. Son règne aboutit à un immense échec. (pp. 253–5)

Behind this analysis lies Duhamel's conviction that true human progress must be moral rather than material. Hence his turning to what he terms 'les ressources du cœur'. His confidence in the possibilities of 'la civilisation morale' is strong, but he does not see it as something that can evolve of its own accord. On the contrary, it will be necessary to devote to it as much energy, as much imagination and as much ingenuity as have been expended on industrial and scientific development.

Even while the war was being fought it was argued by some that war is actually morally desirable, that it is biologically inevitable, etc. Duhamel was aware of such ideas and refers critically to one or two of them. He is quite sure, for example, that war itself cannot contribute to genuine moral development. We shall see shortly that Élie Faure values what he regards as certain positive moral elements in war, but Duhamel sees such ideas as little more than an excuse for moral inaction or a *post hoc* justification of missed opportunities. He is convinced that the profession of killing creates neither the conditions for justice nor the groundwork of moral progress. He is similarly categorical in his rejection of the view that war is a necessary element in the evolution of species, including the human species. He does not really argue a case here but expresses the opinion that any view of war as an aspect of biological necessity implies a determinism and fatalism 'que désavouent et notre sens de l'expérience et notre goût de la perfection' (p. 261). Incidentally, the argument on behalf of the inevitability of war is one which Alain also rejects with some vigour and seeks to refute on rational grounds – as we shall see in the next chapter. Duhamel is especially concerned, however, not simply to counter arguments on behalf of war but to reject the idea that any attempt by humanity to change course again must be doomed to failure. He refuses to believe that Western man has placed himself under a form of industrial and technological determinism, just as he refuses to accept the view that 'l'humanité est, précisément, trop sénile, trop évoluée pour qu'il soit encore capable de renoncer en quoi que ce soit à ses traditions intellectuelles invétérées, à ses acquis scientifiques et aux mœurs qui en découlent' (p. 262). And he believes that post-war political life will show itself to be thoroughly bankrupt if it does not seek to change basic attitudes or fails to encourage the nation to meet the moral perils of peace with the same resolution and faith it displayed in meeting the more obvious material perils of war. Moral reform and 'le règne du cœur' are vitally necessary and Duhamel refuses to believe that men, schooled by the experience of war, are incapable of meeting this challenge. Indeed, history shows us that men have changed their conception of culture and civilization at various times in the past. There is no sound reason why they should not do so again. Duhamel says that he is not advocating an impossible return to a pre-industrial society. Furthermore, he is not claiming that society was ideal in earlier times. What he is asserting is that an earlier society held the right values. Men must now see to it that these values are made active in society and given genuine and practical expression, in accordance with changed circumstances, after the war. He asks that the values of industrial civilization should be made subservient to these values of what he calls 'moral' civilization. Humanism must dominate technology. 'Qu'espérez-vous donc de l'avenir, si vous n'y faites pas la part de l'âme?' (p. 269). Mechanization, commercial competition, material luxury, a life of speed and technical complication – 'l'engrenage industriel moderne' (p. 274) – are goals which have ended in a European massacre and which must be renounced.

It is clear that Duhamel's teaching was largely unheeded and his ideals unfulfilled. Even though some of his ideas have been revived again in recent years under the increasing pressure of highly sophisticated technology, his expression of them can be dismissed as vague, facile, and lacking a cutting edge. Nevertheless, it would be difficult to disagree with the general spirit of his response to the Great War: 'Il faudra toutes nos valeurs, toutes nos définitions, tout notre vocabulaire' (p. 265). All these things have of course changed since 1918. But it seems clear that they have changed more in spite of men than as a result of their considered choice and decision. This is precisely the outcome against which Duhamel warned and which he strove, unsuccessfully, to prevent.

Like Duhamel, Élie Faure (1873–1937) originally qualified as a doctor. Around the turn of the century he was associated with socialist and revolutionary circles in Paris and with the anarchist *L'Ennemi du peuple*. In 1902 he began to contribute art criticism to *L'Aurore*—the Dreyfusard daily which published Zola's 'J'accuse' and of which Clemenceau was the political editor. Between 1905 and 1909 he taught courses in the Université Populaire which he had helped to found and these lectures formed the basis of his ambitious and distinctive five-volume history of art. He is best remembered now as an original art historian who attempted to place works of art in a much wider cultural and historical context. His approach was to influence that of Malraux. When war broke out Faure, as a reserve officer, was called up at once as a *médecin aide-major* and had a full and busy career as an army surgeon. In July 1915 he was briefly invalided home from the front, returned to the Somme in the spring of 1916, and early in 1917 was back in Paris.[15] His experience of war was broadly similar to that of Duhamel though his response to this experience turned out to be very different.

In 1917 Faure published his only novel, *La Roue*. War is not its primary subject but serves as a background to the domestic drama between the main protagonists Pierre and Elizabeth. His first essays on war, collected in *La Sainte Face,* appeared in 1918 and earned him the adjective 'belliciste' from Paul Souday, reviewing the book in *Le Temps* of 20 June 1918. The most complete expression of his theories on war is found in *La Danse sur le feu et l'eau*. He wrote this work in two months (August and September 1918) in the spare time available from his military duties. He wrote of it in a letter: 'J'étais en proie à un délire sacré. C'est de tous mes livres celui qui m'a donné le moins de mal.'[16] He published it immediately in *L'Europe nouvelle* and it appeared in book form in April 1920, almost exactly a year after *La Possession du monde*. The fact that it represents an emotional and lyrical response to war is suggested by Faure's own allusion to his 'délire sacré', and this is further confirmed by Paul Desanges's reference to the 'magnificence lyrique' of the essay. It is worth quoting Desanges's description at this point: 'On y trouve exposée avec une précision qui n'entrave en rien la magnificence lyrique, une conception non plus morale, statique et finaliste, mais esthétique et dynamique de l'Histoire. Le mouvement, le drame, le jeu des passions et des besoins, les conflits souvent cruels, peuvent seuls entretenir chez les peuples comme chez les individus l'élan vital et la puissance créatrice.'[17]In other words, this is a very different outlook from the pacifist reaction of Duhamel. Where Duhamel emphasizes ethics and spiritual values Faure stresses aesthetics and dynamic strength.

As it happens, Duhamel and Faure knew one another quite well, meeting reasonably frequently in the antique shop run by the former's sister (Madame Charles Vildrac) in the rue de Seine. We have already seen that Faure described Duhamel, a trifle patronizingly, as 'le tendre poète'. The latter accused Faure of expressing, in *La Danse sur le feu et l'eau,* 'des idées dangereuses et qui pouvaient faire beaucoup de mal'.[18] There was a wide divergence of views between the two men, but they seem to have argued courteously enough and to have held each other in considerable respect.

If *La Possession du monde* can seem excessively optimistic in some of its ideas, *La Danse sur le feu et l'eau* may appear unacceptably pessimistic. Faure argues for the full-blooded acceptance of war as an immutable fact of life. He concludes his essay by insisting that conflict is an inherent part of all living and implies that pacifist ideals can only inspire those who refuse to face reality. As regards his general approach to these questions, he shares with Duhamel a deep distrust of rationalism and intellectuality. Rationalism, he says, leads to both scepticism and irony with their associated attitudes of doubt, hesitation, lack of firmness, fear of risk, and fear of ridicule. It results in impotence at the level of practical action. In place of mind, reason, logic, detachment, he asserts the need for instinct, flair, passion, involvement. The distance at which he places himself from the approach of an Alain or a Valéry is clear when he writes: 'Vous verrez l'intelligence pure aboutir, tout droit et tout roide, à faire des représentants les mieux qualifiés de la culture, d'imperturbables crétins.'[19] Faure seeks his values and his inspiration in what he terms 'les profondeurs de l'univers lyrique' (p. 14). Nevertheless, his lyricism and emotionalism are of a very different nature from those of Duhamel. He scorns those 'impulsions aveugles qui poussent le commun des hommes vers des absolus sentimentaux' (p. 142) and is equally dismissive of those who flock to banners bearing such words as Peace, Justice, Liberty – 'mots qui affublent l'horreur de vivre du faux-nez idéologique' (p. 90). Faure appears to see a preoccupation with such details as a form of what Pascal analysed as *divertissement*—a stratagem which men employ to disguise from themselves the apparent pointlessness of their lives. His emphasis on energy and violence, blood and strength, together with his scorn for traditional humane and Christian moral ideals, recalls on many occasions the philosophy of Nietzsche which was quite widely known in France by this time. Such ideas seem scarcely consistent with the more sentimental and idealistic forms of socialism, but they are not at odds with one type of left-wing thought which interested Faure and which involves the admiration of power, violence, and revolutionary action in pursuit of power through violence. Such goals emphasize – as the writings of Drieu la Rochelle and others were to confirm in the 1920s and 1930s – the close psychological identity existing between the politically opposed ideologies of extreme left and extreme right. It will become clear, too, in the pages which follow, that Faure's ideas as an art critic and cultural historian also affected his attitude to war. He sees war as an element of culture, as the fire in which new civilizations are forged, and he suggests that to discuss war and peace in terms of style rather than morality is to discuss their true character and real significance.

La Danse sur le feu et l'eau begins boldly and disconcertingly. Faure interprets war – including the Great War which was still being fought when he wrote his book – as an expression of the power and nobility which mankind possesses and which this type of conflict brings uniquely into play. He proclaims the fertilizing virtues of blood and expresses scorn for the weak and sentimental (as he regards them) who are wholly dedicated to peace and an end of suffering. He takes this view not simply out of natural belligerency but because of his conviction that war and violence, conflict and suffering, are an integral part of life and can no more be totally removed from human experience than breathing. It is also his belief that war, which is a biological fact, fulfils too a vital psychological function since it externalizes passions, in the individual or in the group, which would otherwise fester as a result of being repressed. To lessen externalized violence is to intensify inner turmoil. This is no doubt a version of that 'drive-discharge' model of war discussed by E. J. Leed and referred to in Chapter 1. Faure asserts, in fact, that man does not possess the moral or spiritual maturity necessary to overcome those basic needs to which war and violence minister in a very special way.

Apart from the moral objections which they may have to these views, many readers will find the determinism which they imply unacceptably pessimistic. Relatively few thinkers have regarded war as a wholly unavoidable biological and psychological necessity. Given Faure's position, however, any attempt to judge war in terms of good and bad becomes pointless and irrelevant – and even self-deceiving. Faure says, indeed, that to make a moral judgement of war – or revolution – is equivalent to evaluating a poem according to its ethical content alone. It follows that such labels as pessimism and optimism are also irrelevant. What we must strive to attain, against the weight of traditional ethical teaching, is a realistic attitude to war and the implications of war. Faure is scornfully dismissive of facile and deceptive promises of happiness which try to shield men from the truth of their condition, offering 'un bonheur tranquille des quatre côtés duquel s'élève le mur de la basse-cour' (p. 11). This bold view of war, which sees it as part of a human existence that must remain dangerous and violent, is extended further by the claim that it contributes to the cause of progress. Inevitably he does not mean by 'progress' the moral and spiritual growth outlined by Duhamel. Given his general position, such moral progress would be irrelevant and indeed not progress at all but a pointless attempt to change the nature of reality by attaching a different set of labels to it. War can be said to contribute to the cause of progress in so far as it enables men to understand their true condition, opening their minds to 'l'épouvantable héroïsme de leur destinée sans espoir' (p. 14).

In a chapter on the nature of civilization Faure draws closer to Duhamel on one issue, though from a different set of premises. He rejects the idea that scientific development is in itself a form of civilized progress. He makes two characteristic distinctions when he writes: 'Le progrès scientifique, certes, n'est pas la civilisation. Il n'est pas même *"le progrès"*. Mais il est quand même *un* progrès. Le chemin de fer est malpropre, mais si les circonstances exigent que ce Parisien soit dès le lendemain à Rome, il bénira le chemin de fer' (pp. 23–4). What science or technology actually offer is a number of tools which may well influence society, but whether or not they contribute to progress depends entirely on how these tools are used. Faure accepts, then, that the term 'progress' may occasionally be applied – in a limited way and at one remove, as it were – to possible uses of various scientific discoveries. But he remains sceptical about the term and finds most positive applications of it misleading, particularly in the sphere of art and ethics. As regards art, a painting by Renoir, though it may be more complex than an ancient Egyptian stone carving, does not represent progress in the sense of 'un accroissement simultané de science et de moralité' which most of us attribute to the term. And he continues: 'Le progrès esthétique, entendu au sens vulgaire, c'est-à-dire comme une ascension continue en beauté, en noblesse et en puissance de l'œuvre d'art, a donc toutes les chances d'être à peu près aussi chimérique que le progrès moral, et pour les mêmes raisons' (p. 26). The aesthetician in Faure looks to art not for evidence of progress but for indications of quality and style. Given this characteristic of his thought, and his prejudice against moral judgement, it is not surprising to find him arguing that a civilization is properly defined and characterized not by its moral features but by the *style* which it displays: 'Le style. C'est lui, et rien que lui, qui définit la civilisation. Ou plutôt *une* civilisation . . .' (p. 28). This emphasis on aesthetic quality is expressed again a few pages later in an interesting passage:

La civilisation la plus haute est précisément la plus artiste, l'artiste étant le plus civilisé des hommes, parce qu'il est, de tous les hommes, celui chez lequel le besoin d'ordonner la vie est le plus despotique et le plus soutenu. Si l'on pouvait imaginer une époque, un pays où tout homme serait artiste . . . on obtiendrait la plus fidèle image de ce que peut ct doit être une civilisation. En ce sens, notre dix-neuvième siècle est, à n'en pas douter, l'un des moins civilisés de l'Histoire: riche en artistes, il est très pauvre en style, l'artiste restant isolé. Il n'a pas d'architecture, et l'architecture a toujours été l'expression la plus caractéristique des peuples dits civilisés. (pp. 32–3)

This link between civilization and art is confirmed for Faure by his claim that the greatest artists appear during or just after periods of violent convulsion. He further explains that the artist flourishes at such times because he is, above all, a man of order and equilibrium: 'Son unique fonction est d'établir l'ordre en lui-même, de reconnaître chez les autres artistes un besoin d'ordre analogue, et, par insensibles passages, de réunir son ordre propre à l'ordre des autres artistes, pour créer avec eux le style qui définit leur civilisation' (p. 32). Once again it is style, not morality, which defines a given civilization. One can see how Faure could apply this principle to the slave-based civilizations of Greece and Rome or to the socially unjust structure underlying the artistic glories of seventeenth-century France.

It is essential to Faure's argument that he should demonstrate war to be a necessary part of this civilization whose quality is to be assessed in terms of its art rather than its ethics. He first insists that war – and indeed revolution – make possible the transition from a worn-out civilization to a new, alternative pattern of social and cultural norms and ideas. War, or revolution,[20] is to be seen as 'le passage sanglant d'un mythe à un autre mythe, d'une forme de civilisation usée à une forme de civilisation qui se propose à l'expérience' (p. 37). But both phenomena are also a more immediate and integral – if cruel – part of civilization since they externalize the passions and aims of a particular period and then sanction, through bloodshed and through victory or defeat, the essential features of the new civilization that emerges. On this basis war is described as 'partie intégrante et active de la civilisation' (p. 38) and the claim is made that war, which is 'une stylisation de la violence', takes on the style of the particular period in which it occurs. War is described as being 'logique avec César, cartésienne avec Turenne, à la fois rationaliste et romantique avec Napoléon.' He continues: 'L'Histoire de Tite-Live, les voies dallées, les aqueducs correspondent à la première. A la seconde l'architecture des Mansards, les jardins de Le Nôtre, les tragédies de Racine et les murailles de Vauban. A la troisième la critique de Montesquieu et de Voltaire portée par la passion et le sentiment de Jean-Jacques et de Diderot' (p. 38).

This is a suitable point at which to state the obvious and to say that Élie Faure's conception of war (as indeed his conception of art) depends very heavily on broad generalizations, ill-defined terms, assertions masquerading as arguments and a Spengler-like cultural synthesis which must leave the specialist dazed by the assumptions made and the connections claimed. What he offers in *La Danse sur le feu et l'eau* is much more a secular credo than a set of properly supported arguments. His distinctive view of war depends on a series of doubtful biological analogies, an extremely unclear conception of civilization, a number of artistic dogmas which many artists and art historians would reject, etc. It is noticeable too that some of his most firmly proclaimed generalizations lack any supporting detail and are presented as self-evident truths that need no further demonstration. For example, he states unequivocally: 'L'influence fécondante de Marathon et de Salamine sur l'art grec du Ve siècle est trop évidente' (p. 50). Broad, ringing statements like this, or the passage above on the 'style' of different wars, make his book initially challenging and exciting, but they can also be very misleading if not quickly recognized for what they are. He uses the same type of dramatic generalization, in a chapter entitled 'La Tragédie, mère des arts', in order to reinforce his claim not only that war and art are essential elements of civilization but that war and violence are prerequisites of artistic quality.

A typical passage fastens on to one very broad principle of explanation without any concern for detail and ignoring all other ways of accounting for the phenomenon in question:

A partir de 1215, pendant tout le XIIIe siècle et le commencement du XIVe, la guerre civile, à Florence, rougit le pavé . . . La nuit, on entend monter, brusquement, des cris d'assassiné. Or Cimabué naît en 1240, Dante en 1265, Giotto en 1266, Taddeo Gaddi en 1300, Pétrarque en 1304, Boccace en 1313, Orcagna en 1329. Après une éclipse survient, aucun grand nom n'apparaît. Mais que la guerre se rallume entre nobles et manants et atteigne son apogée vers le milieu du XIVe siècle pour durer jusqu'à sa fin, voilà que l'énergie spirituelle se retrempe dans le drame et qu'en trente ardentes années Ghiberti, Brunelleschi, Donatello, Angelico, Andrea del Castagno, Paolo Uccello, Masaccio, L.-B. Alberti, Filippo Lippi, tous nés entre 1374 et 1408, définissent les tendances implacables de l'idéalisme italien. (pp. 59–60)

Faure explains this alleged phenomenon by saying that the violence of war, both civil and foreign, shakes individuals and whole peoples out of their accustomed rut, releasing new energies and encouraging new perspectives. He is being consistent when he goes on to castigate the attempt made by various theorists to distinguish between 'just' and 'unjust' wars in relation to civilized values. Given his general position, he is bound to claim that the moral evaluation of war is pointless and irrelevant – a form of moral equivocation which he despises. War should be seen not as meeting or failing to meet a set of rather doubtful moral criteria, but as the necessary prelude to an upsurge in artistic activity and to new and exciting aesthetic experiments.

It is ironical that Faure should have expressed these ideas at this particular time. It is precisely to these early decades of the twentieth century that one would turn for evidence against his theory. The so-called 'modern movement' in the arts, with all that it implies of vigour and novelty, existed in a very distinctive way before the Great War; it was not a consequence of it. Significant experimental work was done before 1914 by such artists as Picasso, Braque, Mondrian, and Matisse; by Strauss, Schoenberg, Ravel, and Stravinsky; by Strindberg, Proust, Pound, and the Marinetti of the Futurist Manifesto. It was also during the period before 1914 that influential 'modernist' writings were published by Freud, Jung, Sorel, Pareto, Weber, Durkheim, Husserl, etc. This situation has caused one critic to write: 'Although the First World War effectively marks the break between the world of the nineteenth century and our own – both in the minds of those who lived through it and of those of us who read about it in the history books – the modern revolution in the arts did not take place during the war or immediately after it, but a decade or so before. *This should make us wary of too facile an identification of art with the culture and society out of which it springs.*'[21]

It is clear that Faure needs to undermine the generally accepted view of morality as thoroughly as possible in order to strengthen his argument in defence of war. In a chapter headed 'De la moralité de l'art' he attempts to do this by insisting that morality, unlike art, is anti-life because it seeks to suppress those elements of existence, such as violence, of which it disapproves. Faure regards this inclination to suppress part of life as indicating weakness and ending in distortion. It is true that human experience is made up of many conflicting and contending forces, but he claims that true strength comes not from eliminating certain of these forces but from accepting all of them and absorbing them into a balanced whole.[22] It is at this point too that he slips in the idea, crucial to his general concept of war, that good derives benefit from the co-existence of evil and that 'le Bien jaillit comme un feu si le Mal est tapi dans l'ombre' (p. 127). The logic of this idea may not seem very secure. More importantly, this is one of several occasions on which Faure invokes the very type of moral distinction which he holds elsewhere to be irrelevant, in order to make his point. It is true that he can only easily use the type of traditional 'moral' vocabulary which is available to him, but on several occasions he does use it positively, as distinct from accepting it reluctantly. The consequence, for the type of statement just quoted, is that it remains thoroughly unsatisfactory. It means either that Faure is ultimately dependent on the very morality he seeks to refute, or that he uses general moral categories in an attempt to conceal the otherwise unacceptable 'jungle law' of his fundamental position. He goes on, on the basis of this type of statement, to argue that morality seeks to congeal and impoverish the dynamic multiplicity of human experience, whereas art profits by, and contributes to, this life-giving, generative movement of contrasting elements. Morality is paralysis; art is creativity. Once more Faure is making moral judgements in the course of apparently rejecting moral criteria. And it is by means of a somewhat specious logic that he goes on to defend aggression by the strong against the weak and to approve the struggle for survival by the fittest which he holds to be inherent in both human life and the life of ideas:

Les peuples vivants, les races vivantes, les classes vivantes, les idées vivantes sont presque nécessairement amenés, par la marche de leur destin, à envahir brutalement les peuples las, les races déchues, les classes repues, les idées fixes, afin de substituer à une attitude morale de défense qui prétend conserver et restreindre, une attitude artiste de conquête qui veut détruire pour reconstruire et dépenser. (p. 132)

It is hardly necessary to point out how close this type of statement comes to a theoretical justification of the worst features of Realpolitik or of the doctrine that might is right. Nevertheless, it is only fair to recognize that Faure is not speaking here in political terms. He repeatedly emphasizes the crucial and prominent role which he sees for art and artists rather than for politics and politicians. Yet this position eventually leads him into a form of unreality which is just as marked as that which he attributes to the moralists like Duhamel. Not least, it encourages him to make largely meaningless and semi-mystical statements such as: 'L'art, et l'art seulement est moral, parce qu'il est l'obéissance au rythme et qu'il use cruellement de tout, même s'il le faut de la guerre, pour retrouver le rythme quand les hommes l'ont perdu' (pp. 135–6).

As Faure sees it, there will always be an inevitable conflict between 'un rationalisme intellectuel épuisé par les plus nobles conquêtes' and 'un mysticisme social alimenté par les plus violents appétits' (p. 201). What he wishes to make clear to his readers is the necessity of holding these opposing forces in balance and the folly of attempting to eliminate all violent and barbaric elements. This is why Duhamel found his ideas to be dangerous; they not only reject but deny the possibility of genuine pacifism. It is Faure's conviction that to seek to create a rationally organized civilization from which war has been banished is to attempt to destroy art, quality, individualism, and invention.[23] He therefore calls for equilibrium, not reduction and exclusion, in all spheres of experience. Indeed, to advocate balance is simply to recognize the facts of existence since 'tout équilibre, par le fait même qu'il existe, suppose des éléments antagonistes qu'on appelle des partis en langage politique, des classes en langage social, des castes en langage religieux, des fonctions en langage biologique, des forces en langage mécanique, des masses en langage plastique' (p. 172).

It is clear that Duhamel and Faure have little in common as far as their individual views of war are concerned. What they do share is a proselytizing zeal for their contrasting ideas. This zeal, inevitably based much more on instinct than on rational analysis, is expressed in both cases by an often lyrical use of language masquerading as logical discourse. These are writers who, as the French say, 'enflent le ton'. Duhamel's detestation of war originates at a level of feeling at which rationality cannot operate. If anything, this intensifies the impact of his writing. Also, his call to 'possess' the world of men, of natural objects and of art is undoubtedly seductive although it depends on a sentimental view of all three areas of experience. And yet Élie Faure, for all his apparent hardness and realism, is also making an emotional rather than an intellectual case for his ideas. He too calls on us to 'possess' the world, yet he regards it not as a world of all-prevailing goodness and delight but one in which cruelty, bloodshed, and irreducible antagonisms contribute to the fundamental 'rhythm' of existence. A modest rationalist, let alone a logician, could easily ridicule the use made by Duhamel of such terms as 'le règne du cœur', 'la pieuse tendresse', 'le salut de l'âme', 'la civilisation morale', etc. The same might be said of the way in which Faure uses such phrases as 'la force seule est morale', 'les racines de l'art . . . s'enchevêtrent dans l'humus engraissé de sang', 'les grandes convulsions biologiques auxquelles on a donné les noms de révolution et de guerre', etc. Both writers claimed, in fact, that they were writing out of a personal vision beyond the reach, and indeed beyond the competence, of logic and rationality.

These very different forms of lyrical self-expression created many admiring disciples. Both books were written with a fervour and verve not easily ignored − especially in the immediate aftermath of the war. They also gave rise to a certain amount of (largely emotional) reaction to which the periodicals of the time testify. What was most necessary, however, was that the voice of reason and everyday practicality should also be heard. This need was met, in some considerable measure at least, by the publication of Alain's *Mars ou la guerre jugée* a year after the appearance of *La Danse sur le feu et l'eau*. For most readers Alain's was a less exciting work. Coolness, realism, logicality and good sense are not normally calculated to raise the reader's temperature. And yet Alain's voice, the voice of detachment and judgement, was indispensable in the immediate post-war era. He made a much more determined attempt to understand the causes and the nature of war, especially as a prelude to a rational form of pacifism. In doing so he exposed the inadequacy of some of the 'human outrage' arguments associated with Duhamel. He also strongly challenged the view, which Faure was by no means alone in adopting, that war is an inevitable constituent of man's blood-stained destiny.

CHAPTER 8

The Intellectual Response (I)
Alain and Rational Pacifism

Alain is the pen-name of Émile-Auguste Chartier (1865–1951) who had a long and distinguished career as teacher, thinker, and essayist. He exercised considerable influence over pupils and public in the years immediately preceeding and following the Great War. He invented no original philosophical system but was the product of a rational and analytical tradition extending from Aristotle to Comte. In many ways he stood for those particularly French values which the catastrophic experience of war appeared to deny or call into question: intellectual lucidity, individual freedom, high culture, and humanism. He opposed many forms of fanaticism and dogmatism and his republican idealism made him the enemy of most manifestations of established authority. As a young man he had become a pacifist by intellectual conviction. The attitude was confirmed and given more practical expression by his experience as a soldier. War service in the artillery also appears to have strengthened his belief in the importance of the humane and rational doctrines associated with the French Radical Party. He was in his late forties when he volunteered for the army and he served in the ranks until invalided out with a foot injury after three years. Unlike many pre-war pacifists, he retained his pacifist beliefs after 1918 even though they were in abeyance, in practical terms at least, between 1914 and 1918. Indeed, these beliefs are the main motivating force behind the typically brief and pungent essays which he began writing during the actual conflict and which he collected and published in 1921 under the title *Mars ou la guerre jugée*. This original edition contained 92 short two-page essays to which a further 21 were added in the second edition of 1936.

Unlike so many reactions to the phenomenon of war, *Mars ou la guerre jugée* expressed neither patriotic fervour nor simple moral outrage. In contrast with the various different forms of emotionalism associated with Duhamel or Faure, Barbusse or Barrès, the tone is one of cool and realistic analysis: 'Je veux penser les choses comme elles sont.'[1] Alain's voice is never strident. His aim is an exact analysis which will dissolve partiality and passion. He puts his own approach succinctly when he writes: 'Je veux seulement qu'on pense la guerre et la paix selon les notions, non selon les passions' (p. 231). At the same time, he is aware of the difficulties such an approach creates since it is not the most direct way to arouse a response in his readers. Alain knows well enough that men are more easily swayed by an appeal to their emotions than by the processes of logic, but his own instincts and gifts led him in the direction of rational persuasion rather than emotional seduction. At the same time we have here the probable explanation of why his book aroused less interest in the post-war years than it deserved to do. For many readers the intellectual tone appeared abstract, the moral position insufficiently partisan. Besides, many who were outraged yet fascinated by dramatic narratives or memoirs of trench warfare were disinclined to make the effort to think hard about the actual causes and consequences of war. Alain argues that it is all too easy, and indeed fundamentally immoral, to hate war rather than attempt to understand its nature.[2] It is in this sense that he was a rational pacifist.

As his starting-point, Alain was determined not to offer his readers any consolation that depended on intellectual dishonesty. In his preface he proposes to separate with care the various elements that go to make up the phenomenon of war, to give each its true name, and to show how these elements are interrelated. The approach is one that recalls the analytical character of the cartesian method. For Alain, too, rational analysis has its own moral status; intellectual honesty is as important as moral integrity – is indeed a form of moral integrity. As a result, a certain strength of character is required not only to express but to accept the consequences of severely rational analysis: '. . . la pensée n'est pas faite pour plaire; non, mais pour déplaire. Non pour flatter, mais pour juger. Et dès que la preuve est assurée d'être reçue, bonne ou mauvaise, il faut examiner la preuve' (p. 167). It is clear from this that Alain, unlike Valéry, did not regard the war as having cast some doubt on the appropriateness and efficacy of reason itself. On the contrary, given the passions associated with war and aroused by it, he argues that only reason can accurately analyse the causes of passion and thereby overcome war.[3] Thus rationality is the basis of Alain's optimism as it is of his pacifism. He did not respond to the experience of war with apocalyptic gloom and foreboding but retained a strong confidence in the humane and pacific properties of reason.

Given the basic characteristics of Alain's thought, it follows that its most appropriate expression is one distinguished by precision and verbal restraint. He argues that simplicity of expression properly honours heroes and equally properly shows war for the disgrace that it is. He adds: 'Si simplement qu'on parle de la guerre, on l'orne trop' (p. 39). At several points in *Mars ou la guerre jugée* he takes the rhetoricians of war to task and summarizes his attitude by the slogan: 'Dégonflez les matamores' (p. 59). His own prose is notably clear, economical and restrained, with a tendency towards the maxim and the lapidary phrase. It is very much in the tradition of that of various seventeenth- and eighteenth-century French *moralistes*. In many ways, too, the psychology expressed in these pages recalls that of the seventeenth century. In this connection Alain describes Descartes as a 'moraliste trop peu lu' (p. 21), referring to the *Traité des passions*. His own book, with its strong emphasis on the will and its confidence that reason can control passion, encourages one to see it as a *Traité des passions guerrières*.[4] It is also noticeable that, despite his subject, Alain almost totally ignores political questions. In the closing essay he says firmly: '. . . aux politiques je n'ai rien à dire; ils jouent leur jeu' (p. 251). Again like the seventeenth-century *moralistes,* he sees what are now widely regarded as economic and political problems in predominantly moral and intellectual terms.

In *Mars ou la guerre jugée* the fundamentally pacifist spirit of the work is closely linked, as we have seen, with a desire to explain the causes of war. In keeping with the non-political emphasis just mentioned a major argument of the book rests essentially on the claim that the causes of war are to be found in the moral passions and not, as is usually argued, in the clash of political and economic interests. Alain expresses his thesis in condensed form when he writes: 'la guerre est réellement un crime passionnel' (p. 85). The essence of war is psychological and, ironically enough, many of the passions which inspire it are noble in themselves. As regards political and economic conflict, this provides the occasion of wars but is not their fundamental cause.

At various points in the book Alain attempts to take this argument further. For example, he asserts that conscious and deliberate intent, as opposed to passion, cannot be the cause of war though, again, it may be the occasion of conflict. He justifies this by claiming that man's desire is for life, not death. Furthermore, he insists that his argument is based on close observation of men in the trenches and he strongly rejects the view that human beings are chiefly motivated by more or less well disguised, but calculated, self-interest ('cet homme, si souvent décrit, qui suit en toutes ses actions les calculs de l'intérêt, je ne l'ai jamais rencontré', p. 78). On the contrary, one of the most remarkable features of human beings is their readiness to act against what reason would define as their own best interests. What makes this not only possible but fairly commonplace is the intervention of various passions – love, hatred, desire for revenge, etc. As the experience of war demonstrated, man can easily be drawn into a vortex of passions 'toujours contraires à l'intérêt et souvent à la conservation' (p. 79).

Alain is perfectly well aware that his interpretation of the causes of war is not one which is generally shared. In an additional essay in the 1936 edition he emphasizes the difficulty of refuting the theory of economic causes and the argument that, for example, unprecedented industrial development forced Germany into war in 1914. In order to argue his case, he adopts a type of analysis reminiscent of Plato and which goes as follows. All men possess a head, a chest, and a stomach. The problem is to decide which of these human parts is the real seat of those passions which initiate war. Of the head Alain simply says that it does not seem to him to cause war though it often allows itself to be persuaded to approve war. The human part which seems strong enough to persuade the head in this way would seem to be the stomach which demands satisfaction by whatever means. If it is starved of food its demands become so imperious that it will induce the head to approve of violence, and even murder, in order to satisfy its hunger. But this violence or killing, he says, is pillage rather than war. Thus 'je ne puis appeler guerre . . . cette chasse sans pitié que la faim, l'avidité, la convoitise, la peur de manquer éperonnent' (p. 71). Such notions animate the bandit, not the warrior. The warrior is defined as one who consciously chooses to be killed rather than retreat, whereas 'l'animal se risque bien quand il a faim; mais il ne résiste pas à une force évidemment supérieure' (p. 71). Hence Alain rejects the view that war is actually caused or initiated by greed, financial interest, territorial expansion, etc. And it follows, given the human model he has used, that the chest or thorax, i.e. the location of the passions, should be regarded as the part of man which brings war into being. The thorax, he adds, is the seat of anger, and anger is a major cause of what may be properly described as war. He also seems concerned to emphasize that anger is, as he puts it, the daughter of wealth rather than poverty. The anger of a well-nourished man is more to be feared than that of an ill-nourished one. This leads towards his assertion that war, or warlike attitudes, are associated with excess and not with deprivation. Alain's view of the nature of war – mainly based, it must be said, on his experience of the years 1914 to 1918 – is summed up in a series of elliptical phrases:

Guerrier n'est pas maigre ni affamé; riche de nourriture et de sang au contraire; et produisant sa force; et s'enivrant de sa force. Défi, mépris, impatience, injure; commencements d'action, signes, poings fermés. Main disposée non pas pour prendre, mais pour frapper. Cherchant victoire, non profit. . . . Voilà mon homme sans tête parti pour l'assaut; non parce qu'il manque de quelque chose, mais parce qu'il a trop. En un combat d'avares, il n'y aurait guère de sang versé. (pp. 71–2)

And because the passions – and not least the passion of anger – feed upon themselves, war can be alarmingly self-generating and difficult to stop: '. . . c'est une raison de frapper, si l'on menace; et si l'on frappe, c'est une raison de frapper encore plus fort. Jeu, dans le fond . . . Non pas tant signe que quelque chose manque, que signe que quelque chose surabonde, qu'il faut dépenser' (p. 71). 'Facts' can be found, or manufactured, to justify passions, thus prolonging and intensifying conflict. According to this theory, indeed, war could be endless and this sense of a self-renewing deadlock was experienced strongly and widely at various points between 1914 and 1918. But the fact is that passions eventually fade and no one, fortunately, has an interest in prolonging war indefinitely.

This analysis of war is clearly open to a series of objections, particularly if it claims to possess universal validity. It seems to work best for the aggressor in any given conflict and it is clearly unsatisfactory as an account of guerrilla war or wars of 'liberation'. Nevertheless, one can see why it takes the form it does. It reflects Alain's more general philosophical and psychological presuppositions and his necessary concentration on the only war which he had experienced directly. One should also say that in so far as his analysis implies a traditionalist view of the motivation of many combatants, and given that he points out elsewhere the unprecedented conditions of war which they experienced, he is explaining the unique character of the Great War which, in its early phases at least, represented a conjunction of chivalric attitudes and technological realities which created quite horrifying slaughter and suffering.

If Alain appears to oppose what is predominantly a left-wing account of war in terms of economic interest, he is equally dismissive of right-wing patriotic simplicities. He argues that patriotism is an inadequate means of accounting for the totality of a national war-effort. If patriotic sentiment were the chief motivating force, individuals would not be willing to profit financially from a war which killed so many of their fellow-countrymen. But in fact it is exceedingly rare to find anyone who is prepared to say: 'Je ne veux point m'enrichir pendant que ma patrie se ruine' (p. 10). On the contrary, thousands make fortunes from war. Although the armaments, clothes, or foodstuffs which they produce are vital to the nation's survival, their patriotism does not oblige them to renounce huge profits in the course of making this effort. These 'heroes of the deposit safe', as Alain names them, are not willing to say: ' . . . c'est assez pour moi d'avoir vécu; c'est trop d'avoir bien vécu; je refuse une fortune née du malheur public; tout ce que j'ai amassé est à la patrie; qu'elle en use comme elle voudra; et je sais que, donnant ces millions, je donne encore bien moins que le premier fantassin venu' (p. 10). This suggests to Alain that where love of country does exist it is probably sustained and intensified by other natural sentiments in time of war, sentiments which the military machine arouses and exploits with psychological insight and skill.

At most, then, patriotism is a subsidiary passion, not an initiating one, in the prosecution of war. It is clear, however, from what has been said above that Alain regards anger, unlike patriotism, as a passion which actually causes war. The other main cause, in his view, is a sense of honour. Indeed, he appears to place honour above anger in his hierarchy of war-creating passions, describing it as 'le vrai moteur des guerres' (p. 53). Honour can conquer fear. It imparts formidable power even to the materially weak. A sense of honour explains the way in which the nation flocked to arms in 1914. This same sentiment enables men to overcome fear in the conventional sense since they fear to betray a virile and masculine honour more than they fear death. This is Alain's explanation of the apparently suicidal courage displayed by so many at the front. Ironically, it is precisely what made possible that devastating sacrifice of human life for which stubborn or incompetent generalship was ultimately responsible, especially between 1914 and 1916.

The two main passions which cause war – honour and anger – are encouraged as we have seen by patriotic sentiments appropriately exploited. They are also sustained by a number of other passions listed by Alain and which include pride, ambition, generosity, self-discipline, impatience, irresolution, and an aesthetic sense. Such a list caused Alain, despite his pacifist convictions, to admit that many – even most – of the passions inspiring war are noble in character. But impatience and irresolution are hardly noble sentiments, while the role of the aesthetic sense in war is perhaps not immediately obvious. Some further brief comments therefore seem to be required.

Irresolution, which is natural to man, is nonetheless a state which he normally finds it difficult to sustain for very long. It is a feeling which demands its own destruction. The mechanism of indecisiveness is such that it seeks, through impatience, to create its opposite, but the decisiveness to which it aspires is based more on impulsive emotionalism than on rational calculation. Irresolution therefore contributes in an apparently paradoxical way to conflict and fighting: '. . . dans le moment même où la délibération est sans remède, la main se lève; non pas malgré l'irrésolution, mais à cause de l'irrésolution' (p. 22). This irresolution is transformed by impatience into aggression.

Alain also associates war with aesthetics in the sense that warlike attitudes and sentiments are stimulated by military parades and processions. He asserts that beauty affects men more than truth and links this with the view that 'la chose militaire est proprement esthétique' (p. 14). For most individuals, in fact, a marching group, especially if accompanied by music, exerts a natural attraction whatever its object or purpose. The aesthetic element is strong, composed as it is of rhythmic movement and martial sound. Both these aspects create excitement at the possibility of participation in a communal enterprise: 'L'homme se sent et se perçoit avec les autres, invincible et immortel. Ce tambour le fait dieu' (p. 13). A contemporary academic analyst of war made a similar point a few years ago: 'la parade militaire est . . . du langage pour l'inconscient.'[5] The military parade or the departure for war speak at a very fundamental level to the observer – and particularly to the young male observer. Parades, bands, and uniformed crowds transfigure – or conceal – the violence, the ugliness, and the suffering of war. They give brilliance and style to the whole military enterprise.[6]

It is clear from what has been said so far that Alain is concerned to understand the origins and nature of war but that such understanding in no way implies approval. His analysis of war and the attractions of military life is cool and detached. He writes out of a realistic assessment of his own experience and avoids the more familiar rhetorical postures. This may seem, at first sight, to sort ill with his declared pacifism. As already suggested, he answers obviously enough that war cannot be effectively opposed until it is adequately understood. Nevertheless a bridge of some kind seems necessary in order to link his detached anatomy of war with his direct advocacy of pacifism. This is provided mainly by some comments on the nature of the state and of the army.

Alain adopts a highly critical attitude towards the state, not least because of its coercive role generally and yet its evident inefficiency in prosecuting war. He is particularly suspicious of 'les grands', 'les importants', those who occupy influential posts in the state system but whose lack of quality, moral or intellectual, makes of the state a headless monster.[7] The result is that 'la circulation des opinions creuses et émouvantes l'emporte naturellement sur la sagesse désirable' (p. 200). War is the occasion for a series of almost unbelievable blunders committed by military chiefs and leading figures in the state. Alain refers severely to 'la suite des erreurs incroyables où sont tombés les militaires, les diplomates, les financiers, enfin toutes les importances' (p. 201). He says in another essay that 'l'importance rend sot' (p. 101), yet these influential fools are the very people responsible for the conduct of war and they become deeply committed to war because of the power which it gives them.[8] In a word, the great ones in the state often stumble into war through error or stupidity and then go on to sustain a war which ministers to their sense of their own importance. 'Les grands' are severely handled throughout *Mars ou la guerre jugée* in a way that sometimes recalls La Bruyère and which contains a number of features reminding one of Sartre's account of the city fathers of Bouville.

It is a short step from the criticism of political leaders generally to army chiefs in particular. Alain makes all the familiar points against the latter: their short-sightedness, their remoteness, their reckless expenditure of human 'material', etc. He goes so far, indeed, as to speak of the army as being divided into 'deux classes ennemies' (p. 175) – officers and other ranks. He writes as one who remained in the ranks himself and bases his two classes on a fundamental difference of outlook between leaders and led. He makes an interesting but highly generalized distinction, prompted in part by Pascal's *'esprit de finesse'* and *'esprit de géométrie',* between what he calls the 'theological' and 'artisanal' minds. The term 'esprit théologique' can be particularly misleading. Alain seems to mean by it the type of mind which is most at home in dealing with human material rather than inanimate objects. The latter are most naturally and most effectively exploited by the 'esprit artisanal'. The conclusion is drawn that the theological mind provides officers and leaders while the artisanal mind produces the bulk of workers or ordinary soldiers:

Ce n'est donc nullement par hasard que les meneurs d'hommes sont religieux. Inverscment, et par la nature même de ses travaux, l'artisan n'est point théologien du tout. Deux idées, l'intrigue et le travail, forment deux classes d'esprits, l'ambitieux et l'industrieux. L'ambitieux espère, prie, promet, menace; l'industrieux observe, mesure, pèse, invente. Le premier règle ses opinions sur ses désirs, et l'autre sur l'objet. Le premier compte sur sa gloire, sur son autorité, sur sa majesté; ce sont ses armes et ses outils. L'autre nettoie sa pioche. (p. 147)

All this is splendidly expressed. Whether it describes any verifiable human realities is doubtful. Alain perhaps carries more conviction when, on the same page, he applies his distinction more specifically to his own military experience:

C'est pourquoi, dans cette guerre totale, le bureaucrate fut soudain porté à la perfection qui lui est propre, par ce képi dont on le coiffa. A partir de là, les erreurs d'enfant, la folle imprévoyance, la négligence, l'infatuation développèrent tous leurs effets. Un bon calculateur, sans aucun grade, fit dire au capitaine que l'avion ennemi n'était pas à quatre mille, mais bien à six mille mètres. 'Je tire quand même, s'écria l'artilleur théologien.

This basic 'two camp' classification being made by Alain is bound to be biased and untrue to the extent that hc fails to distinguish clearly enough between HQ staff behind the lines and the many officers who led their men directly into battle and shared danger and death with them. The 'harvest of corpses' reaped by the tacticians contained thousands of young officers who were just as much victims of self-important bureaucrats as the men they commanded. Nevertheless, there is a repeated emphasis on the split between two opposed groups in any army operation. Alain insists upon its reality, even referring to the 'slavery' which the men experience – 'les meilleurs à la roue, et les pires levant le fouet' (p. 110). The fact that this degree of contrast does not emerge strongly in most novels or memoirs is attributed by him to the outstanding capacity of human beings to accept circumstances once they are convinced that these cannot be altered. In fact, acceptance and courage are claimed to coincide when he writes: 'Quelque pénible que soit la situation d'esclave, elle est pourtant surmontée par cet animal, si naturellement courageux' (p. 175). Although Alain is opposed to war and very far from being 'belliciste', his honesty and his desire to describe things as they are cause him to point out with interest that the experience of war reveals in man psychological mechanisms and moral resources of this kind which peacetime conditions rarely bring into play. The slavery of the common soldier is a reality, but a reality of which he is scarcely aware. This explains the often amazing acquiescence of non-professional soldiers, faced by almost inconceivable demands on their courage and endurance, during 1914–18. It also explains the true nature of the mutinies which did occur in 1917. They were not primarily caused by bad food or unreasonable orders. These factors simply made possible a momentary consciousness of the underlying condition of slavery and it is this consciousness which led to mutinous behaviour. But as usual Alain considers the logical consequences of the point he has been making. He suggests several times (e.g. pp. 137, 151) that once the war has ended and the need to accept the inevitable is no longer present, the 'slaves' may well rebel, socially and politically, against their 'masters'. What Alain foresaw here was the breaking up of pre-1914 social hierarchies, and the growth in socialist political doctrines, which made distinct progress in the 1920s and 1930s and which was further accelerated by the 1939–45 war.

In the light of these ideas one might have expected Alain to inveigh against the more severe and even unjust aspects of military discipline. Perhaps we have already seen enough of his approach, however, to realize that such a response on his part would be uncharacteristic. Consistency and a concern for logic oblige him to take the view that if one accepts modern war one must accept the strict discipline which is inseparable from it, particularly with a part-volunteer, part-conscript army. He admits that in a sense brutal discipline is scandalous, but in the context of war he holds it to be logically necessary since the 'guerrier libre . . . est régulièrement battu' (p. 24). The reason for this is clear enough:

Il faut battre le fer. Toute la force des coups de marteau se retrouve dans la barre. La trempe est encore une violence. Or c'est à peu près ainsi qu'on forge une armée. La nature humaine est ainsi faite qu'elle supporte mieux un grand malheur qu'un petit. En d'autres termes, c'est le loisir qui fait les jugeurs et les mécontents. Si donc le peuple gronde, cela indique, comme Machiavel voulait, que vous ne frappez pas assez fort. N'ayez pas peur; celui qui frappe fort est premièrement craint, deuxièmement respecté, et finalement aimé. (p. 17)

Alain takes his logic to considerable lengths. Like Dorgelès and Barbusse he refers to the execution by firing-squad of alleged deserters or those who disobeyed orders for whatever reasons. Unlike Dorgelès and Barbusse, however, he does not treat this as a subject of moral outrage. Rather, he claims to be astonished by a journalist who reported such an incident in terms of unjustifiable evil. If you accept war, you must also accept such extreme methods of punishment. It is war itself, already existing before execution by firing-squad, which is atrocious and unjustifiable (p. 31).

Such comments make it clear that Alain is impatient with those who base their protest on certain inevitable manifestations of war rather than on the fact of war as such. He argues, indeed, that not to oppose war, not to adopt a radical pacifism, is to be led logically to accept what is morally repugnant. This is the main basis of the pacifist message of *Mars ou la guerre jugée*. One must oppose the phenomenon itself, not the mere epiphenomena to which it gives rise, and this opposition must be based not on emotionalism but on rational understanding.

This is not to say that Alain ignores the conventional moral case against war. Rather, he takes this case for granted so that there are various references to it without its becoming a prominent and central theme of the book. He describes war, in passing, as 'un malheur démesuré (p. 125), 'la grande tuerie' (p. 142) 'le pire des maux humains' (p. 178), 'ce crime sans mesure' (p. 245). Referring to the Great War in particular, he emphasizes the fact that it killed the finest representatives of a generation, yet solved nothing. Elsewhere he says firmly that the various satisfactions which war can bring to the individual – the pleasures of efficiency, enjoyment in handling and commanding men, exultation in victory – are morally bankrupt for the simple reason that 'tout plaisir est vil qui fleurit sur la mort' (p. 61). Such moral strictures were, of course, widely and frequently made during the period. Alain, while certainly not discounting their importance, takes them to be self-evident truths lying beyond debate and question. His rational pacifism takes him rather in the direction of refuting certain arguments in defence of war.

Perhaps the most common of these arguments involves the claim that war is inevitable and ineradicable. This is a view which the pacifist will want, if possible, to refute. Alain accepts that life does contain some inevitable evils in the face of which human beings can only adopt, at best, an attitude of stoical resignation. A basic question is therefore posed: is war one of these 'maux inévitables'? (p. 98). In connection with this idea of inevitability, Alain criticizes a type of scientifically inspired determinism to which the adjective 'enregistreur' rather than 'jugeur' must be applied. This is the outlook which claims that moral judgement is largely irrelevant since war must quite simply be classified as a fact, like birth or death, and must be accepted as such. But according to Alain war is not an integral part of the human condition and in that sense inevitable. On the contrary, it is a humanly induced fact, the result of human opinions and choices. It is created and sustained by human beings who possess the power to avoid or refuse it: ' . . . la guerre est un fait humain et qui dépend des opinions. La guerre résulte d'une opinion commune, juste ou fausse, accompagnée de colère' (p. 211). In this context, then, the most dangerous of all opinions is that which holds that war is imminent or inevitable.

Apart from the misapplied scientific view just mentioned, there is a more emotional form of determinism, a type of philosophic fatalism which also proclaims the inevitability of war. This is an attitude which Alain condemns on several pages. He regards both scientific determinism and philosophical fatalism as the misbegotten children of positivist thought. Despite his acceptance of many of Comte's ideas, he recommends the study of Renouvier, whose doctrine of moral freedom and will makes important points against a rigidly deterministic view of the universe (p. 106). Alain himself appears to be a determinist in so far as he accepts the fact that certain choices have unsuitable consequences. But he is not a fatalist since he believes strongly that men are free in many areas to make these preliminary choices. In *Mars ou la guerre jugée* he sometimes fails to differentiate clearly and adequately between determinism and fatalism. It is between fatalism and war that he established the largest number of links, two of which are fanaticism and the tragic sense.

Alain establishes a relationship between fanaticism and fatalism when he writes: 'Le fanatisme n'est sans doute pas autre chose que le sentiment d'une fatalité effrayante qui se réalise par l'homme' (p. 156). He adds that a fatalist, by definition, cannot prophesy things that the majority of people desire such as happiness or peace. On the contrary, the fatalist traffics in gloom and disaster. Those whom he persuades by his fanaticism thus expect, accept, and even embrace, the worst. To preach the inevitability of war is, for Alain, to ensure that war happens. In this sense 'le fatalisme est guerre' (p. 157). But the element of 'fanatical' doom in fatalism links it with tragedy also. Fatalism draws much of its strength from a tragic sense on the part of men and seems to be confirmed by their tragic experiences. Indeed, those who take a despairing view of life appear both to fear and to desire the tragic dénouement which fatalism predicts. It is important to be clear, however, that natural calamities are not tragic in the strict sense of the term. An earthquake or a flood is a catastrophe rather than a tragedy. Alain therefore argues, as he did in the case of war, that tragedy is a humanly induced phenomenon in its purest and most fundamental form. And so the tragic element in fatalism finds a natural expression in war just as war readily turns to fatalism as the explanation of its existence. War and the tragic sense, converging rapidly and confirming one another, are further intensified by fanaticism. Alain's own summing up of his argument goes as follows: 'Ainsi le sentiment de la fatalité se satisfait dans la guerre, voulue des deux parts, voulue à chaque instant comme la grande preuve, la preuve des preuves, qui justifie toute une vie de désespoir méchant' (p. 158).

This is the framework within which the passions of anger and honour flourish and from which they draw support. It is the mechanism which causes an older generation, not directly involved in the fighting, to appear to scorn justice and peace and to seem ready to sacrifice its own children in war. The greater the horrors to which the attitude of this generation gives rise, the more thoroughly its worst beliefs seem to be confirmed. It finds in the worst abominations of war a justification of its own despairing fatalism. Alain, however, does not express hatred of those who accept war as inevitable. He attempts to understand them in order to expose the narrow fanaticism of their thought and to convince his readers that war, far from being an unavoidable disaster, is willed by human beings and mostly willed unconsciously. If this is understood and accepted it remains possible for human beings to refuse war by a communal act of the will and with the support of a transformed set of values.

Apart from those who argue that war is inevitable others insist that it is a necessary manifestation of moral strength and determination. Alain refers to Proudhon's *La Guerre et la paix* of 1862 as an expression of this viewpoint. Proudhon identifies might with right and, says Alain, slips from the worship of power into the worship of war. He maintains that Proudhon is entirely mistaken in identifying any army, however great its achievements and however apparently justified its cause, with the combination of virtue and phenomenal strength represented by the mythical figure of Hercules. An army composed of thousands of individuals cannot be identified with a single figure, even a mythic one. Indeed, it is clear from Alain's earlier comments on the folly of leaders and the slavery of the led that no modern army has the moral equilibrium, the imperturbability and the controlled passion which he associates with the individual warrior or hero. In an earlier age, no doubt, the code of chivalry encouraged the identification of virtue and strength. But it is one of his repeated claims in this book, particularly in several additions contained in the 1936 printing, that modern war and ancient chivalry are irreconcilable apart, perhaps, from single-handed aerial combat. He says: '. . . nul ne songe plus qu'il est déshonorant de vaincre par le nombre ou par la surprise, ou par de meilleures armes' (p. 63). In other words, the methods and conditions of modern war nullify all attempts to identify it with virtue and honour:

. . . comme jamais celui qui décide n'est celui qui paie, et puisque finalement il n'y a pas un soldat sur mille qui approuve ce qu'il fait et qui puisse se vanter de l'avoir voulu, je ne puis voir en ce brutal mécanisme que la faiblesse déchaînée, les passions triomphantes et la vertu décapitée. Injustice essentielle. Hercule humilié. (p. 219)

A third argument in support of war sees it as an essential means, if an occasional one, of defending legality and justice. Legality has traditionally been associated with violence in the particular sense that it has had to do with imprisonment, deportation, execution, etc. Alain admits this, but he bases his own argument on the conviction that, for 99 per cent of the population, the provisions of legality and justice are accepted and welcomed. Also, in virtually all cases, these things are not imposed by force of arms. Indeed, if legality and justice were imposed by force they would quite simply cease to have any genuine moral content. In some ways this seems a dubious argument. For example, Alain pays no attention to the history of laws. He does not consider the fact that some laws which are now universally obeyed and welcomed had to be imposed initially in the face of much opposition. Be that as it may, he could still claim that constraint does not immediately create true legality and that, on the same model, war cannot serve immediate justice. What he does go on to argue is that war cannot serve the cause of peace. Indeed he asserts that 'les moyens de la force n'approchent point de la paix, mais . . . en éloignent' (p. 229). There are many obvious criticisms to be made of Alain's position but he does at least avoid the apparent inconsistency of many left-wing pacifists, including Barbusse and, at times, Rolland, who attacked militarism but were prepared to contemplate the creation of the social millennium by violent means.

In an essay added to the 1936 edition, Alain writes: 'les artistes en coups et blessures ne trouvaient jamais une nouvelle manière de percer ou de déchirer, sans qu'aussitôt les artistes du pansement missent à l'étude une nouvelle méthode de guérir, correspondant parfaitement à la nouvelle plaie. Les citoyens étaient très contents, d'autant que le ministère de la persuasion, par mille journaux et brochures, leur prouvait qu'ils devaient l'être' (pp. 28–9). The reference here is to a fourth argument which is directed, more particularly, against the distinctive viciousness of war. It says in effect that the new and sophisticated ways of tearing and torturing human flesh need not worry us too much since counter-techniques of cure and renewal are continually being invented. The more war technology advances in the direction of destruction, the more medical science grows in efficacy. A burnt face is not really so bad given the remarkable advances being made in skin grafting. Alain does not have much to say about this kind of argument though he clearly scorns it. Its inadequacy was clear enough to anyone who had seen the awful wounding and horrifying deaths of many of his companions at the front.[9] Alain therefore suggests that such an argument can only be given force by means of propagandist manipulation. Even then, it is likely to impress civilians only.

A final argument, which seeks to excuse the horrors of war on commonsense grounds, arouses Alain's particular contempt. This is the claim that war, by definition, means killing and that to object to killing is at best illogical and at worst subversive. It is a view sometimes expressed nowadays by means of the homely kitchen metaphor stating that 'you cannot make omelettes without breaking eggs'. For Alain, as for so many of his contemporaries who had direct experience of the trenches, this was a typical argument of the ignorant *arrière* or of a remote and inhuman HQ. A more realistic view of the killing only comes from seeing with one's own eyes the rotting corpses of hundreds of young men lying in mud or impaled on barbed wire and Alain characterizes this killing in terms of the paradoxical phrase: 'sauver l'avenir en le massacrant' (p. 118). At the same time, he tends to use emotional rather than logical terms in rejecting the commonsense argument of the inevitability of killing, and even in rejecting the acceptability of suffering. This is partly because the argument itself contains a spurious logic and because pacifism, however rational the case made to support it, can only become a practical reality when it moves men's emotions as well as persuading their minds. We saw earlier that Alain always realized the limitations of human susceptibility to logical proof. In his exposition of his pacifist ideas he is therefore concerned not to allow his basically rational approach to deteriorate into mere abstraction. He must convince his readers intellectually, but he must also attempt to move them to practical response.

Once Alain turns his attention from statements in defence of war to the more positive aspects of his pacifism he simplifies the intellectual aspect considerably. What he has to say, indeed, is based on the clear and straightforward proposition that war is bad and peace is good.[10] War is bad, above all, because it means that people are killed. Alain takes the integrally pacifist view that killing is never justified, whatever the end which it seeks to serve. War is, by definition, a criminal activity: '. . . il n'est pas de fin au monde, pour un homme, qui puisse prendre pour moyen bien clair, inévitable, la mort d'un autre homme; ou bien c'est crime' (p. 206). Killing cannot be used as a source of moral values. Alain therefore calls upon his readers to reject and resist war, not by violence but by going on strike intellectually, as it were. If the individual waits for others to refuse war before doing so himself, war will continue to occur. It must be resisted by mind and heart and this resistance must be decided upon independently by each individual: 'Décide d'après ton gouvernement intérieur et souverainement . . . Nie la guerre, fermement, sans aucune concession d'esprit' (p. 214).

So Alain requires his readers to pay proper attention to their own deepest moral instincts, to recognize these instincts clearly and to act upon them in a practical and forthright way. He claims that a total rejection of war is the instinctive reaction of most men and of relatively simple working people in particular. He holds this instinct to be sound and realistic. It is only a small and sophisticated élite which actually wants war (because of the power and authority it gives them) and this social élite is largely responsible for persuading ordinary people, against their best instincts, that war is necessary. This means that Alain identifies war, in part at least, with the structure of society. His confidence in the practical possibilities of pacifism therefore depends in considerable measure on social change. Although he does not go into political detail on this aspect of his pacifism, he declares roundly and in general terms: 'Résister à la guerre et résister aux pouvoirs, c'est le même effort' (p. 179). The radical implications are clear. This statement could be taken as a brief and precise résumé of Barbusse's political credo. It puts a major responsibility for war on the shoulders of the 'ruling classes' and therefore suggests that the successful elimination of war is a practical possibility requiring both individual moral strength and social revolution.

Finally, since Alain believes firmly in the natural courage, good sense and moral responsibility of the majority of human beings, he is able to take an optimistic view of the future. The problem for the rational pacifist is simply a practical one of finding adequate ways of appealing to these qualities in man so that he can exercise that moral courage which is one of his most distinctive characteristics and which is also his major weapon in the struggle against the crime of war.

CHAPTER 9

The Intellectual Response (II)
Valéry and Analytical Detachment

We have already seen that the attempt to evaluate the catastrophe of 1914–18 took a variety of forms. Duhamel, for example, seized the opportunity to declare the bankruptcy of scientific, industrialized civilization and to ask for its replacement by what he called 'le règne du cœur'. Faure, on the contrary, used a sombre lyricism of violence to interpret war as a form of biological necessity and a regenerating element of culture. In terms of emotional response we might have added Henri Massis who, having written originally in terms of conventional and patriotic heroism, went on to see in the Great War evidence of the undermining of Western values by alien oriental ideas.[1] One writer who made an admirable effort to bring strictly rational criteria to bear on the question was Alain and in so far as Valéry's response can be related to this rather diverse background it goes most readily, at least in terms of analytical method, with *Mars ou la guerre jugée*.

Both Alain and Valéry put their trust in rational analysis and were not prepared to buy optimism at the cost of intellectual dishonesty. Between them they probably represent the most penetrating attempt, in its immediate aftermath, to understand the war. Nevertheless, the verdicts which they reached were very different. Alain, unlike Valéry, did not regard the Great War as having cast serious doubt on the appropriateness and efficacy of reason itself. On the contrary, in view of the passions associated with war he argued that only reason could accurately analyse the causes of war-creating passions and thereby point the way to overcome them. This is the basis of the relative and rational optimism which underlines his pacifism. Valéry, on the contrary, not only questioned the very intellectualism which he preached but entertained no strongly pacifist convictions. His writings on war in general, and this war in particular, are part of a much larger and systematic view of the nature of mind and the development of Western society. This sense of a broad and coherent philosophic doctrine, drawing together many different strands of thought, is less apparent in Alain's assessment of war. In the end, Valéry's is the greater challenge to the reader.

In one way this is surprising since Valéry, unlike Duhamel, Faure, Massis, and Alain, had no direct experience of war at the front. One might expect his analysis to carry less conviction. There is little reference in his writing to the horrifying slaughter and maiming that occurred between 1914 and 1918. He sees war as an intellectualized ethical problem rather than as an experiential nightmare. But given the mass of writing in this latter mode – memoirs, journals, novels, letters, etc. – his approach is all the more distinctive and valuable. He achieved a detachment and an analytical power to which most of his contemporaries, for reasons of personal experience or individual talent, could not seriously aspire.

Apart from this detached and rational approach to the subject of war, Valéry set it in a much longer historical perspective than most of his contemporaries. This was the outcome both of methodological conviction and of an ability to uncover sequence and connection beneath apparent disjunction and singularity. None of the war analysts previously mentioned could produce a comparable sense of the underlying tendencies which issued in the Great War. Nor, indeed, does any one of them have such a clear and accurate vision of how things were to evolve after 1918. One can therefore say that Valéry was able to offer an account of the war which consists of three distinct phases: an analysis of certain dangerous developments before 1914; some relatively brief comments on the war while it was in progress; an examination of the significance of the war and of its likely effects on the future once it had ended.

Valéry's interest in the contemporary world developed early. In addition to various entries in his *Cahiers* up to 1914, two essays are of particular interest. The Sino-Japanese war, which broke out in 1894, led to his writing an essay, 'Le Yalou', in 1895, though it was not published until many years later.[2] A second essay appeared in French in W. E. Henley's *New Review* of January 1897 under the title 'La Conquête allemande'. The subject was the menacing growth of German industrial and military power. It was reprinted in the *Mercure de France* for 1 August 1915 and the title was altered to 'Une Conquête méthodique' in 1924.[3] Neither article, and more especially 'Le Yalou', is a particularly orthodox piece of political reportage. Valéry's scorn for the pragmatic aspects of political action is well known. Even at this early stage in his career he was concerned not with the immediate details of politics but with the wider and more profound meanings to which they provided pointers.[4] His approach, at once complex and profound, is expressed in a letter to Gide of October 1899 in which he refers to 'la tendance principale de mon esprit qui est l'extension, la généralisation perpétuelle'. He continues: 'Il m'est parfaitement impossible de m'attacher à quoi que ce soit de singulier . . . En somme, je ne veux généralement pas voir les choses comme tout le monde. J'en prends d'abord une impression aussi instantanée que possible, puis j'y reviens en tâchant de les retrouver par une suite de conditions indépendantes entre elles et par conséquent plus générales que mon objet.'[5] This is the kind of mental exercise which enabled Valéry to fulfil a virtually prophetic role prior to 1914.

'Le Yalou' has many of the features of a poetic meditation. Valéry employs the device, familiar from Montesquieu to Malraux, of using an oriental figure (in this case a Chinese scholar or sage) as a means of criticizing various features of European life. The main central section is a long, critical, and sometimes enigmatic monologue uttered by the 'Chinois lettré'. War as such is barely mentioned, but it is constantly present as the likely outcome of the various moral and intellectual characteristics of Europe. Behind the oriental setting and the symbolist imagery a warning note is being sounded. The belief is firmly stated that European civilization has taken a wrong, possibly a fatal, turning. The Chinese speaker describes Europe as possessing some of the worst features of childishness: it is untidy and restless, demands continual novelty, is impatient with the past and fearful of death. He draws the conclusion that Europe is incapable of good government. Most of the faults which he finds, however, are not attributed to immaturity (though they show certain characteristics of immaturity) but to the fact that intellect, as distinct from wisdom, has got out of hand. Europeans, in their worship of the 'bête prépondérante' which is the rational mind, have been led to an ill-judged rejection of tradition and to an uncritical faith in the virtues of science.

The Chinese scholar praises the centuries-old traditionalism of his society and the clearly defined place of the individual within this tradition: 'Chaque homme d'ici se sent fils et père, entre le mille et le dix mille, et se voit saisi dans le peuple autour de lui, et dans le peuple mort au-dessous de lui, et dans le peuple à venir, comme la brique dans le mur des briques. Il tient' (Pl. II, p. 1018). He adds that the inertia of this traditionalism – as the West might interpret it – is in fact a manifestation of both wisdom and strength. It contrasts sharply with that betrayal of traditional values and restless preoccupation with constantly changing ideas which, he asserts, characterize the late nineteenth-century European mind. The Chinese speaker also declares that while oriental traditionalism is at one with the slow, deliberate rhythms of nature, Western rationalism has uprooted man from his natural context. Thus 'en détruisant la simplicité des hommes, on avait excité le désir en eux, et changé la notion qu'ils ont d'eux-mêmes' (Pl. II, p. 1019). The result is the creation of unnaturalness and barbarity by apparently natural and civilized means. Valéry thus prepared his readers, intellectually if not morally, for the fact that within twenty years barbarity was to erupt in a Europe which represented civilization in its most advanced form.

In addition to emphasizing the naturalness and the necessity for the individual to fulfil a temporal role in a slowly unfolding tradition, the Chinese scholar in 'Le Yalou' stresses the importance of the individual's spatial role, as it were, within a social hierarchy. Western democracy and egalitarian aspirations leave him unimpressed: 'Vos chefs ne commandent pas, vos hommes libres travaillent, vos esclaves vous font peur, vos grands hommes baisent les pieds des foules, adorent les petits, ont besoin de tout le monde' (Pl. II, p. 1017). With this he contrasts the traditionalist and hierarchical society of the China of his day which he relates, in part, to questions of literacy and the difficulty of the Chinese language:

Ici, pour pouvoir penser, il faut connaître des signes nombreux; seuls y parviennent les lettrés, au prix d'un labeur immense. Les autres ne peuvent réfléchir profondément, ni combiner leurs informes desseins. Ils sentent, mais le sentiment est toujours une chose enfermée. Tous les pouvoirs contenus dans l'intelligence restent donc aux lettrés, et un ordre inébranlable se fonde sur la difficulté et l'esprit. (Pl. II, p. 1020)

On rational grounds Valéry shared this view of his Chinese spokesman. He had little sympathy with the intellectual questioning of traditional values and hierarchical differences which leads to 'progressive' attitudes and 'democratic' practice. It is well known that Valéry was not a democrat in the popular sense of the word. The *Cahiers* prior to 1914 contain such statements as 'la démocratie est une terrible affectation, une pose. Rien de moins vrai' and 'il est impossible d'être démocrate avec esprit'.[6] Later he was to warn against subjecting the individual to the mass or to what he called the 'caprices du nombre'.[7] He believed that the democratization of the intellect must inevitably lead to mediocrity of rational analysis and judgement. His Chinese spokesman sees the West's rejection of tradition and encouragement of equality as creating a potentially explosive mixture of 'idées terribles' and 'cœurs faibles' (Pl. II, p. 1018). There is a hint here of Yeats's vision of the best lacking all conviction ('cœurs faibles') and the worst being full of passionate intensity ('idées terribles').

Valéry's picture of potentially dangerous intellectual and social unrest and confusion among his contemporaries was intensified by his conviction that European science was progressing in an equally perilous way. His Chinese spokesman refers to the need to limit and control scientific growth. He points out that many great inventions of the West (including the invention of gunpowder) took their origins from China. But it was an essential element of Chinese wisdom that these inventions should be given only limited scope: 'Comprends-tu désormais pourquoi elles n'ont pas été poursuivies? Leur perfection spéciale eût gâté notre lente et grande existence en troublant le régime simple de son cours. Tu vois qu'il ne faut pas nous mépriser, car, nous avons inventé la poudre, pour brandir, le soir, des fusées' (Pl. II, p. 1020). The general picture, then, in 'Le Yalou', is of a confused and unbalanced European civilization undergoing a dangerous intellectual mutation and increasingly lacking agreed values and the ability to determine and attain its own goals. This is consistent with the more detailed analysis of Europe which Valéry was to write in 1919 when he set out what he regarded as the main lessons of the Great War.[8]

'Une Conquête méthodique', originally published in 1897, is more directly political in tone. The focus is now primarily on Germany and some aspects of modern life only briefly touched on in 'Le Yalou' are taken further. Also, the danger of war is much more strongly implied. Valéry begins with a fairly rapid account of the military, industrial and commercial strength of Germany, acknowledging a debt to Ernest E. Williams's *Made in Germany* and Maurice Schwob's *Le Danger allemand* – both published in book form in 1896. German strength is seen as the result of a deliberate policy which had been planned in immense detail and executed with determination and skill. This strength, based on systematic thought and systematic action, is in sharp contrast to the general disorder and lack of purpose in Europe at large as described in 'Le Yalou'. The result is that where France and Britain are concerned 'nous luttons contre cette armée comme des bandes sauvages contre une troupe organisée' (Pl. I, p. 937). Although this prospect is a dangerous and alarming one, Valéry feels bound to admire the formal perfection of the method applied by the Germans to all aspects of their national life. It is the outcome of a disciplined and sustained use and application of the intellect. Nevertheless, he analyses in some detail, and with considerable foreboding, the calculated and carefully integrated exercise of a common scientific method in industry, commerce, war, etc. Apart from the dangers implied for relations between France and Germany, he is uneasy about the practical consequences in various spheres of life. He sees rationalistic methodology spreading through social life and even into literature and art. This is the beginning of a developing trend.[9] His argument is that this methodology, despite its formal dependence on the intellect, puts a premium on thoroughness rather than inventiveness, on conscientiousness rather than originality, on obedience rather than initiative, on hard work rather than imagination and flair. It is a system which leaves nothing to chance and, once the method has been created, it proves an ideal framework of operation for the fundamentally mediocre and bureaucratic mind. Valéry claimed that these were precisely the qualities and characteristics concentrated in the machine-like personality of the Prussian general von Moltke:

Pour ce héros glacial, le *véritable ennemi c'est le hasard*. Il le poursuit, et sa force réside dans la méthode uniquement. De là naît une étrange idée. La méthode requiert une véritable médiocrité de l'individu, ou plutôt la grandeur seulement des dons les plus élémentaires, tels que la patience, l'attention départie à tout, sans choix, sans enthousiasme. Enfin, la puissance du travail. Ceci accordé, on obtient un individu qui viendra toujours et inévitablement à bout de n'importe quel homme supérieur. Ce dernier verra d'abord ses idées triomphantes; puis limitées avec une ironique précision; puis, lentement modifiées, perfectionnées selon une logique sans faute comme elle est sans interruption (Pl. I, p. 981)

According to Valéry, this is the type of mind which is tending more and more to dominate modern life. It is a mental ordinariness which is so thoroughly disciplined and so remorselessly applied that, in terms of practical efficacity, it proves superior to genuine intelligence. Bureaucratic determination and technological skill are ushering in the reign of mediocrity.

Valéry warns that the Germans, by applying this new method to military affairs, have significantly altered the character of future wars. The age of heroic, chivalric encounters is past. Referring to von Moltke's revolution in military thinking he writes:

Il fait table rase des idées militaires de son temps. Il n'use que des idées scientifiques et des progrès matériels de ce temps. Il les combine avec le meilleur de la stratégie du passé – c'est-à-dire, avec ce qu'il sera éternellement rationnel de faire à la guerre. Il voit dans l'emploi des chemins de fer l'extension des fameuses marches rapides de Napoléon. Il reprend et perfectionne l'exploitation de toutes les ressources d'un pays envahi. Il fait la guerre où il faut, il terrorise les habitants pour briser le courage général. Il multiplie les moyens d'information, il écoute les indications de l'opinion, celles de la finance, les rumeurs, les journaux, le sentiment des neutres . . . Il est sans passion, sans génie, et dans les papiers. (Pl. I, pp. 980–1)

The last phrase here reminds one that some years later, in his *Cahier* of 1910, Valéry was to re-emphasize the close similarity which he saw between the modern military leader and the manager of any large commercial enterprise. Both are mainly concerned with administration and logistics. Quantity becomes at least as important as quality. Figures and calculations take over from ideals.[10] On the question of numbers and quantity, Valéry goes on to warn that the modern German determination is to organize numerical superiority, not chivalric equality. As in industry and commerce, so in war the aim is 'l'organisation de la prépondérance' (Pl. I, p. 978). Alain was to confirm this view, in retrospect, when he wrote in 1921: '. . . nul ne songe plus qu'il est déshonorant de vaincre par le nombre ou par la surprise, ou par de meilleures armes'.[11] Valéry's picture is of a modern form of warfare which is organized in the utmost detail, which has rejected traditional chivalry, and which is 'total war' in the sense that it is integrated into an industrial and commercial whole. The danger is clear:

Il ne faut pas se dissimuler que, pour les vieilles nations supérieures, la lutte deviendra de plus en plus malaisée. Elle a pris un caractère tel que les qualités mêmes qui étaient considérées parmi elles comme les plus favorables à leur vie, et comme les principaux moyens de leur grandeur, deviennent des motifs d'infériorité. Ainsi, l'habitude de chercher la perfection de l'objet fabriqué, l'encouragement donné à la concurrence intérieure, l'amélioration de la vie des ouvriers sont autant d'obstacles à la lutte. (Pl. I, p. 983)

It was shortly after the publication of these views, in May 1897, that Valéry obtained a post in the French War Ministry which he occupied until July 1900. It is clear that he understood better than most both the danger of war and the need to revise received military theory. There is little evidence, however, that he had much influence on the French government.

In his relatively few comments on the actual progress of the Great War, Valéry showed continuing insight and foresight. In July 1914, just before war was declared, he wrote in a letter to his brother Jules that the outcome of the imminent conflict would not justify the effort made and the probable destruction to be suffered: 'Il est étrange de penser que si la pente s'accentue, dans trois semaines il y aura dix millions d'hommes sous les armes, et la ruine générale commencée. Le résultat à attendre pour quiconque ne correspond pas à l'effort et aux destructions probables' (Pl. I, pp. 37–8). And the following September, when the conviction was widespread in Britain and France that the war would be over by Christmas, he again showed his insight: 'Je crois d'ailleurs à la longueur de la guerre. La libération totale de l'Europe doit se faire.' He added somewhat caustically in a reference to Britain: 'Et quand nous serions tentés d'en finir à moitié chemin, les Anglais, auxquels le Channel permet toute logique, nous prieront d'aller jusqu'au bout.'[12]

We have already noticed that Valéry's 'Une Conquête méthodique', still entitled 'La Conquête allemande', was republished with only the most minor alterations of phrasing and punctuation in September 1915. This was his one public comment on the war appearing between 1914 and 1918. In fact, despite his perceptive response to public affairs in the period before 1914, he made his reputation during the war not as a commentator on the conflict but as a major poet whose work appeared particularly abstract and disengaged in the context of the dramas being acted out on the Western Front. This was a deliberate choice on his part and it seems to have been brought about, in a paradoxical way, by his instinctive preoccupation with the fighting. Early in 1915 he wrote to his wife: 'Je travaille autant que mon cerveau capricieux le daigne. C'est le moyen d'échapper à l'obsession de la guerre' (Pl. I, p. 38).[13] In fact, he was working at 'La Jeune Parque', published in 1917, and his *Album de vers anciens* which finally appeared in 1920. Valéry seems to have been cultivating what he later called, in a *Cahier* entry of 1940, 'un être sans date en moi'. The connection with his ideas in 'Le Yalou' is clear. Furthermore, he was convinced – even in 1914 – that to allow himself to be totally preoccupied by the war would have been to surrender to an emotional obsession which oversimplified the issues and encouraged crude and unsubtle judgements ('Deux ou trois seules grosses couleurs, pas de nuances, comme un drapeau').[14] He attempted to justify his attitude, retrospectively, in a letter of 1929 to Duhamel following a reading of the latter's *Guerre et littérature* with its reference to the Olympian serenity of an unnamed poet during the war:

La guerre vint. Je perdis ma liberté intérieure. Spéculer me parut honteux, ou me devint impossible. Et je voyais bien que toutes mes réflexions sur les événements étaient vaines et sottes. L'angoisse, les prévisions inutiles, le sentiment de l'impuissance me dévoraient sans fruit. C'est alors que l'idée en moi naquit de me contraindre, à mes heures de loisir, à une tâche illimitée soumise à d'étroites conditions formelles. Je m'imposai de faire des vers, de ceux qui sont chargés de chaînes. Je poursuivis un long poème.

Et voici où je voulais en venir. Voici le souvenir où m'a reconduit tout à l'heure votre mot sur l'Olympienne Sérénité:

Ce poème (qui fut appelé la *Jeune Parque*) présente toutes les apparences des poèmes qu'on aurait pu écrire en 1868 comme en 1890. 'Tout se passe' comme si la guerre de 1914–1918, pendant laquelle il a été fait, n'avait pas existé.

Et moi, pourtant, qui l'ai fait, je sais bien que je l'ai fait *sub signo Martis*. Je ne me l'explique à moi-même, je ne puis concevoir que je l'ai fait qu'en fonction de la guerre.

Je l'ai fait dans l'anxiété, et à demi contre elle. J'avais fini par me suggérer que j'accomplissais un devoir, que je rendais un culte à quelque chose en perdition. Je m'assimilais à ces moines du premier moyen âge qui écoutaient le monde civilisé autour de leur cloître crouler, qui ne croyaient plus qu'en la fin du monde; et toutefois, qui écrivaient difficilement, en hexamètres durs et ténébreux, d'immenses poèmes pour personne. Je confesse que le français me semblait une langue mourante, et que je m'étudiais à le considérer *sub specie aeternitatis* . . .

Il n'y avait aucune sérénité en moi. Je pense donc que la sérénité de l'œuvre ne démontre pas la sérénité de l'être. Il peut arriver, au contraire, qu'elle soit l'effet d'une résistance anxieuse à de profondes perturbations, et réponde, sans la refléter en rien, à l'attente des catastrophes.[15]

Inevitably, of course, Valéry made some scattered comments on the war in letters and in his *Cahiers*. The most practical and important of these is a letter of 29 September 1915 written to Victor Cambon and emphasizing the need to reorganise the French army. If Valéry's comments on his writing of 'La Jeune Parque' during the war recall his attitude in 'Le Yalou', the letter to Cambon follows naturally enough from his analysis of Germany in 'Une Conquête méthodique'. It includes the following passage:

Il y a quelques années, je songeais à une réforme très intime de notre armée.

Il s'agissait de parer à notre déficience croissante d'effectifs. Je voyais en imagination une telle organisation, une adaptation si poussée de ses fonctions, que mon armée chimérique eût été à celle existante ce que celle-ci est à un troupeau.

J'en ai entretenu quelques officiers qui ont été étonnés, mais enfin qui n'ont pas bondi. Depuis que le système Taylor a paru, je me suis avisé que mon système militaire lui ressemblait vaguement. Si j'eusse été Allemand, sans doute aurais-je approfondi et publié cette première idée. Peut-être lui aurait-on fait un sort.

Mais j'ai eu, depuis toujours, la sagesse de ne tourner mes entreprises que vers l'intérieur. Mes déceptions intestines me suffisent! (Pl. I, p. 1789)[16]

A letter of the same period to André Fontainas adds further details: 'J'avais mon système très révolutionnaire fondé sur une division du travail très étudiée – une armée sportive-technique, obtenue par des reclassements des effectifs, une profonde modification de la notion de grade, des exercises, etc. . . . Je regrette de ne l'avoir rédigé, ce projet, ni publié en ce temps. Je serais compris aujourd'hui'.[17] Since this last letter refers to these ideas as dating from five or six years earlier, they clearly crystallized in Valéry's mind nearly a decade after his experience at the Ministry of War.

These references to military reorganization, associated in Valéry's mind with questions of strategy and tactics, make this an appropriate point at which to desert chronology for a brief period. In 1931, in his speech of welcome to Marshal Pétain on the latter's election to the French Academy, Valéry inevitably dwelt on Pétain's contribution to war theory. An intellectual sympathy existed between the two men precisely because of the new thinking about war which both expressed. Pétain's realistic appraisal of the changed circumstances of industrialized and total war is emphasized. As is well known, he opposed the concept of the *attaque à outrance* and the throwing of wave upon wave of infantry troops against the machine-gun and the flame-thrower. Valéry quotes a number of his maxims including 'le feu tue' and 'le canon conquiert, l'infanterie occupe'. The comments contained in this speech are also of considerable interest because of the light they throw on Valéry's own ideas – ideas which, although expressed in 1931, varied little from those he had put forward before and during the war itself.

At an early stage in the speech the distinctive characteristic of the Great War as a war of attrition is emphasized. Pétain is described as having been particularly well equipped, temperamentally and intellectually, to recognize and exploit 'le caractère stationnaire, dilatoire, en quelque sorte, d'une guerre de peuples, caractérisée par un équilibre, à durée indéterminée, de puissances et de résistances profondes' (Pl. I, p. 1101). But he also recognized the vital role being played by increasingly sophisticated weapons. Here he was well in advance of his more traditionally-minded military contemporaries. While Valéry says of the latter that 'les progrès des engins les touchaient peu', he emphasizes the fact that Pétain understood the demands made on military tactics by a 'combat tel que l'armement à grande puissance exige qu'on le conçoive' (Pl. I, pp. 1105 and 1108). The Great War turned out to be of such a new and complex nature that, as Valéry had foreseen and Pétain had demonstrated, it amounted to a 'sorte de corps à corps technique et intellectuel' (Pl. I, p. 1110).

Although Valéry continued to point to the intellectual and moral confusion which preceded and followed the war, he was disinclined in 1931 to speak in terms of a thoroughly disabling and enfeebling decadence. He seems to have regarded the war, indeed, as providing evidence that decadence was by no means all-pervasive:

On nous a assez dit que nous étions un peuple en décadence, qui ne fait plus d'enfants, qui n'a plus de foi en soi-même, qui se décompose assez voluptueusement sur le territoire admirable dont il jouit depuis trop de siècles.

Mais cette nation énervée est aussi une nation mystérieuse. Elle est logique dans le discours; mais parfois surprenante dans l'acte.

La guerre? dit la France, – *Soit.* (Pl. I, p. 1112)

Similarly, he regarded Verdun as an occasion when men, said to be irremediably softened and weakened by the deification of scepticism and pleasure, scaled the very heights of heroic energy and self-sacrifice. All this was achieved in the course of a war which, says Valéry, 'se résume en tâtonnements sanglants, dans une confusion de nouveautés et de traditions, au milieu de conditions jusque-là inconnues, qui déconcertaient les plus habiles' (Pl. I, p. 116).

Finally, having emphasized the way in which a kind of disguised war – the so-called *paix armée*—extended from 1875 to 1914 and made the eventual outbreak of hostilities inevitable, Valéry looks to the future with considerable foreboding. He finds every evidence that in 1931 there are those who are consciously contemplating a new war despite the 'terrifiants souvenirs' of 1914–18. Dorgelès had concluded in 1919, in Chapter 11 of *Les Croix de bois:* 'Allons, il y aura toujours des guerres, toujours, toujours . . .'. With a similar sense of helplessness Valéry saw humanity, a mere dozen years after the signing of the Armistice, as 'un essaim d'absurdes et misérables insectes invinciblement attirés par la flamme' (Pl. I, p. 1128).

Returning now to Valéry's comments while the war was still in progress, two may be mentioned briefly. In a letter to his nephew Jean, on the occasion of the latter's mobilization in November 1917, he emphasized the debilitating effect which the war was having on Europe 'maintenant qu'elle a à peu près détruit toute sa façade de durée, et son apparence immuable' (Pl. I, p. 40). In seeking to destroy one another, Britain and France on the one hand, and Germany and Austria on the other, were undermining above all the strength and the example of European civilization. Valéry regarded the war not only as destructive in this sense but as the wrong means of settling affairs satisfactorily. It could not be an effective way of solving problems since it used violence and crude strength in response to difficulties which demanded 'l'analyse la plus fine et des essais très prudents'.[18] Here, as in most of his comments, Valéry had nothing to say about the slaughter and the suffering. This certainly does not mean that he was insensitive to such matters, but it does emphasize that his own distinctive contribution was to be in mainly intellectual terms and in an analysis of the meaning of the war for the future of Europe. This analysis is contained in his best-known comments on the war – his two articles entitled 'La Crise de l'Esprit', and the associated 'Note (ou l'Européen)' in which various ideas in the original articles are developed further.

In the *Cahier* for 1926 Valéry made a simple but important distinction between 'dramatic' and 'functional' historical events. A war, particularly one of such destructive power as the Great War, comes into the first category in terms of its form. It is concentrated in time and sharply positive in impact. 'Functional' events, on the other hand, have much less precise limits, are more 'normal' in character, and operate in a more diffuse and unremarkable way. Valéry adds that dramatic events 'ont en général un intérêt infiniment moindre'.[19] In the case of the Great War, however, he sees it as possessing characteristics of both kinds of event in a unique and striking way. Its form is dramatic, but its essence is functional. The war therefore calls for analysis and interpretation; its importance arises above all from the very special way in which it focuses and dramatizes certain underlying and 'functional' developments of modern European civilization. Valéry can be said, in fact, to analyse the war less for what it is than for what it portends. And as we shall see, whereas most commentators saw the war as a savage and senseless interruption of normality, he interpreted it as evidence of a fundamentally changing world.

It follows from this that Valéry is dealing as much with future possibilities as with recent events. His response to the Great War is essentially speculative. This attitude is not only necessitated by his approach to history but encouraged by his conception of war. He insists that when men embark on war they cannot know, or control,. the eventual consequences. This seems to have been particularly true of the 1914–18 period and Valéry makes the point with a homely but striking image: 'On frappe sur un clou et le clou s'enfonce. Mais il y a dans le mur un conducteur électrique – qui peut, touché, donner *n'importe quels* effets'.[20] These effects are regarded by Valéry as being especially important and demanding close investigation.

As for the motivation behind his attempt to interpret the meaning of the war, this was amply provided by the shock, which Valéry shared with his contemporaries, at the contrast between late-nineteenth-century self-confidence and the shattering of illusions between 1914 and 1918. In a frequently quoted letter to the Belgian symbolist writer Albert Mockel he wrote in May 1918: 'Mais quelle époque! Notre génération aura comme un destin bien étrange: jamais enivrements intellectuels plus puissants, plus variés que ceux, il y a 30 ans, que nous connûmes! . . . et nous voici pourtant dans une catastrophe indéfinie, songeant qu'une civilisation est chose aussi frêle qu'une vie humaine.'[21]

The two articles or letters entitled 'La Crise de l'Esprit' first appeared in English, in Middleton Murry's *Athenaeum,* with the titles 'The Spiritual Crisis' (11 April 1919) and 'The Intellectual Crisis' (2 May 1919). They appeared in French, with the single title 'La Crise de l'Esprit', in the *Nouvelle Revue Française* of 1 August 1919. As regards the associated 'Note', this is the text of a lecture given at the University of Zurich in 1922. All three articles were published together in *Variété* of 1924.[22] The famous opening phrase – 'Nous autres, civilisations, nous savons maintenant que nous sommes mortelles' (Pl. I, p. 988) – echoes the final phrase of the comment to Mockel quoted above. Valéry made it clear that he regarded arguments about the precise meaning of 'civilisations' and 'mortelles' as a waste of time. His statement was a way of saying that he and his contemporaries were passing through a particularly critical phase of history.[23] What made the war such a crucial event was, above all, the way in which it called into question the intellectual and moral assumptions of the Belle Époque and, indeed, of the whole European tradition.

This is the main subject of the first article with its description of what Valéry calls 'l'agonie de l'âme européenne'. He outlines the many aspects of Europe's apparent death-throes in a series of striking phrases:

Les faits . . . sont claires et impitoyables. Il y a des milliers de jeunes écrivains et de jeunes artistes qui sont morts. Il y a l'illusion perdue d'une culture européenne et la démonstration de l'impuissance de la connaissance à sauver quoi que ce soit; il y a la science, atteinte mortellement dans ses ambitions morales, et comme déshonorée par la cruauté de ses applications; il y a l'idéalisme, difficilement vainqueur, profondément meurtri, responsable de ses rêves; le réalisme déçu, battu, accablé de crimes et de fautes; la convoitise et le renoncement également bafoués; les croyances confondues dans les camps, croix contre croix, croissant contre croissant; il y a les sceptiques eux-mêmes désarçonnés par des événements si soudains, si violents, si émouvants, et qui jouent avec nos pensées comme le chat avec la souris, – les sceptiques perdent leurs doutes, les retrouvent, les reperdent, et ne savent plus se servir des mouvements de leur esprit.

L'oscillation du navire a été si forte que les lampes les mieux suspendues se sont à la fin renversées. (Pl. I, pp. 990–1)

This is the intellectual and moral state of affairs which war had revealed with particular clarity and urgency. But it was a state of affairs that had existed for some time; it was, after all, diagnosed by Valéry in the 1890s. The war could be regarded as a very severe illness which had simply brought home to the patient the fact of his own long-standing ill health. The exact stage which the progress of this ill health had reached was not, however, easily determined. Indeed, Valéry points out that the limits of military or economic crises are more easily defined than those of moral or intellectual ones. He is therefore more concerned to issue a very general warning at this stage than to attempt to outline future developments with any precision.

The crisis which Valéry describes has two main elements. Traditional intellectual ideals and traditional moral standards have both been called in question. At this point Valéry's conservatism and anti-modernism come to the fore as he associates the collapse of firm and generally accepted values with the moral and intellectual pluralism of Belle Époque intellectuals. In answer to his own question: 'Et de quoi était fait ce désordre de notre Europe mentale?' he replies: 'De la libre co-existence dans tous les esprits cultivés des idées les plus dissemblables, des principes de vie et de connaissance les plus opposés. C'est là ce qui caractérise une époque *moderne*' (Pl. I, pp. 991–2). A paragraph later he continues vigorously: 'Eh bien! l'Europe de 1914 était peut-être arrivée à la limite de ce modernisme . . . Combien de matériaux, combien de travaux, de calculs, de siècles spoliés, combien de vies hétérogènes additionnées a-t-il fallu pour que ce carnaval fût possible et fût intronisé comme forme de la suprême sagesse et triomphe de l'humanité?' This is the situation which the war has both revealed and reinforced.

The complex interaction of intellectual and moral factors is emphasized in another well-known passage:

. . . les grandes vertus des peuples allemands ont engendré plus de maux que l'oisiveté jamais n'a créé de vices. Nous avons vu, de nos yeux vu, le travail consciencieux, l'instruction la plus solide, la discipline et l'application les plus sérieuses, adaptés à d'épouvantables desseins.
Tant d'horreurs n'auraient pas été possibles sans tant de vertus. Il a fallu, sans doute, beaucoup de science pour tuer tant d'hommes, dissiper tant de biens, anéantir tant de villes en si peu de temps; mais il a fallu non moins de *qualités morales.* Savoir et Devoir, vous êtes donc suspects? (Pl. I, p. 989)

What is intellectually approved may lead to unacceptable moral conclusions and what is morally ratified may lack a convincing intellectual basis. The war has shown that rationality is incapable of preventing barbarity while the moral arguments of pacifism lacked decisive intellectual power in 1914. The events and experiences of the war have dealt a series of severe blows to received ideas so that intellectual achievements (*Savoir*) raise awkward moral difficulties – the concentration of human ingenuity on destructive ends – and moral assumptions (*Devoir*) create intellectual problems – the contribution of duty and industriousness to manifestly evil and aggressive purposes. At the end of the first article Valéry sees the European intellectual as a modern Hamlet meditating uncertainly on the life and death of intellectual verities and moral certainties. In the midst of immediate post-war euphoria Valéry and his more perceptive contemporaries saw Europe as even more confused, weak and lacking in clear objectives than the Europe described in 'Le Yalou'.

The second letter, also entitled 'La Crise de l'Esprit', is less obviously and less directly linked with the war. Nevertheless, it contains some of Valéry's most characteristic thoughts on the weakness of Europe to which the Great War contributed. He begins with the axiom that peace is more complex than war and therefore less easily understood. This is due, at least in part, to the fact that fundamental trends or changes of direction receive less dramatic expression in peacetime and are less easily identified. The suggestion seems to be, indeed, that it is one of the functions of war to clarify what is happening over a much longer period than that of its own duration. Valéry, as he meditates on the war, goes on to describe the change that he sees taking place in the role of Europe in the world. He is little concerned with specific economic or political changes. His purpose is to analyse the immediate post-war situation in purely intellectual terms, claiming that world affairs interest him strictly 'sous le rapport de l'intellect'.

The cultural centrality of Europe throughout so many centuries is a striking fact: 'aucune partie du monde n'a possédé cette singulière propriété *physique*: le plus intense pouvoir *émissif* uni au plus intense pouvoir *absorbant*' (Pl. I, p. 995). Given the smallness of Europe in physical terms, and its relatively limited natural resources, the 'miracle' of Europe's long intellectual and moral dominance must be due to the qualities possessed by its inhabitants. On the map it merely constitutes 'un petit cap du continent asiatique', yet it has proved to be 'la perle de la sphère, le cerveau d'un vaste corps'. The qualities of mind and character which appear to have given Europeans their traditional pre-eminence probably include 'l'avidité active, la curiosité ardente et désintéressée, un heureux mélange de l'imagination et de la rigueur logique, un certain scepticisme non pessimiste, un mysticisme non résigné (Pl. I, p. 996). Whatever the precise nature of these qualities, the important point for Valéry is the traditional and notable disparity between Europe's physical limits and her centuries-old moral and intellectual ascendancy. This leads him to propose a 'fundamental theorem' which is the central point of his article and to which the war had drawn particular attention. He argues that this predominance is rapidly being lost. Quality is being forced to yield to quantity; numerical strength is becoming the real means of influencing the world. Status based on quality alone is being rapidly replaced by status based on size. Although Valéry does not say so, his 'theorem' would seem to be confirmed by the growing 'great power' status of the USA and USSR after 1918, and the relative decline of western European countries.

It is clear from what he says that he regards the real instrument of this change as being neither politics nor economics. The true source of Europe's power has been the development of science by generations of researchers – a development that goes back to the mental disciplines of the early Greek geometers. In the course of the industrial revolution above all, scientific activity ceased to be an end in itself and a largely disinterested pursuit of knowledge. Increasingly applied on a large scale to industrial and commercial ends, it became 'moyen de puissance, moyen de domination concrète, excitant de la richesse, appareil d'exploitation du capital planétaire' (Pl. I, p. 998). Put another way, 'le savoir, qui était une valeur de consommation, devient une valeur d'échange.' As soon as applied science and technology became commodities which non-European countries could purchase or imitate, the balance of influence in the world began to change. The factor which counted most in terms of practical influence was no longer intellectual originality but '*la grandeur matérielle brute, les éléments de statistique, les nombres,—population, superficie, matières premières*'. The Great War itself, as we have seen, was finally less a matter of heroism and skill than a question of superior material resources.

For Valéry, this gradual diffusion of science outside Europe was a factor likely to be of the utmost importance in shaping the future of the world. It corresponded, at an international level, to the increasing diffusion of culture within nations which, in turn, involved 'l'accession à la culture de catégories de plus en plus grandes d'individus'. It was a form of international democracy and as such it made Valéry uneasy. While admitting that it is difficult to be sure whether or not these trends represent a decline, his final comments in this article suggest that he distrusts a world in which quantity and materialism play the dominant role. But he does question whether such developments are inevitable, suggesting that they may be reversed if the effort made is sufficiently great and carried out at an individual level:

Le phénomène de la mise en exploitation du globe, le phénomène de l'égalisation des techniques et le phénomène démocratique, qui font prévoir une *deminutio capitis* de l'Europe, doivent-ils être pris comme décisions absolues du destin? Ou avons-nous quelque liberté *contre* cette menaçante conjuration des choses?

C'est peut-être en cherchant cette liberté qu'on la crée. Mais pour une telle recherche, il faut abandonner pour un temps la considération des ensembles, et étudier dans l'individu pensant, la lutte de la vie personnelle avec la vie sociale. (Pl. I, p. 1000)

The Great War, then, far from solving fundamental problems, appeared to Valéry to reveal their pressing nature more clearly and to leave Europe less capable of dealing with them. And the very quality of intellect which he so deeply admired seemed to be fashioning its own eventual downfall.

The 'Note' of 1922 expands several aspects of the two 'Crise de l'Esprit' letters. The mood is sombre. The opening paragraph both repeats the earlier picture of post-war disarray and contains a sense of foreboding that appears to have increased during the intervening three years (as it was to do, even more markedly, by 1931):

L'orage vient de finir, et cependant nous sommes inquiets, anxieux, comme si l'orage allait éclater. Presque toutes les choses humaines demeurent dans une terrible incertitude. Nous considérons ce qui a disparu, nous sommes presque détruits par ce qui est détruit; nous ne savons pas ce qui va naître, et nous pouvons raisonnablement le craindre. Nous espérons vaguement, nous redoutons précisément; nos craintes sont infiniment plus précises que nos espérances; nous confessons que la douceur de vivre est derrière nous, que l'abondance est derrière nous, mais le désarroi et le doute sont en nous et avec nous. (Pl. I, p. 1000)

This experience of certain fear and uncertain hope is directly linked with the war ('toutes les choses essentielles de ce monde ont été affectées par la guerre'). And Valéry adds that what he calls the 'resonance' of war will reverberate throughout the remaining lives of all men and women of his generation.

The damage done by the war, in terms of economics, politics and social life, is obvious. But Valéry is primarily and characteristically concerned with the damage suffered by the intellect. It was suggested above that intellect appeared to him to be fashioning its own downfall with increasing certainty during the first two decades of the twentieth century. He now writes specifically: 'L'Esprit est en vérité cruellement atteint; il se plaint dans le cœur des hommes de l'esprit et se juge tristement. Il doute profondément de soi-même' (Pl. I, p. 1001). In order to explain these views further he makes a series of observations on the subject of man.

Man is distinct from other living beings in the sense that he is dissatisfied with what already exists and is preoccupied with what might come to exist in the future. This is something like that 'divine discontent' of which others have written. Man is constantly searching for ways to fashion reality according to his own dreams and ideals. Hence Valéry says of man that 'il contient ce qu'il faut pour se mécontenter de ce qui le contentait . . . Il ne forme pas un *système fermé* de besoins, et de satisfactions de ses besoins. Il tire de la satisfaction je ne sais quel excès de puissance qui renverse son contentement' (Pl. I, pp. 1001–2). It is this restless intellectual dissatisfaction which is the source of man's greatest achievements – of civilization, progress, science, art. A page or two later, however, it becomes clear that this account of man is regarded by Valéry as a description of European man only. In fact he divides human beings into two distinct groups and while he associates a peculiarly fruitful discontent with the intelligentsia of Europe, he recognizes a second category of human beings 'qui occupe la plus grande partie du globe, demeure comme immobile dans ses coutumes, dans ses connaissances, dans sa puissance pratique; il ne progresse plus, ou ne progresse qu'imperceptiblement' (Pl. I, p. 1005). The description of this latter group recalls the account of oriental wisdom given in 'Le Yalou' and

Valéry cannot now oppose it without displaying considerable inconsistency. In fact, he appears to have been very undecided at this time. Instinctively he admired the restless, searching type of mind, but realized that it could lead to the kind of moral bankruptcy of which the war had furnished a particularly stark example. But equally instinctively he found intellectual quiescence unattractive, yet he admired its outcome in terms of ordered wisdom. His dilemma is clear when he writes: 'Il faut que notre pensée se développe et il faut qu'elle se conserve. Elle n'avance que par les extrêmes, mais elle ne subsiste que par les moyens. L'ordre extrême, qui est l'automatisme, serait sa perte; le désordre extrême la conduirait encore plus rapidement à l'abîme' (Pl. I, p. 1006). This short paragraph sums up that crisis of the rational intellect which became a continuing preoccupation with Valéry from the end of the Great War onwards. The war had demonstrated in a dramatic way the capacity of intelligence to become self-destructive, to perish as a result of its own virutes. The sustained rejection by the intellect of existing conditions, be they social, economic, or technical, and its formal coherence and order leading to practical incoherence and disorder, make it as much an object of suspicion as an instrument of progress. Such are the real terms of Valéry's deep-seated practical conservatism which coexisted with a non-conservative recognition that radical and irreversible change had come about in the modern world. It was an intellectual dilemma that could not fail to give a pessimistic tone to much of his post-war thought.

He returned to this theme on numerous occasions in such works as *Propos sur l'intelligence* (1926), *Regards sur le monde actuel* (1931), *La Politique de l'esprit* (1933), and his unfinished *Mon Faust* (1946). In this last work, for example, Faust tells Mephistopheles that the original truths by which man lived for so long have disappeared. Men have learned that 'l'intellect à lui seul ne peut conduire qu'à l'erreur et qu'il faut donc s'instruire à le soumettre entièrement à l'expérience. Toute leur science se réduit à des pouvoirs d'agir bien démontrés' (Pl. I, p. 301). In such passages Valéry anticipates the need for a revaluation of the claims of rationality as traditionally understood. It is not a far step from this point to a recognition of certain assumptions of phenomenological and existential thought. As thinkers in the seventeenth century had to free themselves from the abstractions of medieval scholasticism, so twentieth-century thinkers have increasingly rejected the total claims made on behalf of the rational intellect by Cartesian/Newtonian abstraction. Intellectual knowledge has been reduced to the level of the personal, even the accidental, because it is 'an achievement of the whole, inalienable psycho-physical person' and not 'the work of a disembodied intellect'.[24] Valéry himself did not carry his argument this far, but his prolonged meditation on the fundamental meaning of the Great War led him to conclusions resembling those on which this new epistemology is largely based.

CHAPTER 10

Malraux and the Reinvention of Man

We have just seen that Valéry maintained a cartesian rigour and abstraction in his response to the contemporary world. Nevertheless, because of the disquieting applications of a certain kind of intellect which he associated particularly with Germany before and during the Great War, he experienced an unease which finally called in question the very instrument of his own enquiry. To this extent his vision comes close to being deeply pessimistic, if not ultimately nihilistic. Pure mind represents perfection for Valéry, but its application to human affairs must be far from perfect since being, or existence, necessarily involves imperfection and impurity. One is reminded of his statement, in 'Ébauche d'un serpent', that '. . . l'univers n'est qu'un défaut/Dans la pureté du Non-être!' and of the closing invocation, in the same poem, of 'l'étrange Toute-Puissance du Néant!'

Such ideas encouraged Valéry, as he considered the impact of the Great War, to expose dangerous developments in the modern western world by using its own highest cultural aspirations as his standard of judgement. They led him towards a vision which prompts Roulin to describe him as one of the first twentieth-century thinkers to have sounded the knell of European civilization.[1] And yet, because he was so totally identified with European cultural values, his critique of his times remains a limited one. He was unable to detach himself so thoroughly from tradition as to be able to uncover the full drama of the situation. It is true that he showed signs of moving in this direction – in 'Le Yalou' for example – but a fully radical analysis, freed from any reliance on values regarded as wholly discredited by the experience of the war, had to wait for a new generation and a more original point of view. In this sense André Malraux turned out to be a major spokesman of the new generation. He was particularly qualified, intellectually and temperamentally, to adopt a new and wide-ranging focus. In doing so he established a new conceptual vocabulary – *angoisse, absurdité, révolte, authenticité,* etc. – which was to dominate intellectual debate before and immediately after the second World War.

Malraux is the one writer, among all those discussed in these pages, who was not an adult when war broke out in 1914. He reached the age of eighteen in 1919, four months after the signature of the Treaty of Versailles. He therefore experienced the war as a highly intelligent adolescent confined to the *arrière*. There is little explicit reference to the war in his two works which will be discussed here: *La Tentation de l'Occident* of 1926 and the essay, 'D'une jeunesse européenne', published in 1927. Nevertheless the implications of the Great War are present – indeed prevalent – in both works. The war, rather like Flaubert's description of God in the created world, is 'présent partout, visible nulle part'. It may be an exaggeration to claim that, had there been no war, these two works could not have been written. Nonetheless it seems certain that without the war they would have taken a different form and contained different emphases.[2]

In general, then, it is appropriate to end this account of various responses to the Great War with a closer look at some of Malraux's early ideas. As already suggested, he takes over from Valéry in a number of ways. He expands and deepens our understanding of 'la crise de l'esprit' and goes further in arguing the need for a total reappraisal and redefinition of man. Furthermore, he acts as an important link. He reveals the continuity between post-1918 disarray and pre-1939 anxieties. Valéry had offered a hint, and Malraux now adds abundant confirmation, that the philosophical and moral turmoil intensified and dramatized by the Great War had set up ripples which quickly spread outwards to form the existentialist and absurdist swirls and eddies of the 1930s and 1940s. The texts of 1926 and 1927 show how the crisis emphasized by the catastrophe of war was bound to be extended into our own times. It follows that these same writings pose problems which remain unsolved despite the fact that they were brought into focus at the end of the first quarter of this century. And they do much to establish Malraux's status as a major analyst of twentieth-century metaphysical and moral anguish and confusion.

In choosing his title, *La Tentation de l'Occident,* Malraux had in mind Spengler's work. This latter had appeared in a French translation, under the title *La Décadence de l'Occident,* in 1923. *La Défense de l'Occident,* published by Massis in 1927 and reviewed by Malraux in the *Nouvelle Revue Française* of that year, may be taken as echoing both Spengler and Malraux himself in its choice of title. And all three works, of course, confirm the sense of crisis and the concern for European civilization and culture which preoccupied some of the most original minds in Europe during the immediate aftermath of the war. As for Malraux's long essay, 'D'une jeunesse européenne', there is a similarity between his title and that of *Le Jeune Européen* published by his friend Drieu la Rochelle in the same year. It has been pointed out too that some of the most characteristic phrases of *La Tentation de l'Occident* 'could almost have come straight from current periodicals or from the early essay *Mesure de la France*' which Drieu published in 1922.[3]

It is clear, then, that such works represent a movement away from the thoroughly documented horrors of war itself to a closer consideration of the civilization which failed to prevent them and which, in certain perverse ways, attempted positively to glory in them. This was not the first time, however, that the civilized assumptions and cultural norms of the early twentieth century had been called in question. Before the outbreak of war in 1914, writers and artists identified with the 'Modern Movement' had challenged the intellectual, moral and aesthetic canons of the age. Indeed, many features of the Great War appeared to confirm and fulfil the aims and prophecies of the more violent and destructive manifestations of the avant-garde while creating the disarray in which experiment and innovation flourish. Not least, the war accelerated and intensified certain attitudes associated with Dadaism and subsequently with Surrealism. Dadaism, which its founder Tristan Tzara described as a state of mind, was opposed to 'systems', represented a violent break with artistic and moral tradition, and emphasized the importance of spontaneity and individual freedom in the midst of what Jean Arp called 'the slaughterhouses of the world war' and 'the curious madness of these times'. As for Surrealism, the apparent collapse of the claims of reason after 1914 encouraged Breton to stake a claim for 'automatisme psychique pur'. The impact of war also seems to be present in his later and celebrated statement, in his novel *Nadja* (1928), that if beauty is not *convulsive* it will not be beauty.

It is of particular relevance to mention such ideas here since Malraux originally moved in avant-garde literary circles and his own earliest works bear their imprint. *Lunes en papier* (1921) and *Royaume farfelu* (1928) are surrealist fictions which belong to the new world and the new sensibility intensified by war and emphasizing pain, death, insanity, imprisonment, incoherence, and violence.

Neither *La Tentation de l'Occident* nor 'D'une jeunesse

européenne' is written in a surrealistic style. At the same time, both are far removed from traditional discursive modes. There is no question of using strictly logical and sequential procedures to call in question logic and order. On the contrary, structure and style are essentially elliptic, disjunctive, cryptic, visionary. This inevitably creates problems since any attempt to analyse such works must involve some rearrangement of the contents and will do less than justice to their distinctive tonality and artistic impact. While 'D'une jeunesse européenne' is cast in the form of an essay, *La Tentation de l'Occident* consists of letters exchanged between a young Frenchman, A. D., travelling in China, and a young Chinese, Ling, travelling in Europe. The fact that the letters contain little in the way of closely reasoned argument or direct replies and genuine debate may be taken as indicating – at a formal level – the metaphysical isolation and alienation which are major subjects of speculation by both correspondents.

The picture of twentieth-century western man which emerges from Malraux's two texts makes them significant documents of post-war despair and poses questions which continue to haunt many thinkers today. As one would expect, Malraux was up to date. He wrote out of an awareness that the 'classical' view of human nature had been thoroughly challenged by the writings of Darwin, Marx, Bergson, and Freud. Marx had opened up new perspectives for revolutionary action; Bergson had called in question the whole status of the rational mind; Freud focused attention on the unconscious and the nature of instinctual drives. Freud's *L'Introduction à la psychanalyse* was the first of his works to be translated into French (in 1921). The Freudian revelation appears to lie behind Malraux's claim, in 'D'une jeunesse européenne', that 'il faut oser maintenant regarder en nous-mêmes' or that 'Le Moi, palais du silence où chacun pénètre seul, recèle toutes les pierreries de nos provisoires démences mêlées à celles de la lucidité.'[4]

The writings of Freud can also be used to account for the lack of correspondence between rational intention and subsequent behaviour. This is something which the war had dramatized in the sense that human rationality had proved incapable of preventing enormous slaughter and a four-year denial of reason. There are echoes of this problem at several points in *La Tentation de l'Occident*. For example, Ling writes: 'Je crois que les passions que vous éprouvez organisent moins le monde en faveur de leur objet qu'elles ne vous désagrègent.'[5] In the following letter A. D. admits: 'Avec quelque force que je veuille prendre conscience de moi-même, je me sens soumis à une série désordonnée de sensations sur lesquelles je n'ai point prise, et qui ne dépendent que de mon imagination et des réactions qu'elle appelle' (*T.O.*, pp. 72–3). Again he states in the final letter of the book: 'Avec une détresse calme, nous prenons conscience de l'opposition de nos actions et de notre vie profonde' (*T.O.*, p. 158). Malraux does not show any signs of becoming a thoroughgoing Freudian but uses the insights of Freud as evidence of the absence of inner unity and lack of true self-knowledge which characterize himself and his contemporaries. Going beyond Freud he interprets the self-division of western man not simply as a psychological fact but as the expression of a fundamental metaphysical dilemma. He writes in a well-known (and italicized) passage: '. . . *au centre de l'homme européen, dominant les grands mouvements de sa vie, est une absurdité essentielle*' (*T.O.*, p. 57).

According to Malraux then, western man is both self-estranged and alienated on a cosmic scale. He possesses a self which is psychologically split and metaphysically meaningless. The post-war world therefore poses a pressing question: 'Quelle notion de l'Homme saura tirer de son angoisse la civilisation de la solitude?' (*J.E.*, p. 134). Man is no longer satisfied or convinced by the civilization which his self-division has created – a civilization already characterized by Valéry as 'mortal'. He is tormented by both lack of belief and a need for conviction. It was this dilemma, which he referred to as a 'nouveau mal du siècle', which Marcel Arland described in 1924: 'Aucune doctrine ne nous peut satisfaire; mais l'absence de doctrine nous est un tourment'.[6] Three years later Paul Morand suggested the existence of a direct link between the Great War and the new *mal du siècle* when he observed: 'Aujourd'hui les Français [savent] que tout ce massacre a été vain, que, huit ans après, il ne reste rien des principes au nom de quoi l'on se battait, mots usés pour avoir été trop portés au cimier des casques.'[7]

The general sense that western civilization is based on false premises and empty values, together with a renewed awareness of the importance of the non-rational element in human experience, prompted some intellectuals of the period to seek answers to their problems in oriental thought. Romain Rolland, for example, wrote in 1922: 'Nous sommes un certain nombre en Europe, à qui ne suffit plus la civilisation d'Europe. Des fils insatisfaits de l'esprit d'Occident, qui se trouvent à l'étroit dans la vieille maison . . . nous sommes quelques-uns qui regardons vers l'Asie.'[8] It is partly against this background that *La Tentation de l'Occident* should be read. Malraux sets out the stereotyped contrast of the period between the practical man of the West who finds meaning in action and the contemplative man of the East who seeks union with the cosmos. Western man attempts heroically to impose his will on the world; oriental man finds wisdom and serenity in a merging of the self with the totality of being. Ling expresses the distinction clearly:

Entre l'esprit oriental et l'esprit occidental s'appliquant à penser, je crois saisir d'abord une différence de direction, je dirais presque de démarche. Celui-ci veut dresser un plan de l'univers, en donner une image intelligible, c'est-à-dire établir entre des choses ignorées et des choses connues une suite de rapports susceptibles de faire connaître celles qui étaient jusque-là obscures. Il veut se soumettre le monde, et trouve dans son action une fierté d'autant plus grande qu'il croit le posséder davantage. Son univers est un mythe cohérent. L'esprit oriental, au contraire, n'accorde aucune valeur à l'homme en lui-même; il s'ingénie à trouver dans les mouvements du monde les pensées qui lui permettront de rompre les attaches humaines. L'une veut apporter le monde à l'homme, l'autre propose l'homme en offrande au monde. (*T.O.*, pp. 112–13)

The prospect of serene detachment from the world and the promise of deep inner contentment were bound to tempt some of those who had just emerged, disturbed and disillusioned, from four years of mechanized killing and moral confusion. As we have seen, however, Malraux was not immediately identified with the war generation and his spokesman A. D. rejects the temptation of the Orient. He finds eastern philosophies as arbitrary and as false as the intellectual systems of the West. In particular, eastern mysticism claims that direct contact with the absolute is a reality, but A. D. regards this alleged absolute as nothing more than intense subjective experience: 'Dans l'extase, le penseur ne s'identifie pas à l'absolu comme l'enseignent vos sages; il appelle absolu le point extrême de sa sensibilité' (*T.O.*, p. 122). More generally, there is strong emphasis on the fact that the vision of the world associated with the East is crumbling quickly under the pressure of European ideology. A. D. reports a long conversation with Wang-loh, a venerable Chinese sage who describes the best minds in China as being both conquered and disgusted by European values. Wang-loh goes on to speak of a 'confucianisme en miettes' and notes, with sorrow, the tendency of young people in China to adopt alien western attitudes towards action and physical force. He adds that whereas the status of force is a very low one in Confucianist thought, 'la Chine, qui en fit jadis un auxiliaire vulgaire, la recherche aujourd'hui, et lui apporte, comme une offrande aux dieux méchants, l'intelligence de toute sa jeunesse' (*T.O.*, p. 136).

It is clear then that for Malraux oriental thought can suggest some lessons to the West but has no definitive solutions to offer. He does not propose to follow in the steps of Romain Rolland. He wrote part of *La Tentation de l'Occident* while in the Far East, but he sees oriental mysticism less as a genuine intellectual temptation than as a way of pointing up more clearly the nature of western man's crisis. He is not presenting eastern thought as an alternative or as a solution. At best it casts an oblique light on the philosophical absurdity at the heart of twentieth-century European man's experience. We turn therefore to his main undertaking in these two texts: an analysis of the crisis of the West in the course of which he traces a development which begins with the death of God and moves through the death of man and the failure of individualism to nihilism and absurdity. He sees Europe, in the aftermath of war, as a 'grand cimetière où ne dorment que des conquérants morts' (*T.O.,* p. 159) while in the 'Postface' to his novel *Les Conquérants* he still maintained twenty years later: 'Le drame actuel de l'Europe, c'est la mort de l'homme'.

The ultimate roots of modern man's disorientation and experience of anguish are traced by Malraux to the eighteenth century. Alienation and a sense of the absurd are seen as inevitable features of the post-Christian world ushered in by the Enlightenment and the 'death of God'. Malraux emphasizes the way in which Christianity shaped and characterized traditional European civilization in terms of its account of the nature of man, the nature of ultimate reality, and the relationship between them. Since these three elements underpin any civilization, their collapse – in this case the collapse of the Christian interpretation of the world – led to a gradual disintegration of the forms of European civilization which had persisted into the seventeenth century. Most important, however, as far as Malraux's analysis is concerned, is his claim that with the increasing rejection of Christianity a coherent view of man's experience of the world also began to break up. As he was to comment much later: '. . . tout au long de l'histoire l'homme s'est accordé à lui-même à travers ce qui le dépasse.'[9] Once man is not at one with the cosmos he cannot be at one with himself. It is noticeable too that Ling, as he scrutinizes the Christian iconography of the West, is struck by the harmony which it displays even in representations of the crucifixion: 'Votre foi, jadis, disposait habilement le monde, et, quelque hostilité qu'elle éveille en moi, je ne puis voir sans respect les figures presque barbares où s'est pétrifiée, grâce à elle, une grande souffrance harmonieuse' (*T.O.,* pp. 24–5). Christianity, then, gave meaning to man's experience of the world and taught reconciliation with his lot.

It is noticeable in Ling's comment just quoted that he has no wish to conceal his hostility to Christianity even though he is impressed by the nature of its contribution to European civilization. His attitude is perhaps not far removed from Malraux's own. Malraux shows a very clear understanding of the harmonizing and integrating functions of Christianity. For example, the Christian concept of an immortal soul created by God, together with the doctrine of the Incarnation, gave permanence and meaning to individual personality and denied the possibility of metaphysical isolation. Malraux is aware, then, of what was lost by eighteenth-century rationalism and the eventual 'death of God'. He is even conscious of the 'temptation' which Christianity still offers. There is no doubt, however, that he strongly resists this temptation even as he acknowledges its reality. The 'incroyance passionnée' which Camus saw as characterizing a number of twentieth-century intellectuals describes Malraux's position particularly well. In his last letter A. D. sees the imperfections of the ideals invented by men to replace Christian values in a post-Christian world – the secular humanist values of justice, truth, heroism, etc. Nevertheless, despite this admission and despite his view that Christianity offers a set of values above those of secular humanism, he rejects the former. In fact, he adopts an apparently contradictory position which refuses to accept the Christian faith while accepting its superiority: 'Certes, il est une foi plus haute: celle que proposent toutes les croix des villages, et ces mêmes croix qui dominent nos morts. Elle est amour, et l'apaisement est en elle. Je ne l'accepterai jamais; je ne m'abaisserai pas à lui demander l'apaisement auquel ma faiblesse m'appelle' (*T.O.*, p. 159). This is an attitude which the writer admits to be based more on intense pride than on intellectual conviction.

What strikes one here, indeed, is the fact that the refusal of Christianity involved is so arbitrary and so passionate. It is typical of other crucial passages in Malraux, and also in the work of Camus and Sartre, where the assertion of disbelief – what has been called 'postulatory atheism' – is no less non-rational, even capricious, than the expression of faith and Christian conviction which it rejects. We have seen that there is no serious attempt here to explain or justify it on exclusively rational grounds. Nor is it to be accounted for at that popular level of understanding which simply asserts, in a sweeping generalization, that 'science has disproved Christianity'. On the other hand, disbelief as an emotional option rather than as a rational conviction almost certainly has a lot to do with problems for Christian belief posed by the Great War: the spectacle of both opposing sides believing that the same God will bless their arms; the justification of killing in what were often explicitly religious terms; the apparent impossibility of reconciling the 'martyrdom of man' on the Western Front with belief in an omnipotent God of love and justice.[10] In connection with this last point it is no doubt significant that the problem of evil occurs in so many forms in the writings of Malraux's generation.

In 'D'une jeunesse européenne' Malraux suggests that the dominant role of Christian metaphysical attitudes throughout so many centuries in Europe meant that they could not disappear entirely overnight. The presence of a vestigial Christianity in the post-1918 world causes him to write: 'Notre époque, où rôdent tant d'échos, ne veut pas avouer sa pensée nihiliste, destructrice, foncièrement négative' (*J.E.*, p. 148). Those who have accepted secular humanism as a 'progressive' replacement of Christianity are unwilling to recognize that their own beliefs and confidence, as well as those of Christians, have been put under the severest strain by the phenomenon of the Great War. They may even be inhibited, by persisting traces of that Christianity which they claim to have rejected utterly, from facing the full consequences of their own secular assumptions. But Malraux concedes that those who, like himself, 'ont découvert la vie au lendemain de la guerre', are led to question, if only secretly, 'la pensée des plus grands d'entre eux' (*J.E.*, pp. 148, 148–9). The war thus implied much more than a challenge to the Christian tradition. It called in question most forms of secular confidence as well. In addition, the persistence of sometimes unconsciously Christian ways of seeing and interpreting experience means that many declared non-Christians still tended to look at the world through Christian spectacles, as it were. As Malraux puts it: '. . . notre première faiblesse vient de la nécessité où nous sommes de prendre connaissance du monde grâce à une ''grille'' chrétienne, nous qui ne sommes plus chrétiens' (*J.E.*, p. 137). In this way a natural reluctance to acknowledge unpalatable truths, together with persisting if often unconscious Christian suppositions, prevented most of Malraux's elders – and indeed many of his contemporaries – from recognizing the desperate nature of Western man's metaphysical condition. Many failed to see that the war had at least as much to say about the 'death' of man as about that of God.

The 'death of man' is the second stage noted by Malraux on the road to full and final recognition of dereliction and absurdity. The 'death of God' had meant, of course, that meanings, attributes, and capacities previously associated with divinity were claimed on behalf of man. The Greeks had regarded man as the measure of all things. Post-Christian secularism puts him back at the centre of the universe, claiming for him independence and mastery, and regarding him as the source – and arbiter – of values. As Malraux puts it, 'l'homme prend en lui-même la place qu'il donnait à Dieu', and this new secular religion is described as 'une sorte de passion de l'Homme' (*J.E.* p. 138). Much later, in *Les Voix du silence,* he claimed that as a result of this altered outlook an eighteenth-century rationalist was much further removed from Racine, for example, than Racine himself from the twelfth-century Saint Bernard.[11] Belief grew rapidly in man's capacity for moral progress without transcendental aid. Progress and scientific knowledge became synonymous concepts. By the nineteenth century there existed a confidence that man could solve in wholly secular terms, or else show to be false, the problems raised earlier by Christian thought. The omniscience and omnipotence assigned to God in earlier ages were within human grasp. As Malraux puts it, 'un élan dirige tout le xixe siècle, qui ne peut être comparé, pour la puissance et l'importance, qu'à une religion' (*J.E.,* p. 138). It is the failure, in turn, of this secular religion which ushered in what he regarded as the fundamentally tragic twentieth century and what he describes as 'une démence qui se contemple' and 'le soir européen . . . lamentable et vide' (*T.O.,* pp. 70 and 81). We saw in the previous chapter that Valéry suspected something of the kind in 1919 as he meditated on the character of the Great War and the 'crisis of the intellect'. Seven years later Malraux could write with considerable assurance:

Notre civilisation, depuis qu'elle a perdu l'espoir de trouver dans les sciences le sens du monde, est privée de tout but spirituel. Chacune des générations qui, depuis un siècle, se sont succédé [*sic*] en Europe, a dû travailler plus de vingt ans pour modeler le monde à l'image de son désir; et ce désaccord inévitable de la pensée et de la sensibilité n'est pas l'une des moindres causes du trouble que nous observons. (*J.E.,* p. 145)

The events of 1914–18 had proved a major and crowning example of the divorce between rational, secular aspiration and moral outcome.

The objection might well be made, at this point, that to speak of the 'death of man', simply because the Great War appeared to signal the collapse of the highest humanist ideals and assumptions, is greatly to over-dramatize the situation. At most, it could be said, one is talking of a moral failure which, however great, was not necessarily either total or inevitable. This was a widespread view. Much optimism and determination were expressed in the 1920s; we have seen something, for example, of the moral optimism of Duhamel and the political deter-mination of Barbusse. But this was certainly not the view of Malraux.

On the contrary, and by analogy with Nietzsche's earlier account of the 'death of God', he expresses his concept of the 'death of man' very positively through Ling (and italicizes the phrase):

La réalité absolue a été pour vous Dieu, puis l'homme; mais *l'homme est mort,* après Dieu, et vous cherchez avec angoisse celui à qui vous pourriez confier son étrange héritage. Vos petits essais de structure pour des nihilismes modérés ne me semblent plus destinés à une longue existence . . .
  Quelle conscience pouvez-vous prendre de cet univers sur lequel s'est fait votre accord, et que vous appelez réalité? Celle d'une différence. La conscience totale du monde est: mort, et vous l'avez bien compris. Mais la conscience que vous en prenez est ordonnée, et, par conséquent, esprit. Pauvre appui, reflet dans l'eau qui se calme . . . (*T.O.,* pp. 128–9)

The precise meaning of this passage is not easily grasped. It depends for much of its effect on the lyrical, visionary flavour which is characteristic of *La Tentation de l'Occident* at large. However, read within the wider context of Malraux's thought at this time, it seems to say that all pursuit of absolutes is bound to fail in the modern world. As man increasingly came of age (as the rationalists would have it) God as an absolute idea gradually ceased to command men's allegiance. Man, having replaced God as the absolute value of a secular, rationalist world, similarly failed increasingly to retain confidence as the highest secular ideals proved as unsatisfactory and unconvincing as the earlier religious ones. This is the stage reached by the post-1918 world which Malraux is examining and of which he is a part.

He seems to suggest, in fact, that no concept of man can any longer be underpinned by a privileged relationship with the cosmos and that claims on behalf of man's autonomy and authority are doomed to defeat. When man is regarded as the source and standard of all values, he mistakenly assumes that the intellectual pattern which he imposes on reality also constitutes the substance of that reality. Hence the contrast, in the last passage quoted above, between reality which involves continual change and certain death, and the categorizing, immobilizing tendencies of the human mind. The resulting similarity between modern physics and modern metaphysics is clearly expressed in 'D'une jeunesse européenne':

. . . que devient un monde qui est ma représentation si je n'ai que peu d'intérêt pour moi-même et si je tiens pour essentiellement mensongère la volonté *d'édifier* cette représentation?
  . . . le monde se réduit à un immense jeu de rapports, que nulle intelligence ne s'applique plus à fixer, puisqu'il est dans leur nature même de changer, de se renouveler sans cesse. Il semble que notre civilisation tende à se créer une

métaphysique d'où tout point fixe soit exclu, du même ordre que sa conception de la matière. (*J.E.,* pp. 151–2)

Just after a comment by A. D. to the effect that 'de singuliers visages se découvrent au miroir des guerres' (*T.O.,* p. 157), Malraux adds significantly:

Pour détruire Dieu, et après l'avoir détruit, l'esprit européen a anéanti tout ce qui pouvait s'opposer à l'homme: parvenu au terme des ses efforts . . . il ne trouve que la mort. Avec son image enfin atteinte il découvre qu'il ne peut plus se passionner pour elle. Et jamais il ne fit d'aussi inquiétante découverte . . . Il n'est pas d'idéal auquel nous puissions nous sacrifier, car de tous nous connaissons les mensonges, nous qui ne savons point ce qu'est la vérité. (*T.O.,* pp. 158–9)

The negativity emphasized here is perhaps the most obvious manifestation of what Malraux calls man's 'death'. Having emptied the world of fundamental meaning in order to replace God by man, human beings have finally discovered that man rapidly loses significance, even value, when placed in a philosophical context which denies absolutes, stresses relativity, refuses to recognize fixed points of reference and requires man to create meaning for himself from his own inner resources. Total metaphysical isolation, together with the inescapable fact of mortality, seems to deny the possibility of man possessing universal meaning or value. Hence the 'death' of man.

In presenting the 'death of man' as a consequence of the 'death of God', Malraux traces a development which is the reverse of that envisaged by Nietzsche. As already noted, however, he is certainly not expressing regret or nostalgia. He is not suggesting that man has taken a wrong turning, as it were, by rejecting an account of the universe made meaningful by religious faith. On the contrary, he is simply noting what he is bound to regard as inevitable stages along the path to realistic self-awareness. Self-awareness involves the concept of individualism and the self is the ultimate source to which one looks for meaning and value. The consciousness of solitude and mortality, intensified by awareness of man's 'death', makes the self, or individualism, the next stage on the path to realism. It is inevitable, in these circumstances, that individualism should be a recurrent theme in *La Tentation de l'Occident.* And it is appropriate since individualism in the West has traditionally been contrasted with fusion of the self with the One in eastern thought.

A strong sense of the individual, set over against the world, is seen by Malraux as a major gift of the ancient Greeks to European civilization: 'Les Grecs ont conçu l'homme comme un homme, un être qui naît et meurt' (*T.O.,* p. 50). For many centuries, however, Christianity ensured that the self was seen in fundamental relationship to God and shared, through the fatherhood of God, a common allegiance with other selves. For Malraux, however, the most significant feature of the twentieth-century post-Christian world is a return to individualism, an individualism without apparent meaning since there is no God and man is cut off from other men. It is this individualism of the isolated, meaningless self, living in a world without transcendence and faced by the certainty of death, which gives rise to the distinctive vocabulary of *La Tentation de l'Occident* with its repeated use of such terms as 'douleur', 'crainte', 'désordre', 'désagrégation', 'absurde'. Such terms characterize the failure of individualism rendered inevitable by man's 'death' and expressed succinctly in the statement: 'Après la mort du Sphinx, Œdipe s'attaque à lui-même' (*T.O.,* p. 51). Indeed, the self tends to disintegrate, as a concept, within a meaningless world: 'Rien de défini, ni qui nous permette de nous définir' (*T.O.,* p. 71). Nevertheless, this experience of individualism is a mystery, even a paradox, since an undeniable sense of selfhood persists at the heart of apparent disintegration. Thought and feeling become irreconcilable:

Vouloir donner au moi de la précision, c'est le contraindre à se disperser en probabilités. D'où vient donc la difficulté que nous éprouvons à affirmer sa disparition lorsque nous le voyons s'effacer sous nos yeux? De ce qu'au plus profond de nous-même est le sentiment de notre existence distincte dans l'instant. La conscience d'être *un* est l'une des données irréductibles de l'existence humaine, et peut-être la seule intangible. (*J.E.,* pp. 143–4)

The self, which constitutes the very core of individualism, becomes the source of the most passionate and dogged attempts to overcome isolation and create meaning and value. In the case of modern western man action has been the chief means by which he has sought to reconcile negative thought with positive feeling and to hold together a disintegrating individualism. He has attempted to create meaning and purpose in his life by recourse to action. At the same time, action in a world without agreed absolutes and shared values is exceptionally dangerous. Indeed, because of his preoccupation with what Malraux terms 'la preuve du geste', modern man has found himself called upon to experience '(le) plus sanglant destin'. War and bloodshed have been one outcome of man's need to force meaning upon the world, and to create purpose for himself, through violent action. The exercise of the will and the attainment of domination are central concerns of twentieth-century man. But it is also clear that he has found himself obliged to use will-power and dominance negatively; there is no agreed and universal truth which they can serve.

Malraux does not claim, of course, that warfare is the only outcome of man's need to assert himself through action. Eroticism – perhaps a subordinate form of warfare none the less – is a more common means by which the individual seeks to assert his will and achieve dominance. Erotic pleasure, which increasingly displaces love as the individual's avowed goal, is regarded by Ling (with doubtful justification) as characterizing western rather than oriental man. It also represents an effort to reconcile thought and feeling and is 'a desperate attempt to be at the same time oneself and *the other*'.[12] The individual can only believe in his own existence, can only be convinced that he has a place in the world, when his will is served and his domination acknowledged by his sexual 'victim'. In fact, the road from eroticism to sadism is a short one.

While Malraux is not inclined to underestimate the importance, perhaps even the positive value, of eroticism, he is also aware of its limits. The individual can never be wholly 'the other', and erotic pleasure is constantly threatened by the passage of time and the inevitability of death. At best it offers a temporary alleviation of man's solitude and his (still unsatisfied) need for meaning. At worst, and according to Ling, it reveals the final stage of the journey to total self-knowledge – the ultimate awareness that the individual's existence is characterized by meaninglessness. Ling writes to A. D.:

L'homme passionné est en désaccord avec le monde qu'il a conçu, comme avec celui qu'il subit, et qu'il ait prévu la passion n'y saurait rien changer. L'homme qui veut aimer veut s'échapper, et cela est peu; mais l'homme ou la femme qui veulent être aimés, qui veulent faire perdre à un autre être, en leur faveur, sa soumission à cet accord me paraissent obéir à une nécessité si puissante que j'y trouve cette conviction: *au centre de l'homme européen, dominant les grands mouvements de sa vie, est une absurdité essentielle.* Ne le pensez-vous pas? (*T.O.,* p. 57)

One is strongly reminded here of Pascal's *divertissement,* with its claim that much human activity amounts to an attempt – conscious or unconscious – by the individual to hide his own inner void from himself.

This last stage on the way to self-knowledge – the absurd – is particularly characterized for Malraux by the facts of mortality and human transience. These features of man's experience appear to deprive the individual's life of genuine meaning. They also explain his feverish attempts to create meaning, in concert with others, by resort to war, eroticism, political and social action, etc. *L'absurde* is thus a term used to describe a situation in which the world experienced by man possesses no absolute meaning, and in which those worlds which he creates through his own efforts prove equally void. His experience is doubly meaningless. He is doubly alienated and apparently superfluous. All those systems of thought, from early Christianity to nineteenth-century 'scientism', which have claimed to contain a coherent account of man's relationship to the universe, are necessarily false. They are mere instances of the deeply solipsistic tendencies of the human mind.

In the light of these ideas the Great War takes on a distinctive character and may be interpreted in a distinctive way. It becomes, in fact, a dramatization of this form of absurdity. It was fought by both sides on behalf of traditional values which were presented as absolutes to the contending armies: patriotism, nationalism, truth, courage, justice, etc. The fact that millions of lives were sacrificed to these absolutes argues a startling failure, or a wicked unwillingness, to recognize the nature of intellectual and moral relativism. Again, the war showed particularly clearly to the intellectuals of Malraux's generation that man proves incapable of establishing 'des rapports constants entre les principes qu'il a acceptés et ses actions' (*J.E.,* p. 140). There was, inevitably, an unbridgeable gap between the ideals of the warring parties in 1914 and the methods which they employed in pursuit of those ideals. Much of the protest literature written during the fighting arose precisely from an acute awareness and experience of this gap. Such experience, sharpened and intensified by war, was further interpreted by Malraux as part of a general and quite basic 'opposition de nos actions et de notre vie profonde' (*T.O.,* p. 158).

The war played a special role in diffusing more widely and more rapidly than would otherwise have been likely a sense of metaphysical crisis and a consciousness of the need to re-examine (and replace) the religious and secular accounts of man sanctioned by a long European tradition. The problem facing the post-war generation was expressed by Malraux in another statement of 1926 published in *Les Nouvelles littéraires*:

Le premier présent de notre génération, j'ai la conviction que c'est la proclamation de la faillite de l'individualisme, de toutes les valeurs, de toutes les attitudes, de toutes les doctrines qui se justifient par l'exaltation du Moi. Le fait capital de l'Occident, à nos yeux, dans l'ordre intellectuel, c'est la nécessité où se trouve presque toute la jeunesse européenne de rompre avec l'effort d'un siècle, bien que sa sensibilité n'en soit pas encore complètement détachée. Toute la passion du xxe siècle attachée à l'homme, s'épanouit dans l'affirmation véhémente du moi. Eh bien, cet homme et ce moi, édifiés sur tant de ruines et qui nous dominent encore, que nous le voulions ou non, ne nous intéressent pas. D'autre part, nous sommes décidés à ne point écouter l'appel de notre faiblesse, qu'il nous propose une doctrine ou une foi . . . L'objet de la recherche de la jeunesse occidentale est une notion nouvelle de l'homme.[13]

It is this new notion of man, this necessity to 'reinvent' man, which preoccupied Malraux in his subsequent writings and which fascinated many of his contemporaries. For Malraux, the war had not created a new situation. But it did reveal an existing situation, recognized by few, with startling clarity and novelty. Furthermore, the violence and the suffering which it brought in its train meant that some men underwent a trauma that was deep enough to enable them to break with the past and see the basic features of the human condition with new eyes. The intellectual history of the western world since the 1920s confirms this fact. It consists of a bewildering variety of attempts, including the fighting of further wars, to find an answer to the death of God and the death of man which received such destructive expression in the Great War of 1914–18.

The so-called 'dark lyricism' of Malraux, which characterizes the two early works discussed above, is used to strengthen the argument that the Great War was a turning-point in western man's awareness of his true metaphysical condition. We have seen that the picture which emerges is one of modern man moving through the 'metallic kingdoms of the absurd', seeking a path among the ruins of Christian beliefs and humanist claims, estranged and isolated from the ground of being, from other beings, and from himself. Corresponding to this metaphysical picture, but in more direct and perhaps more simple terms, the Great War has also been seen as a turning-point in the social and ethical history of European civilization. Indeed, it is not difficult to demonstrate that the war brought the social and the ethical into a sharp and disillusioning relationship with one another. It is obvious, for example, that newly perceived material realities forming part of an increasingly industrialized society presented a disturbing challenge to various traditional moral ideas.

We noted in the very first chapter of this study that many men in 1914 looked forward to a war as a potential form of moral transformation for society, or as a means of release from the social constrictions of peacetime attitudes and norms. But we also saw that, in the end, technological warfare appeared to an increasing number of participants as nothing other than a peculiarly dramatic and condensed image of the new industrial society. War was seen with growing frequency as an integral part of that society and not as a counter-experience, strength-ened by fraternity and a sense of shared dangers, which might somehow have served to redeem a materialistic and profit-centred civilization. As E. J. Leed puts it: 'The voyage of the soldier beyond the boundaries of his home was a voyage to the place where the contradictions of industrial, capitalist society were most densely impacted. It was a voyage to the place where inequalities of wealth and status became inequalities of sacrifice and suffering.'[14] Whether or not this statement is objectively true is certainly open to debate. But there can be little doubt that many combatants saw the war in this light. The more they went on leave and noted the contrast between civilian life and life in the trenches, the more they saw the striking difference between their own lives and those of home-based profiteers and playboys as a paradigm of their position on the margins of peacetime industrial society. The war appeared to dramatize and to intensify social aliena-tion. The hierarchies associated with an increasingly industrial and urban civilization were never quite the same again. After 1918 they were to be increasingly challenged.

At a different though related level, and as suggested in earlier chapters, war also seemed to destroy a number of the old moral certainties. The contrast between the home front and the battlefront itself bred scepticism and cynicism. Furthermore, the propagandist exploitation and simplification of great and resounding moral absolutes left them meaningless and generally repellent. Moral indifference or moral relativism followed. The 'années folles' of the 1920s seem an inevitable consequence. We are in the world of E. M. Forster's 'every-thing exists, nothing has value'. It is worth adding briefly that Bergson's doctrine of flux was invoked in certain circles to explain, in an appar-ently acceptable intellectual manner, moral relativism and the loss of traditional, absolute values. Julien Benda went so far as to blame Bergson for what he termed the post-war 'adoration du contingent' and 'mépris de l'éternel'. Bergson replied, without much success, that an important distinction had to be made between an explanatory prin-ciple (which was what his philosophy offered) and a rule of conduct (which formed no part of his intention).[15] There were those who continued to confuse these two things, however, and it is significant that already in 1927, the year in which Benda's *Trahison des clercs* was published, the case for absolutes made in this work appeared outmoded and increasingly indefensible.

It would certainly be wrong to suggest that the Great War was the sole and initiating cause of the trends just mentioned. But it increased awareness of them and probably accelerated them. Without the Great War there would not have been so rapid a growth in philosophical nihilism, social dissent, ethical relativism, and the contending political ideologies of fascism and communism. These developments were widely experienced as a crisis within the mind and spirit of twentieth-century man. They were seen as part and parcel of a new emergency of which war was an external manifestation. George A. Panichas implies too direct a causal connection when he describes such things as 'the legacy of the Great War'. But he describes very accurately the post-war state of affairs – a state of affairs which the Great War helped to dramatize and confirm – when he writes of 'the alienation, the meaninglessness, the cynicism, the hate, the despair, the confusion, the suspicion, the fear, the doubt that possess modern man even in the midst of his triumphs in science and technology'.[16] It was after 1918 that modern man set out again 'in search of a soul'. The direction which this search was to take was affected in a fundamental way by the catastrophe of 1914–18.

Notes

CHAPTER 1   Heroic Enthusiasm

1   C. E. Montague, *Disenchantment* (London, 1968; first publ. 1922), p. 10.

2   Edmund Gosse, *Inter Arma* (London, 1916), p. 3.

3   See E. F. Benson, *The Outbreak of War, 1914* (London, 1933), p. 23: 'It was simply impossible to believe in disturbances when all over the green heart of the country there lay, like sunlight out of a clear sky, this stabilized tranquillity.'

4   P.-H. Simon, *L'Esprit et l'histoire* (Paris, 1954), p. 22. It is of some interest to contrast with this French description E. F. Benson's very English and very romantic pastoralism which follows the phrase quoted in the previous note: 'The harvest promised a bumper yield, there was no such thing as· unemployment, labourers' cottages stood festooned with honeysuckle, there were beehives in their front gardens, and when the day's toil was over the bees dropped out of the sky to gather their honey, and the young men of the village played cricket on the green, or sauntered with their girls in the deep lanes, or went bathing in the lake among the woods. Their elders sat outside the public-house with their pewters of cheap beer, or tended their allotments. Sunday morning saw the church full of broad-cloth and best-hats, and of a pleasant bumble of congregational singing, and Sunday afternoon saw the village dozing in a roast-beef somnolence. All individuals, naturally, are liable to the pains and distresses of mortality, but never did the community seem more secure, nor the national machine working so smoothly.'

5   A. Schinz, *French Literature of the Great War* (New York, 1920), p. 5.

6   See J.-J. Becker, *Comment les Français sont entrés dans la guerre* (Paris, 1977), esp. pp. 125–45.

7   G. Guy-Grand, *Le Conflit des idées dans la France d'aujourd'hui* (Paris, 1921), p. 121.

8   Cf. Raoul Girardet, *Le Nationalisme français (1871–1914)* (Paris, 1966), p. 18: 'Le nationalisme des "nationalistes" de la fin du 19e et du début du 20e siècle, même s'il s'obstine dans la fidélité aux provinces perdues, n'est plus un nationalisme conquérant, un nationalisme d'expansion. Il est avant tout mouvement de défense, repli, reserrement sur lui-même d'un corps blessé.'

9   See, e.g., K. W. Swart, *The Sense of Decadence in Nineteenth-Century France* (The Hague, 1964), esp. Ch. VII.

10   K. W. Swart, op. cit., pp. 210–11.

11   J. Barzun, *Darwin, Marx, Wagner: Critique of a Heritage* (London, 1942), pp. 351–2.

12   Quoted in R. Garguilo, *La Genèse des Thibault de Roger Martin du Gard* (Paris, 1974), p. 397. The fact that such a view of war was not confined

to France is indicated, for example, by P. Wust, *Crisis in the West* (London, 1931), pp. 41–2: 'On December 31st, 1913, the eminent Berlin lawyer, Joseph Kohler, wrote the preface to a book that bore the title *Recht und Persönlichkeit*. At the end of this preface he triumphantly spoke of the victory won by the modern mind. With particular pride he pointed out that war, like private revenge, had been, so to speak, left behind, thanks to the great strides made by modern reason which, as Comte had already said, must finally succeed in abolishing all irrational outbursts of violence. The fury of war, in Kohler's opinion, had been banished to the Far East, where it was lingering out its last days.'

13   Becker, op. cit., pp. 277 ff.
14   Ibid., pp. 313–28.
15   A. Philonenko, *Essais sur la philosophie de la guerre* (Paris, 1976), pp. 165–76.
16   See E. J. Leed, *No Man's Land. Combat and Identity in World War I* (Cambridge, 1979), pp. 5–6.
17   Ibid., p. 6.
18   See, e.g., Stanley Cooperman, *World War I and the American Novel* (Baltimore, 1967), p. 45 and E. J. Leed, op. cit., pp. 21, 30, 48, 58 ff., 63–4, 66, 70, 95.
19   Charles Péguy, *Œuvres en prose, 1909–1914* (Paris, Pléiade, 1968), p. 988.
20   Ernest Psichari, *L'Appel des armes* (Paris, 1913).
21   Leed, op. cit., p. 194.
22   A. Marwick, *The Deluge* (London, 1961), p. 84.
23   Leed, op. cit., p. 21.
24   See, e.g., W. M. Maxwell, *A Psychological Retrospect of the Great War* (London, 1923).
25   In 1911 Henri Massis, in co-operation with Alfred de Tarde and under the joint pseudonym of 'Agathon', had published their severely critical *L'Esprit de la Nouvelle Sorbonne*.
26   Péguy, op. cit., p. 1211.
27   Ibid., p. 1254.
28   Ibid., p. 1257.
29   Ibid., p. 1233. Péguy attributed the defeat of 1870 to bad leadership. In 'Notre Jeunesse' of 1910 he had written: 'En 1870 même, au mois d'août, si une armée française, comme elle était, avait été remise aux mains d'un Napoléon Bonaparte, tous les tiroirs et toutes les préparations, toutes les fiches et tous les registres d'un de Moltke seraient aujourd'hui la risée des historiens mêmes' (op. cit., p. 622).
30   Psichari's dedicatory note reads: 'A celui dont l'esprit m'accompagnait dans les solitudes de l'Afrique, à cet autre solitaire en qui vit aujourd'hui l'âme de la France, et dont l'œuvre a courbé d'amour notre jeunesse, à notre Maître CHARLES PÉGUY, ce livre de notre grandeur et de notre misère.'
31   Ernest Psichari, *Œuvres complètes* (III) (Paris, 1948), p. 331.
32   Ernest Psichari, *L'Appel des armes* (Paris, 1913), p. 16. Further page references to this novel are given in brackets in the text.
33   Psichari discusses these ideas, outside their fictional context, in a long and interesting letter to Mme G. Favre dated 30 Sept. 1912. At one point he exclaims: ' . . . quelle différence entre les pères et les fils!' See *Œuvres complètes* (III), pp. 235–7.

34   Sainte-Beuve in the *Revue des deux mondes* for 15 Oct. 1835. In a letter to Péguy dated 18 Aug. 1910 Psichari tells his friend that his library in the desert consists of several issues of Péguy's *Cahiers de la quinzaine,* Pascal's *Pensées,* Bossuet's *Sermons,* Dupuy's *Table des logarithms,* the *Règlement de l'artillerie de campagne* and *Servitude et grandeur militaires.* See *Œuvres complètes*(III), pp. 182–3.

35   Micheline Tison-Braun, *La Crise de l'humanisme* (2 vols.) (Paris, 1958 and 1967), Vol. I, p. 454.

36   Léon Riegel, *Guerre et littérature* (Paris, 1978), p. 58.

37   Psichari, *Œuvres complètes* (III), p. 230.

38   Alfred de Tarde (his name is sometimes printed as Alfred Tarde) is mistakenly called Alexis de Tarde by Becker, op. cit., and Albert de Tarde by Tison-Braun, op. cit.

39   Psichari, *Œuvres complètes* (III), pp. 231–2.

40   Ibid., pp. 232.

41   Agathon, *Les Jeunes Gens d'aujourd'hui* (Paris, 1913), p. ii. Further page references to this work are given in brackets in the text.

42   For some further comments on this point see Becker, op. cit., pp. 30–4.

43   Other *enquêtes* around this period include Henriot in *Le Temps* (April–June 1912) later published under the title *A quoi rêvent les jeunes gens*; Faguet, 'Enquête sur la jeunesse' in *Revue hebdomadaire* (March–July 1912); Bertaut in *Le Gaulois* (June 1912). The *Revue française* ran an enquiry into the influence of Barrès (July–August 1913) and the *Grande revue* surveyed the influence of Bergson (February–April 1914).

44   This point is clearly made, and the whole 'generational setting' of the enquiry is well described, in Robert Wohl, *The Generation of 1914* (London, 1980), especially pp. 5–18.

45   Psichari, *Œuvres complètes* (III), p. 232.

46   Massis and Tarde wrote, for example: 'Nous avons trouvé, chez maints jeunes hommes, une opposition ferme, résolue, nullement aggressive, à la thèse essentielle de *l'Action française*, et cela, non point pour des raisons strictement politiques, mais parce que l'attitude intellectuelle, le mode de raisonnement des disciples de Maurras, heurtent et leur intime croyance, et leur goût des réalités, étant établi que la politique est un problème, non d'idées pures, mais de faits, et que les sentiments sont les moins négligeables des faits . . . S'il n'y a de jeunesse, en effet, qu'ardemment patriote, il y a une jeunesse démocrate. C'est la plus nombreuse et, sinon la plus agitée, sans doute la plus vraiment réaliste' (p. 100).

47   Wohl, op. cit., p. 40.

48   Ibid., p. 249.

49   Ibid., p. 17.

50   Roland N. Stromberg, 'The Intellectuals and the Coming of War in 1914', *Journal of European Studies,* Vol. 3 (June 1973), p. 109. In the final paragraph of this same article Stromberg comments (p. 122): 'The martial spirit of the intellectuals in 1914 seems strange today to the fashionably pacifist young, and has seemed strange since 1918. It is true that intellectuals supported World War II, but they did so for the most part without relish for war itself, coming only reluctantly and in most cases belatedly to believe that Hitlerism had to be overcome by force. In 1914 they gladly embraced war virtually for war's sake. In fact, the mood which sent idealistic youth off to

war in 1914 was very like that which impels the present younger generation into the streets to protest against war. The youth movements which poured their energies into World War I were quite like today's in fundamentals: in their accusatory attitude toward the older generation, their desire to escape the trammels of convention, their fuzzy but powerful idealism and Utopian aspiration to remake the world. They sought a grand cause and found it in the heroism and renewing power of a military crusade.'

51   Romain Rolland, 'Au-dessus de la mêlée', *Journal de Genève*, 15 Sept., 1914. See also Romain Rolland, *Au-dessus de la mêlée* (Paris, 1926; first publ. 1915), p. 45.

52   Ibid., p. 42.

CHAPTER 2   Saying the Unsayable

1   The forecasts of Sorel are particularly striking. In October 1908 he had written: 'L'Europe est, par excellence, la terre des cataclysmes guerriers . . . Malheureuse Europe! Pourquoi lui cacher ce qui l'attend? Avant dix ans, elle sombrera dans la guerre et l'anarchie'. In December 1912 he added: 'L'Europe, ce cimetière, est peuplée par des peuples qui chantent avant d'aller s'entretuer. Les Français et les Allemands chanteront bientôt.' Quoted in J. B. Duroselle, *La France et les Français, 1900–1914* (Paris, 1972), p. 383.

2   J. Norton Cru, *Témoins: essai d'analyse et de critique des souvenirs de combattants édités en français de 1915 à 1918* (Paris, 1929), p. 342. The same problem had been expressed as follows in 1920 in relation to British writers: 'Those young writing-men who had set out in a spirit of adventure went back to Fleet Street with a queer look in their eyes . . . because there was no code of words which would convey the picture of the wild agony of peoples, that smashing of all civilized laws . . .' (Philip Gibbs, *Realities of War* (London, 1920, revised edn. 1929), pp. 11–12).

3   See both *Essai sur les données immédiates de la conscience* (1888) and *Le Rire: essai sur la signification du comique* (1900).

4   Valéry, *Œuvres II* (Paris, Pléiade, 1960), p. 878.

5   Valéry, *Œuvres I* (Paris, Pléiade, 1957), p. 1172.

6   A. E. Pilkington, *Bergson and his Influence: a Reassessment* (London, 1976), p. 125.

7   The late Stanley Cooperman, in his excellent study of the American novel and the Great War, took the opposite view. He argued strongly, though probably mistakenly, that the Great War was unprecedented in the strictest sense of the word – unprecedented in nature and not simply in degree. He also explained why the Second World War was not unprecedented in the same sense: 'The machine slaughter and danse-macabre absurdity of World War I . . . had no parallel – and for this reason its impact differed in nature no less than degree from the impact of previous war experiences. Crane's Henry Fleming [in *The Red Badge of Courage*, 1895] was in a "universal situation" and so could discover himself on the proving ground. Boyd's William Hicks [in *Through the Wheat*, 1923], on the other hand, and the Word War I protagonists as a group, found themselves in a situation which for them was in essence non-human and non-universal; there could be no "generic" recognition because the machine genre of their environment, of

death itself, was without precedent. Only when this machine genre had been assimilated culturally, emotionally and imaginatively could war again become a "universal situation"; like the drawing-room or office, industrial plant or courtroom, war could then – and only then – be taken simply as material upon which a drama of human values could be based' (Stanley Cooperman, *World War I and the American Novel* (Baltimore, 1967), p. 214).

8   Jacques Rivière, *A la trace de Dieu* (Paris, 1925), p. 136.

9   Léon Werth, *Clavel soldat* (Paris, 1919), p. 244.

10   See Marc Ferro, *The Great War 1914–18,* translated by Nicole Stone (London, 1973), p. 227. There are also some details of casualties in Theodore Ropp, *War in the Modern World* (Durham, North Carolina, 1959), esp. pp. 227–34 and 248–6. Ropp calculates that the French lost 955,000 men for the five months of 1914. 'In 1915 the losses were 1,430,000 men, and yet in all of 1915 the British and French did not gain more than three miles at any one point' (p. 228). There are also useful details and tables in Colin Dyer, *Population and Society in Twentieth-Century France* (London, 1978), pp. 37–47.

11   Quoted in Leed, op. cit., p. 29.

12   H. M. Tomlinson, 'War books', *Criterion,* 9, No. 36 (April, 1930), p. 419.

13   Quoted in Leed, op. cit., p. 30.

14   Ibid., p. 193. Leed continues a few lines later: ' . . . the disillusioning realization of the inherent similitude of industrial societies and the wars they wage – something that is a commonplace to us – eviscerated, drained, and confounded the logic upon which the moral significance of war and the figure of the warrior had been based. "Total war" was nothing but the assertion that there was no such thing as two realities, two sets of rules, two levels upon which life might be lived and experienced. In war combatants learned that there is *only* an industrial world, the reality of which defined them in war much more than it had in peace. In the trenches men learned that mechanized destruction and industrial production were mirror images of each other.'

15   Quoted in Jacques Loreilhe, *Léon Bloy, son œuvre, sa mission* (La Rochelle, 1929), p. 42.

16   *Journal de Léon Bloy,* Vol. 3 (Paris, 1963), p. 194.

17   Ibid., p. 313.

18   Quoted in Michael Roberts, *T. E. Hulme* (London, 1938), p. 30.

19   Marc Boas-Boasson, *Au soir d'un monde: lettres de guerre* (Paris, 1926), quoted in J. Norton Cru, op. cit., p. 499.

20   Jean Galtier-Boissière, *En rase campagne 1914. Un hiver à Souchez 1915–16* (Paris, 1917), quoted ibid., p. 140.

21   Details of the use of chlorine, phosgene, and mustard gas are given in J. F. C. Fuller, *The Conduct of War 1789–1961* (London, 1972; first publ. 1961), pp. 172–4.

22   Adrien Bertrand, *L'Appel du sol* (Paris, 1916), pp. 12–13.

23   Ibid., pp. 19–20.

24   Charles Péguy, *Œuvres en prose 1898–1908* (Paris, Pléiade, 1959), p. 684.

25   Bertrand, op. cit., pp. 190 and 187.

26   P. Chaine, *Les Mémoires d'un rat* (Paris, 1917), p. 110. The same phenomenon of small units blindly manipulated by a huge, impersonal machine is expressed by various English writers. In *Marlborough and Other Poems* (Cambridge, 1916) Charles Sorley begins an untitled poem with the haunting lines:
>   A hundred thousand million mites we go
>   Wheeling and tacking o'er the eternal plain,
>   Some black with death – and some are white with woe.
>   Who sent us forth? Who takes us home again?

27   It is only honest to point out that one of the most distinguished wartime novelists, Roland Dorgelès, rejected this emphasis on the unprecedented nature of the Great War. Writing in 1949 he described it as 'la dernière guerre aux mesures humaines'. He added: 'Notre guerre à nous ne différait pas tellement des batailles de jadis. En août 1914, on a formé le carré comme la garde à Waterloo; des Saint-Cyriens se sont offerts aux balles en arborant leur panache, comme pour se battre à Fontenoy . . . ' (R. Dorgelès, *Bleu Horizon. Pages de la Grande Guerre* (Paris 1949), p. 43). These features of war in August 1914 which Dorgelès picks out were of course those which proved particularly inadequate and irrelevant. Furthermore, his own most famous war novel, *Les Croix de bois* (1919), conveys a picture of the war in keeping with what has been said about its unprecedented nature for those who fought in it.

28   A. Kazin, *On Native Grounds* (New York, 1942), p. 184. Edmund Gosse in *Inter Arma* (London, 1916), pp. 11–12, says of the last four books which he received from France before war was declared: 'The sentiment of confidence, of uninterrupted peace, is curiously spread over these four books, and unites them, in spite of their mutual unlikeness, in one haze of serenity.' The books in question were: Francis Vielé-Griffin, *Voix d'Ionie*; Jacques Vontade, *Un Voyage;* Henri de Régnier, *Romaine Mirmault*; Paul Bourget, *Le Démon de midi.*

29   Cooperman, op. cit., p. 7.

30   Ibid., p. 241.

31   Charles Péguy, *Œuvres en prose 1909–1914* (Paris, Pléiade, 1968), p. 126.

32   J. Norton Cru, op. cit., p. 37, produces figures to indicate the very high incidence of deaths among those members of the 'professions libérales' who fought in the war. The proportion of dead to mobilized in this group, as against the corresponding figure for agricultural workers for example, is given as 209/124. Edmund Gosse, in an essay of 1917 reprinted in *Selected Essays (Second Series)* (London, 1928), wrote p. 70: ' . . . the holocaust of victims, poets and historians, painters and sculptors, musicians and architects, has been heart-rending. . . . A year ago the *Revue critique,* one of the most serious and original journals of Paris, announced the losses it had endured. It was conducted by a staff of forty scholars; by the summer of 1916 this number was reduced by twenty-seven; thirteen had been killed, eleven severely wounded, three had disappeared.'

33   Gosse, op. cit., pp. 82–3.

34   Tomlinson, loc. cit., p. 409.

35   R. Dorgelès, *Souvenirs sur les Croix de bois* (Paris, 1929), pp. 21 and 36.

Another relevant comment, though in fictional form, occurs in the final chapter of Barbusse's *Le Feu*:

'Paradis, le dos plié sous des tapis de terreau et de glaise cherchait à rendre l'impression que la guerre est inimaginable, et incommensurable dans le temps et dans l'espace.

– Quand on parle de toute la guerre, songeait-il tout haut, c'est comme si on n'disait rien. Ça étouffe les paroles. On est là, à r'garder ça comme des espèces d'aveugles . . .

Une voix de basse roula un peu plus loin:

– Non, on n'peut pas s'figurer.'

36 Alain, *Mars ou la guerre jugée* (Paris, 1936), p. 39.

37 Ibid., p. 127.

38 Quoted by A. E. Pilkington, op. cit., p. 5. Chapters I and III of Pilkington's book contain a very good exposition of the attitudes to language of Bergson and Valéry.

39 It is noticeable that the critical judgements passed in J. Norton Cru's otherwise admirable – and in any case indispensable – *Témoins* are distorted by his insistence that a war novel cannot be good unless it contains detailed and circumstantial historical accuracy.

40 The spirit of Vigny's *Servitude et grandeur militaires* pervades Bertrand's *L'Appel du sol* as it did Psichari's *L'Appel des armes*. Zola's presence is often clear in Barbusse's *Le Feu*.

41 Tomlinson, loc. cit., p. 404.

42 Malcolm Bradbury, 'The Denuded Place: War and Form in *Parade's End* and *U.S.A.*', in Holger Klein (ed.), *The First World War in Fiction* (London, 1976), p. 193.

CHAPTER 3 Critical Approaches to Great War Fiction

1 Examples from France would include Montherlant, *Le Songe* (1922), Kessel, *L'Équipage* (1923), Giono, *Le Grand Troupeau* (1931), Céline, *Voyage au bout de la nuit* (1932), Drieu La Rochelle, *La Comédie de Charleroi* (1934), Romains, *Prélude à Verdun* and *Verdun* (1937).

2 See n. 35 to Ch. 2 above.

3 Duhamel, in *Vie des martyrs, 1914–1916* (Paris, 1917), writes on the final page: 'Il ne suffit pas de porter le couteau bienfaisant dans la plaie, ou d'en renouveler les linges avec exactitude et adresse. Il faut encore, sans en rien altérer, pouvoir retracer dans sa vérité et sa simplicité votre histoire de victimes émissaires, l'histoire de ces hommes que vous êtes pendant la douleur.'

4 Klein, op. cit., p. 4.

5 Maurice Rieuneau, *Guerre et révolution dans le roman français de 1919 à 1939* (Paris, 1974), pp. 8–9.

6 Paul Fussell, *The Great War and Modern Memory* (London, 1975), p. 130.

7 The point is well made by John Flower in Klein, op. cit., p. 59: 'We do not find in this early war literature . . . the kind of careful interweaving of themes and images which Giono achieves in *Le Grand Troupeau* (1931) nor

the sustained, highly personalized, even fantasied, reaction to war which Drieu offers us in *La Comédie de Charleroi* (1934).'

8   Cooperman, op. cit., p. 194.

9   See ibid., pp. 198 ff. I am much indebted to Cooperman's full account of this debate. An interesting, and very different, interpretation is to be found in Kenneth Burke's 'War, Response and Contradiction' in his *The Philosophy of Literary Form* (New York, 1957, revised and abridged ed.), pp. 201–20.

10   C. E. Carrington, 'Some Soldiers', in G. A. Panichas, *Promise of Greatness. The War of 1914–1918* (London, 1968), pp. 158–9.

11   Fussell, op. cit., p. 36.

12   Rieuneau, op. cit., p. 23. This point is also well made by René Pomeau, 'Guerre et roman dans l'entre-deux-guerres', *Revue des sciences humaines* (janvier–mars, 1963), pp. 77–95.

13   See Dorgelès, op. cit., p. 33: ' . . . ne pas raconter *ma* guerre, mais *la* guerre'.

14   J. Norton Cru, *Du Témoignage* (Paris, 1930, new ed. Paris, 1967), pp. 104–5.

15   According to A. Schinz, op. cit., p. 30, *Le Feu* sold 230,000 copies in the two years following its publication.

16   The last three words of the epigraph to Vigny's *Servitude et grandeur militaires* – the 'Ave, Caesar, morituri te salutant' of Suetonius – are used by Bertrand as the title of his sixth chapter.

17   André Bertrand, *L'Appel du sol* (Paris, 1916), p. 231. Further page references are given in the text.

18   Henri Barbusse, *Le Feu* (Paris, 1928; first publ. 1916), p. 243. Further page references are given in the text.

19   Burke, loc. cit., p. 205

20   Ibid., p. 206.

21   Ibid., p. 209 (Burke's italics).

CHAPTER 4   Maintaining Decorum

1   B. Cadwallader, 'The Temptation of the East: the Sense of Crisis in French Writers of the Twenties as Reflected in the Opposition between Europe and the East, with particular Reference to the Writings of André Malraux and Pierre Drieu la Rochelle', unpubl. D Phil. thesis, University of Sussex, 1976.

2   In an article of 1922 reprinted in *Réflexions sur la littérature* (Paris, 1938), p. 147, Albert Thibaudet classifies *Gaspard* as 'pompier' or conventional and banal.

3   Dorgelès, *Bleu Horizon,* pp. 50–1.

4   René Benjamin, *Gaspard* (Paris, 1915), pp. 112–13. Further page references are given in the text.

5   Bertrand was mobilized in the cavalry in August 1914 and wounded in September. He possibly spent less than a month at the front. He died, as a result of his wounds, in 1917.

6   Quoted in Cooperman, op. cit., p. 8. Near the end of *L'Appel du sol* Vaissette gets sufficiently close to this point to admit: 'Nous savons maintenant la fragilité de nos bonheurs périssables . . .' (p. 281).

7   See Cooperman, *passim.*

8   Gabriel-Tristan Franconi, *Un Tel de l'armée française* (Paris, 1918), p. 103. Further page references are given in the text.
9   In 1914 Poincaré appealed for national solidarity in the face of war, the so-called *union sacrée*. Clericals and anti-clericals, monarchists and republicans, intellectuals and manual workers were called upon to unite in defence of France. The *union sacrée* was also reflected in the broad coalition which characterized the French cabinet in the early years of the war.
10   Fernand Divoire, *Gabriel-Tristan Franconi* (Abbeville, 1921), p. 14.
11   Klein, op. cit., p. 99. Holger Klein, in an interesting essay entitled 'Projections of Everyman', links together Henry Williamson's *The Patriot's Progress,* Ernst Wiechert's, *Jedermann,* and Franconi's novel.
12   Dorgelès, in *Bleu Horizon,* p. 170, recalls that Franconi himself, in his pre-war Montmartre days, 'faisait alors grand étalage de ses opinions terroristes et parlait constamment d'attentats, de bombes vengeresses.'

CHAPTER 5   Expressing Protest (I)

1   Irving Howe, *Politics and the Novel* (New York, 1957), p. 16.
2   Ibid., p. 19.
3   Cooperman, op. cit., p. 44.
4   Henri Barbusse, *Le Feu,* p. 233.
5   Ibid., p. 330.
6   Ibid., pp. 340–1.
7   Henry de Montherlant, '*La guerre à vingt ans* de Philippe Barrès', *Revue hebdomadaire,* no. 38, 20 September, 1924, pp. 356–7.
8   By late 1918 *Le Feu* had sold close on 250,000 copies. This figure had risen to 370,000 by 1928. N. 15 of Ch. 3 above indicates that Schinz had calculated the first of these figures to be 230,000.
9   The remaining page references to *Le Feu* in this chapter are given in the text.
10   At the same time Barbusse, through one of his characters, declares himself against 'modified' protest: 'Ce serait un crime de montrer les beaux côtés de la guerre, murmura un des sombres soldats, même s'il y en avait' (p. 347).
11   Henri Barbusse, *Paroles d'un combattant: articles et discours 1917–1920* (Paris, 1920), p. 7.
12   e.g. 'Le conférencier de Chicago m'accuse d'avoir dit que peu de prêtres ont porté le sac. Je maintiens formellement cette affirmation', ibid., p. 68.
13   Henri Barbusse's *Staline* (Paris, 1935) includes this explanatory phrase which conveys the atmosphere of the book: 'Beaucoup de légendes courent sur Staline et, en dehors d'une minorité d'élites conscientes, on le considère comme une sorte de despote oriental, de dictateur imposant son autorité même à son entourage direct. Ces absurdités se démolissent par une relation objective et historique des faits. Je pense qu'il n'est pas mauvais de démentir, par la narration d'anecdotes vécues, ces accusations inconsidérées d'ambitions personnelles, d'arbitraire et de cruauté' (quoted by Annette Vidal, *Henri Barbusse, soldat de la paix* (Paris, 1953), p. 328).
14   Frank Field paraphrases Barbusse's position as follows: 'As for Rolland's objections to the use of violence these, by definition, were irrelevant: there could not be any errors of calculation in the 'social geometry

of revolution' to be found in the programme of the Clarté movement since there is no fundamental difference between the laws of society and the laws of science. No one within Clarté was advocating any unnecessary use of force to achieve a just society, but it must be remembered that society, as it was at present constituted, was itself an instrument of violence in the hands of the capitalist classes; if anyone was inclined to dispute this fact they had only to look at the origins and development of the First World War to see that this was true. The question at issue was not whether the exploited should be permitted to use violence to achieve their aims, but whether they should be permitted to use violence as a legitimate means of self-defence against the forces which had plunged the continent into war on one occasion and would do the same again unless the peoples of Europe brought their activities to an end. The violence of the masses must be seen, not as an act of aggression, therefore, but as the only means left to the people to disarm their leaders (in *Three French Writers and the Great War: Studies in the Rise of Communism and Fascism* (Cambridge, 1975), pp. 58–9). In contrast to Barbusse's arguments, Romain Rolland had written in 1915: 'Faites la paix en vous d'abord: . . . Ce n'est pas en faisant la guerre à la guerre que vous la supprimerez, c'est en préservant de la guerre votre cœur, en sauvant de l'incendie l'avenir qui est en vous. . . . Soyez la paix vivante au milieu de la guerre' (in *Les Précurseurs* (Paris, 1919), p. 33).

15   Roland Dorgelès, *Bleu Horizon* (Paris, 1949), p. 43.

16   Page references to *Vie des martyrs* and *Civilisation* in this chapter are given in the text. They refer to the 'Livre de poche' editions of both works.

17   It is said that Duhamel treated about 4,000 wounded men and performed over 2,000 operations at the front. See L. Clark Keating, *Critic of Civilization: Georges Duhamel and his Writings* (Kentucky, 1965), p. 26.

18   Georges Duhamel, *La Possession du monde* (Paris, 1923: first published 1919), pp. 254–5.

CHAPTER 6   Expressing Protest (II)

1   Rieuneau, op. cit., quotes from a letter which he received from Dorgelès dated 30 Oct. 1964 (pp. 31–2).

2   Quoted by A. Dubeux, *Roland Dorgelès: son œuvre* (Paris, 1930), p. 30.

3   Dorgelès, *Souvenirs sur les Croix de bois* (Paris, 1929), p. 27.

4   Ibid., p. 33.

5   Ibid., p. 27.

6   Ibid., p. 8.

7   Ibid., p. 25.

8   Dorgelès, *Les Croix de bois* (Paris, 1919). As he cleans Demachy's leggings Sulphart exclaims, without any trace of irony: 'C'est la bonne vie' (p. 84). This and the remaining page references – mainly given in the text – are to the 'Livre de poche' edition of Dorgelès's novel.

9   'Faire la guerre n'est plus que cela: attendre. Attendre la relève, attendre les lettres, attendre la soupe, attendre le jour, attendre la mort . . . Et tout cela arrive à son heure: il suffit d'attendre . . .' (p. 318).

10   e.g. Ibid., pp. 262–3, 272, 290, 407.

11   Ibid., pp. 272, 283.

12   See *Souvenirs sur les Croix de bois:* ' . . . j'étais persuadé que mes Croix

de bois étaient un ouvrage subversif, que sa gaieté était outrageante, sa pitié séditieuse, et je tremblais à la pensée que cette diatribe pût tomber sous les yeux de mes chefs' (pp. 55–6).

13   See n. 26 to Ch. 2.

14   e.g. Rieuneau, op. cit., ch. 8, sees *Clavel soldat* as directly descended from *Le Feu* in a chapter which he entitles: 'La Postérité du *Feu*: révolte et pacifisme'.

15   It is only fair to add, however, that Werth was identified for some time after 1918 with Barbusse's 'Clarté' movement.

16   See Ch. 3, p. 54.

17   Maurice Merleau-Ponty, *Humanisme et terreur* (Paris, 1947).

18   See Ch. 3, pp. 43, 45.

19   Léon Werth, *Clavel soldat* (Paris, 1919), p. 9. Further page references are given in the text.

20   Werth writes: 'Si on parlait à un soldat de la beauté du danger, il rirait . . . On l'accepte, on le subit, on l'affronte, si un ordre est donné. Mais chacun rêve du moyen de l'évader' (p. 167).

21   This is why Werth's pacifism is more integral, at the theoretical level, than that of Barbusse.

22   Although not strictly about pacifists, there is much useful information on this point in R. N. Stromberg, loc. cit.

CHAPTER 7   The Emotional Response

1   Jacques Rivière, *A la trace de Dieu* (Paris, 1925), p. 131. Rivière was taken prisoner as early as 24 August 1914. Ch. 5 of *A la trace de Dieu* is entitled 'Sens de la guerre' and consists of notes written between 1914 and 1917. Rivière's views are of considerable interest but they are, of course, those of a virtual non-combatant.

2   See Henri Massis, *Le Sacrifice, 1914–1916* (Paris, 1917), *passim*. This volume also contains essays on Péguy and Psichari.

3   See Victor Giraud, *Pro Patria: La Banqueroute du scientisme: En marge de la guerre* (Paris, n. d.), *passim*. This volume was published in 1917.

4   Quoted in Massis, op. cit., pp. 149–50. But see also n. 31 to Ch. 1 above.

5   P.-H. Simon, *Georges Duhamel* (Paris, 1946), p. 32. Quoted in L. Clark Keating, *Critic of Civilization: Georges Duhamel and his Writings* (Kentucky, 1965), p. 39.

6   Georges Duhamel, *La Possession du monde* (Paris, 1923), p. viii. This work first appeared in 1919, but all page references here and in the text are to the revised and corrected edition of 1923.

7   Duhamel declares: 'C'est au cœur qu'il faut s'adresser. C'est à tous les cœurs généreux que l'on doit faire appel' (p. xiv). It is his purpose to 'honorer plus que jamais les ressources fidèles et incorruptibles de la vie intérieure' (p. xv).

8   'C'est en vain que la destruction, le désordre et la mort ont tenté d'interrompre le colloque sublime et familier que tout être poursuit avec la meilleure partie de lui-même. Ce colloque va reprendre, il reprend, au sein même de la bataille, parmi les odeurs et les gémissements de l'hôpital' (pp. xviii–xix).

9   Élie Faure, *La Danse sur le feu et l'eau* (Paris, 1920), p. 82.

10   See H. Massis, 'Le Cas de M. Georges Duhamel', *Revue universelle,* VIII (1922), 738–61.

11   The earlier debate about the nature and status of science was continued in the post-war years and was much influenced by the fact that scientific skills contributed so much to the killing (and no doubt in part to the healing) that went on during the war. Nevertheless, an intelligent and detailed case against science is not easily found, apart from the fundamental arguments put forward by Valéry (see Ch. 9 above). Many of the defenders of traditional humane values such as Victor Giraud (see n. 3 above) claimed to be attacking not science as such but the misunderstanding and misapplication of science which they called 'scientisme'. Some of the most interesting brief comments are to be found in Lucien Romier, *Explication de notre temps* (Paris, 1925), esp. pp. 167–71. Romier argues that pure or theoretical science lacks that power of social cohesion which a religion or political system must provide: 'La science ne crée pas de lien collectif, parce qu'en tant qu'effort de recherche, elle est essentiellement personnelle, mouvante, et que ses résultats, toujours provisoires, impliquent des constatations, non des obligations.' As regards the applied sciences, their influence on society is notable, but Romier insists that they cannot in themselves affect its *moral* fabric. He therefore concludes: 'Il est donc absurde de conférer à la science, qu'il s'agisse de la connaissance des faits ou de leur utilisation pratique, une portée éducative.' Nevertheless, through admiration for the methodology of science and the qualities of mind which it requires, Romier describes the theoretical scientists as forming a moral and civic élite. He concludes with a statement from which Duhamel would hardly dissent; ' . . . il faudra restaurer, pour la science, le prestige de la recherche désintéressée, et, pour les techniques, le souci de la qualité.'

12   'Me voici quand même sûr que le bonheur est le but de la vie. Cette certitude m'est venue surtout de l'intérieur, et non pas des événements, et non pas du spectacle des autres hommes. Comme toutes les certitudes intérieures, elle est obstinée, indéfectible, agressive même. Toutes les objections semblent faites pour la fortifier' (p. 4).

13   The relevant passage from Pascal's *Pensées* is the following: 'Nous connaissons la vérité, non seulement par la raison, mais encore par le cœur; c'est de cette dernière sorte que nous connaissons les premiers principes, et c'est en vain que le raisonnement qui n'y a point de part, essaye de les combattre. Les pyrrhoniens, qui n'ont que cela pour objet, y travaillent inutilement. Nous savons que nous ne rêvons point; quelque impuissance où nous soyons de le prouver par raison, cette impuissance ne conclut autre chose que la faiblesse de notre raison, mais non pas l'incertitude de toutes nos connaissances, comme ils le prétendent. Car la connaissance des premiers principes, comme qu'il y a espace, temps, mouvement, nombres, [est] aussi ferme qu'aucune de celles que nos raisonnements nous donnent. Et c'est sur ces connaissances du cœur et de l'instinct qu'il faut que la raison s'appuie, et qu'elle y fonde tout son discours' (Br. 282; L. 110).

14   Addressing the present, Duhamel writes: ' . . . lorsque tu n'auras plus, pour nous, que de la colère et de la haine, que de l'avarice et de la cruauté, il faudra bien que chacun de nous t'abandonne et retourne à ses refuges' (p. 204). An earlier passage is also relevant: 'Plus je vois les hommes qui, depuis quatre ans, mènent aux armées une vie inhumaine, et mieux je comprends le sens de leur incroyable patience: entre l'avenir et le souvenir, ils ont l'air de laisser passer un orage. . . . On sent, dans leurs propos, que ces deux

existences illuminées se cherchent et se rejoignent sans cesse par-dessus l'abîme sanglant' (pp. 180–1).

15 Details of Faure's career will be found in Paul Desanges, *Élie Faure: regards sur sa vie et sur son œuvre* (Geneva, 1963).

16 Quoted in Desanges, op. cit., p. 131.

17 Ibid., p. 132.

18 Ibid.

19 Élie Faure, op. cit., p. 180. Further page references are mainly given in the text.

20 Faure distinguishes somewhat sententiously between revolution and war: ' . . . la Révolution est une guerre sans style, la guerre une révolution sans vie. Et leur rôle profond est que l'une tend à susciter la vie quand le style n'a plus de vie et l'autre à recréer le style quand la vie n'a plus de style. Par là, la révolution et la guerre me paraissent avoir été les facteurs les plus cruels, certes, mais jusqu'ici les plus nécessaires, de la civilisation' (Ibid., p. 39).

21 G. D. Josipovici, 'The Birth of the Modern: 1885–1914' in John Cruickshank (ed.), *French Literature and its Background, 6: The Twentieth Century* (London, 1970), p. 2. My italics.

22 Faure writes: 'La morale ne comprend pas qu'une société, comme une œuvre d'art, comme un cœur, doit être un composé vivant d'éléments antagonistes, vices, vertus, idées, passions, énergies, faiblesses, enthousiasmes et dégoûts dont les oppositions et les contrastes jouent et entrent les uns dans les autres par des passages mystérieux' (p. 135).

23 'Ce que je sais, ce que je sens plutôt, c'est qu'une telle civilisation me semble à peine concevable. Et j'aurais peur qu'elle devînt, par sa lucidité cruelle, sa précision, sa prévision, sa détermination mathématique, même sans drame, même sans guerre, mille fois plus atroce que la nôtre, envisagée sous ses plus terribles aspects. Le bonheur unanime tuerait la joie, tuerait l'espoir, tuerait la générosité. Tout étant au même niveau, rien n'aspirerait à monter. L'intelligence, tournant à vide dans son cercle de diamant, rejoindrait l'inconscience, et tout ce qui fait la noblesse de l'homme ensanglanté qui tend vers un dieu intérieur impossible à saisir, s'abîmerait dans la perfection métaphysique du néant. S'il faut choisir entre ce rationalisme absolu, qui fixerait la civilisation, et le mythe toujours vivant et toujours renouvelé qui la poursuit dans toutes les formes du chemin sans l'arrêter jamais en image définitive, c'est le mythe que je choisis' (p. 34).

CHAPTER 8   The Intellectual Response (I)

1 Alain, *Mars ou la guerre jugée* (Paris, 1936), p. 205. All further page references to this work are given in the text and also refer to the 1936 edition.

2 Cf. 'il est plus vite fait de haïr la guerre que de savoir ce que c'est' (p. 113) and 's'indigner sans comprendre, c'est cela qui rend méchant' (p. 222).

3 Alain quotes Spinoza: 'Une passion cesse d'être une passion dès que nous en connaissons adéquatement les causes' (p. 12).

4 Micheline Tison-Braun, op. cit., Vol. 2 (p. 172), says rather sharply: '[Alain] met sa coquetterie à analyser les passions de l'homme moderne dans la langue de Descartes et de la Rochefoucauld.'

5 A. Philonenko, op. cit., p. 165.

6 See ibid., p. 164.

7   This attitude is associated with Alain's low view of politicians. He writes: 'Si j'écrivais quelque ouvrage politique, je lui donnerais comme titre: *Léviathan, ou l'Animal sans Tête'* (p. 201).

8   'L'élite trouve trop d'avantages dans cet ordre resserré que la guerre impose' (p. 105).

9   Nevertheless, consideration must no doubt be given to the kind of point made in a review-article in the *Times Literary Supplement* for 12 June 1930 and in which one of the books reviewed happened to be the English translation of Alain's work:

'The Great War, it is not to be denied, had many features more terrible than the majority of former wars. The enormous numbers engaged, the length of a conflict in which there were no winter quarters and active operations were frequently carried on in very bad weather, the larger proportion of that conflict during which the conditions were those of siege warfare, the shattering effect upon the nerves of high-explosive shells fired in unlimited quantities, the fact that battle casualties were greater than in most wars, though not than in all – these aspects were all in some degree peculiar to the last war. But in exchange there were some great compensations. Let us think only for a moment of those inventions of medical science: the antiseptic, the anaesthetic and the antitoxin. . . . The amount of pain and mortality avoided by the use of these three boons is almost incalculable. . . . [Otherwise] the deaths from disease on the Western Front would have exceeded those from bullet and shell.'

10   'C'est que la paix est le bien, et la guerre le mal' (p. 97).

CHAPTER 9   The Intellectual Response (II)

1   See Henri Massis, *Le Sacrifice, 1914–1916* (Paris, 1917) and *Défense de l'Occident* (Paris, 1927).

2   The text of 'Le Yalou' is printed as part of *Regards sur le monde actuel* in the Pléiade edition of Valéry's *Œuvres II* (Paris, 1960), pp. 1016–21. Details regarding composition and publication are given on p. 1551. Quotations from works reprinted in this volume and the Pléiade *Œuvres I* (Paris, 1957) are followed in the text by the indication Pl. I or Pl. II, with the appropriate page reference in brackets.

3   The text of 'Une Conquête méthodique' is printed as part of *Variété* in Pl. I, pp. 972–87.

4   Cf. Valéry's comment of 1944: ' . . . les événements sont l'écume des choses, mais c'est la mer qui m'intéresse' (*Propos me concernant,* p. 4).

5   *Correspondance d'André Gide et de Paul Valéry, 1890–1942* (Paris, 1955), pp. 355–6.

6   *Cahiers, 1,* p. 316 and *Cahiers, 2,* p. 179. Further comments on Valéry's attitude to democracy may be found in E. Gaède, *Nietzsche et Valéry: essai sur la comédie de l'esprit* (Paris, 1962), esp. pp. 347–9.

7   Pl. II, p. 963.

8   Cf. Pierre Roulin, *Paul Valéry, témoin et juge du monde moderne* (Neuchatel, 1964): ' . . . le Valéry d'après "la Grande Guerre" est déjà presque tout entier dans celui d'avant la guerre' (p. 33).

9   Roulin's comment is enlightening: 'Nous sommes donc autorisés à voir dans *Une Conquête Méthodique* la description de l'application de la

méthode scientifique à un domaine qui lui semblait jusque-là fermé, celui de l'économie. Mais l'analyse minutieuse que Valéry fait du mécanisme allemand a encore une portée plus générale que celle de nous donner une synthèse de l'économie modern en générale; à travers ce système, c'est l'analyse de la Méthode appliquée à une grande échelle, c'est donc celle d'un aspect important du monde moderne, exemple d'une vaste organisation scientifiquement menée.

Pour Valéry, le système économique allemand est le premier exemple de ce qui caractérisera le monde moderne: c'est-à-dire l'application méthodique, rationnelle, puissante, à grande échelle des lois de l'esprit, de la raison, sorte de totalitarisme logique consistant dans l'application intégrale de la méthode à quelque forme d'existence que ce soit' (p. 75).

10   'Ressemblance grande entre le chef militaire moderne et le monteur d'affaires – Maniement des masses, grand orchestre – données numériques, calcul mental et mémorial' (*Cahiers, 4*, p. 471).

11   Alain, *Mars ou la guerre jugée* (Paris, 2nd edn. 1936), p. 63.

12   Letter to André Fontainas, printed in Paul Valéry, *Lettres à quelques-uns* (Paris, 1952), p. 102.

13   A letter of the same year to A. Coste contains this passage: 'Maintenant c'est la guerre . . . J'ai d'abord souffert de ne rien faire. Le temps était trop tendu pour continuer des exercices de longue haleine; savez-vous ce que je fais: je redouble, repeins et vernis d'anciens vers. Cela est chinois et ridicule, mais cela est traditionnel: à chaque terrible époque humaine on a toujours vu un monsieur assis dans un coin qui soignait son écriture et enfilait des perles . . .' (ibid., pp. 103–4). Valéry appears to see himself here as following the doctrine of his own Chinese spokesman in 'Le Yalou'.

14   See *Cahiers, 5*, p. 372. Valéry adds here: 'Celui qui est loin du feu pense au feu . . .'.

15   *Lettres à quelques-uns*, pp. 179–80. In 1940 Valéry looked back to this period and again saw himself as preserving important and seriously threatened values by writing 'La Jeune Parque' at the time he did (see *Cahiers, 23*, p. 736). Also, in *Mélange*, which was first published in 1939, he wrote firmly: 'Il n'est pas mauvais que certains hommes aient la force d'attacher plus de conséquence et de prix à la détermination d'une lointaine décimale ou de la position d'une virgule, qu'à la nouvelle la plus retentissante, à la catastrophe la plus considérable, ou à leur vie même . . . Je ne regrette point quatre années passées à tenter chaque jour de résoudre des problèmes de versification très sévères' (Pl. I, p. 304).

16   'Le système Taylor' is a reference to F. W. Taylor (1856–1915) who was a distinguished American engineer. He is now best known for his contributions to the theory of business organization. In *The Principles of Scientific Management* (1911) and several others works, he set out a modern system of management which has since been widely adopted in the interests of business efficiency and increased productivity.

17   *Lettres à quelques-uns*, p. 122.

18   *Cahiers, 6*, p. 869.

19   *Cahiers, 9*, p. 900.

20   *Cahiers, 12*, p. 141.

21   *Lettres à quelques-uns*, p. 129.

22   For further details regarding publication see Pl. I, pp. 1790–2.

23   Cf. letter of 29 July 1934 to Paul Desjardins: 'Le titre même de l'étude et l'ensemble des idées qu'elle contient me semble montrer assez clairement que j'entends décrire une "phase critique", un état de choses opposé fortement à celui que l'on représente par les noms de "régime" et de "développement régulier" ' (*Lettres à quelques-uns*, p. 223).

24   See Marjorie Grene, *The Knower and the Known* (London, 1966), p. 82 and *passim*. See also the general thesis of Michael Polanyi, *Personal Knowledge* (London, 1958) and his insistence – against the idea of objectivity and certainty – that 'into every act of knowing there enters a passionate contribution of the person knowing what is being known' (p. viii).

CHAPTER 10   Malraux and the Reinvention of Man

1   Roulin, op. cit., p. 195.

2   Joseph Hoffman, in *L'Humanisme de Malraux* (Paris, 1963), places these early works under the shadow of the Great War when he writes: '[Malraux] s'éveille . . . à la vie intellectuelle pendant les années de l'immédiate après-guerre, dans un climat profondément marqué par cette grande tourmente qui, pendant quatre années, ravagea l'Europe toute entière. La guerre finie, on commence à mesurer la portée de cette grande convulsion du monde occidental et l'ampleur de ses conséquences. Une guerre se terminait où, pour la première fois, les plaies des vainqueurs étaient aussi grandes que celles des vaincus. Le trouble s'était emparé des esprits et les valeurs traditionnelles étaient fortement ébranlées . . . on commence à s'interroger sur l'homme lui-même et sur l'image que l'Occident s'en était faite' (pp. 10–11).

3   C. Jenkins, *André Malraux* (New York, 1972), p. 30. Hoffmann, however, sees in *La Tentation de l'Occident* 'une profusion d'images toutes barrésiennes' (op. cit., p. 23).

4   André Malraux, 'D'une jeunesse européenne' in *Écrits* (Paris, 1927), pp. 147 and 142. Further page references to this essay are given in brackets in the text, preceded by the letters *J.E.*

5   André Malraux, *La Tentation de l'Occident* (Paris, 1972; first publ. 1926), p. 58. Page references are to the 'Livre de poche' edition of 1972 and are given in brackets in the text, preceded by the letters *T.O.*

6   Marcel Arland, 'Sur un nouveau mal du siècle', *Nouvelle Revue Française*, no. 125, 1 Feb. 1924, p. 156.

7   Paul Morand, *Bouddha vivant* (Paris, 1927), p. 13.

8   Romain Rolland's introduction to A. Coomaraswamy, *La Danse de Çiva* (Abbeville, 1922), p. 7.

9   Quoted in 'Rencontre avec Malraux', *Les Nouvelles littéraires,* 3 Apr. 1952.

10   These questions, as they affected British combatants and the British public, are well discussed in Alan Wilkinson, *The Church of England and the First World War* (London, 1978).

11   See André Malraux, *Les Voix du silence* (Paris, 1951), p. 466.

12   V. Brombert, *The Intellectual Hero: Studies in the French Novel, 1880– 1955* (Philadelphia and New York, 1961), p. 174.

13   In 'André Malraux et l'Orient', *Les Nouvelles littéraires,* 31 July 1926.

14   E. J. Leed, op. cit., p. 207.

15   For a useful discussion of this debate see Pilkington, op. cit., esp. pp. 184, 185, and 199–202.
16   G. A. Panichas (ed.), *Promise of Greatness: The War of 1914–1918* (London, 1968), p. xxvi.

Selective Bibliography

(Sections (A) and (B) below list only those works which are discussed or referred to in the preceding pages)

(A) *Fiction between 1915 and 1919*

René Benjamin, *Les Soldats de la guerre: Gaspard,* Paris, Fayard, 1915
Henri Barbusse, *Le Feu (Journal d'une escouade),* Paris, Flammarion, 1916
Adrien Bertrand, *L'Appel du sol,* Paris, Calmann-Lévy, 1916
Georges Duhamel, *Vie des martyrs, 1914–1916,* Paris, Mercure de France, 1917
　　　　　　　Civilisation, 1914–1917, Paris, Mercure de France, 1918
Gabriel-Tristan Franconi, *Un Tel de l'armée française,* Paris, Payot, 1918
Roland Dorgelès, *Les Croix de bois,* Paris, Albin Michel, 1919
　　　　　　　Le Cabaret de la Belle Femme, Paris, Albin Michel, 1919
Léon Werth, *Clavel soldat,* Paris, Albin Michel, 1919

(B) *Works of Analysis between 1917 and 1927*

Henri Massis, *Le Sacrifice, 1914–1916,* Paris, Plon-Nourrit, 1917
Victor Girard, *Pro Patria: la Banqueroute du scientisme: en Marge de la guerre,* Paris, Bloud & Gay, n. d. [1917].
Georges Duhamel, *La Possession du monde,* Paris, Mercure de France, 1919
Paul Valéry, 'La Crise de l'esprit', *Nouvelle Revue Française* (1 Aug. 1919), pp. 321–37
Élie Faure, *La Danse sur le feu et l'eau,* Paris, Crès, 1920
Alain, *Mars ou la guerre jugée,* Paris, NRF, 1921 (revised and enlarged edition: NRF, 1936)
G. Guy-Grand, *Le Conflit des idées dans la France d'aujourd'hui,* Paris, Rivière, 1921
Marcel Arland, 'Sur un nouveau mal du siècle, *Nouvelle Revue Française* (February 1924), pp. 149–58
Jacques Rivière, *A la trace de Dieu,* Paris, Gallimard, 1925
Lucien Romier, *Explication de notre temps,* Paris, Grasset, 1925
André Malraux, *La Tentation de l'Occident,* Paris, Grasset, 1926
　　　　　　　'D'une jeunesse européenne' in André Chamson (ed.), *Écrits,* ('Les Cahiers verts'), Paris, Grasset, 1927, pp. 129–53
Henri Massis, *Défense de l'Occident,* Paris, Plon, 1927

(C) *Other Miscellaneous Writings, 1913–1926*

'Agathon' (Henri Massis and Alfred de Tarde), *Les Jeunes Gens d'aujourd'hui,* Paris, Plon, 1913
Ernest Psichari, *L'Appel des armes,* Paris, Oudin, 1913
Romain Rolland, *Au-dessus de la mêlée,* Paris, Ollendorff, 1915

Paul Adam, *La Littérature et la guerre,* Paris, Crès, 1916

Edmund Gosse, *Inter Arma,* London, Heinemann, 1916

Pierre Chaine, *Les Mémoires d'un rat,* Paris, L'Œuvre, 1917

Jean Galtier-Boissière, *En rase campagne 1914. Un hiver à Souchez 1915–16,* Paris, Berger-Levrault, 1917

Albert Schinz, *French Literature of the Great War,* New York, Appleton & Co., 1920

C. E. Montague, *Disenchantment,* London, MacGibbon & Kee, 1968 (first published 1922)

Jean Vic, *La Littérature de guerre* (5 vols.), Paris, Les Presses françaises, 1917–24

Marc Boas-Boasson, *Au Soir d'un monde: lettres de guerre,* Paris, Plon, 1926

(D) *General Background*

Jacques Barzun, *Darwin, Marx, Wagner. Critique of a Heritage,* London, Secker & Warburg, 1942

Jean-Jacques Becker, *1914: Comment les Français sont entrés dans la guerre,* Paris, Presses de la Fondation Nationale des Sciences Politiques, 1978

E. F. Benson, *The Outbreak of War, 1914,* London, Peter Davies, 1933

Bernard Bergonzi, *Heroes' Twilight: a Study of the Literature of the Great War,* London, Constable, 1965
    'Before 1914: Writers and the Threat of War', *Critical Quarterly,* No. 6 (Summer 1964), pp. 126–34

J. K. Bostock, *Some Well-Known German War Novels, 1914–1930,* Oxford, Blackwell, 1931

Kenneth Burke, *The Philosophy of Literary Form,* New York, Vintage Books, 1957

J. V. L. Casserley, *The Retreat from Christianity in the Modern World,* London, Longmans Green, 1952

Owen Chadwick, *The Secularization of the European Mind in the Nineteenth Century,* Cambridge, Cambridge University Press, 1976

I. F. Clarke, *Voices Prophesying War, 1763–1984,* London, Oxford University Press, 1966

Stanley Cooperman, *World War I and the American Novel,* Baltimore, Johns Hopkins Press, 1967

Benjamin Crémieux, *Inquiétude et reconstruction: essai sur la littérature d'après-guerre,* Paris, Corrêa, 1931

J. Norton Cru, *Témoins: essai d'analyse et de critique des souvenirs de combattants édités en français de 1915 à 1928,* Paris, Les Étincelles, 1929

M. Curtis, *Three against the Third Republic. Sorel, Barrès and Maurras,* Princeton, Princeton University Press, 1959

Jean David, *Le Procès de l'intelligence dans les lettres françaises au seuil de l'entre-deux-guerres,* Paris, Nizet, 1966

Jacques Desmaret, *La Grand Guerre, 1914–1919,* Paris Hachette, 1978

Roland Dorgelès, *Souvenirs sur les Croix de bois,* Paris, La Cité des livres, 1929
    Bleu horizon, pages de la Grande Guerre, Paris, Albin Michel, 1949

J. B. Duroselle, *La France et les Français, 1900–1914,* Paris, Éd. Richelieu, 1972

Colin Dyer, *Population and Society in Twentieth-Century France,* London, Hodder & Stoughton, 1978

L. L. Farrar, *The Short-War Illusion,* Oxford, Clio Press, 1974

Marc Ferro, *The Great War 1914–18,* London, Routledge & Kegan Paul, 1973

Frank Field, *Three French Writers and the Great War: Barbusse, Drieu la Rochelle, Bernanos: Studies in the Rise of Communism and Fascism,* Cambridge, Cambridge University Press, 1975

John F. C. Fuller, *The Conduct of War, 1789–1961,* London, Methuen, 1975

Paul Fussell, *The Great War and Modern Memory,* London, Oxford University Press, 1975

Robert Gibson, 'The First World War and the Literary Consciousness' in John Cruickshank (ed.), *French Literature and its Background* (Vol. 6): *Twentieth Century,* London, Oxford University Press, 1970, pp. 55–72

Raoul Girardet, *Le Nationalisme français, 1871–1914,* Paris, A. Colin (Collection 'U'), 1966

M. S. Greicus, *Prose Writers of World War I,* London, Longman, 1973

Frederick J. Hoffman, *The Mortal No: Death and the Modern Imagination,* Princeton, Princeton University Press, 1964

Alfred Kazin, *On Native Grounds,* New York, Harcourt, 1942

Holger Klein (ed.), *The First World War in Fiction,* London, Macmillan, 1976

E. J. Leed, *No Man's Land. Combat and Identity in World War I,* Cambridge, Cambridge University Press, 1979

Arthur Marwick, *The Deluge,* London, Bodley Head, 1961

Chester W. Obuchowski, *Mars on Trial: War as seen by French Writers of the Twentieth Century,* Madrid, Turanzas ('Studia Humanitatis'), 1978

George A. Panichas (ed.), *Promise of Greatness: the War of 1914–1918,* London, Cassell, 1968

Gabriel Perreux, *La Guerre de 1914–1918,* Paris, Hachette, 1964

———— *La Vie quotidienne des civils en France pendant la Grande Guerre,* Paris, Hachette, 1966

Alexis Philonenko, *Essais sur la philosophie de la guerre,* Paris, Vrin, 1976

A. E. Pilkington, *Bergson and his Influence: a Reassessment,* Cambridge, Cambridge University Press, 1976

René Pomeau, 'Guerre et roman dans l'entre-deux-guerres', *Revue des sciences humaines,* fasc. 109 (Jan.–Mar., 1963), pp. 77–95

Herbert Read, 'The Failure of War books' in *A Coat of Many Colours,* London, Routledge, 1945

P. Renouvin, *La Crise européenne et la première guerre mondiale (1914–1918),* Paris, PUF, 1969

Léon Riegel, *Guerre et littérature: le bouleversement des consciences dans la littérature romanesque inspirée par la Grande Guerre,* Paris, Klincksieck, 1978

Maurice Rieuneau, *Guerre et révolution dans le roman français de 1919 à 1939,* Paris, Klincksieck, 1974

Theodore Ropp, *War in the Modern World,* Durham (NC), Duke University Press, 1959

Pierre-Henri Simon, *L'Esprit et l'histoire: essai sur la conscience historique dans la littérature du xxe siècle,* Paris, A. Colin, 1954

Roland N. Stromberg, 'The Intellectuals and the Coming of War in 1914', *Journal of European Studies,* Vol. 3 (June, 1973), pp. 109–22

K. W. Swart, *The Sense of Decadence in Nineteenth-Century France,* The Hague, Nijhoff, 1964

G. M. Thomson, *The Twelve Days, 24 July to 4 August 1914,* London, Hutchinson, 1964

Micheline Tison-Braun, *La Crise de l'humanisme* (2 vols.), Paris, Nizet, 1958 and 1967

H. M. Tomlinson, 'War books', *Criterion,* No. 36 (Apr. 1930), pp. 402–19

Eugen Weber, *The Nationalist Revival in France,* Berkeley, University of California Press, 1959

Alan Wilkinson, *The Church of England and the First World War,* London, SPCK, 1978

Robert Wohl, *The Generation of 1914,* London, Weidenfeld & Nicolson, 1980

Peter Wust, *Crisis in the West,* London, Sheed & Ward, 1931

Index